# RUTH
## ANCESTOR OF CHRIST

**RUTH AND ESTHER: WOMEN OF FAITH**

# ESTHER
## THE QUEEN WHO SAVED HER PEOPLE

# RUTH
## ANCESTOR OF CHRIST

**RUTH AND ESTHER: WOMEN OF FAITH**

# ESTHER
## THE QUEEN WHO SAVED HER PEOPLE

Paula Massie Oneal, D.Min.

**Studio of Books LLC**
5900 Balcones Drive Suite 100
Austin, Texas 78731
*www.studioofbooks.org*
Hotline: (254) 800-1183

Ordering Information:
Special discounts are available on quantity purchases by corporations, associations, and others. For details, contact the publisher at the address above.

Printed in the United States of America.

ISBN-13:  Softcover    978-1-964864-10-5
          eBook       978-1-964864-11-2

Library of Congress Control Number:

*This book is dedicated to the glory of God in loving memory of my beloved son, Robert Eugene John Massie (Bobby) Oneal. He was a man of faith and a loving son, husband, and father. I was indeed blessed to be his mother.*

# Table of Contents

# BIBLICAL REFERENCES

Unless stated otherwise, scripture quotations are from the HOLY BIBLE, NEW INTERNATIONAL VERSION ® (NIV), copyright © 1973, 1978, 1984, 2011 by International Bible Society. Zondervan Publishing House.

Other versions of the Bible have been used to show differences in translations.

These include the following:

American Standard Version (ASV) Public Domain.

Amplified Bible (AMP) Copyright © 2015 by The Lockman Foundation, La Habra, CA 90631.

Authorized (King James) Version (AKJV) Cambridge University Press, the Crown's patentee in the UK.

BRG Bible (BRG) Blue Red and Gold Letter Edition™ Copyright © 2012 BRG Bible Ministries.

Christian Standard Bible (CSB) The Christian Standard Bible. Copyright © 2017 by Holman Bible Publishers.

Common English Bible (CEB) Copyright © 2011 by Common English Bible.

Complete Jewish Bible (CJB) Copyright © 1998 by David H. Stern.

# ACKNOWLEDGMENTS

I WOULD LIKE TO THANK THE FOLLOWING MINISTERS, family members, and Christian friends whose advice, prayers, and encouragement made this book possible.

**Pastor Larry Bowlin:** Senior Pastor, Tyrone Covenant Presbyterian Church (PCA), Fenton, MI. (former Pastor of Providence Presbyterian Church, Murphy, NC).

**The Rev. Bert Daly:** Rector, St Mark's Episcopal Church, Starke, Florida.

**Rev. Mike Moreau:** Senior Pastor, Central Presbyterian Church (PCA), Kingstree, SC. (former pastor of Providence Presbyterian Church, Murphy, NC): Proofreader and Advisor.

**Rev. Dr. Sharon Gottfried Lewis:** Episcopal Priest in the Diocese of Southwest Florida, Founder and Executive Director of Amazing Love Healing Ministry

**Nicholas Sommer:** Director of Youth and Family, Grace Presbyterian Church (PCA), Blairsville, GA.

**Renate Craig:** Editor and proofreader

**Nosha Oneal and Khyree Oneal:** Proofreaders, Advisors, Encouragers, Computer experts, and much-loved grandsons

**Rachel Whitener** (Director of Learning Resources), **Deborah Kenyon and Katrina Miller** (Librarians), **Donnie Morrow** (Learning Management Systems Administrator), Tri-County Community College, Murphy, NC.

**Pauline Hebb, and Pam Baker**, Proofreaders.

**Áine Massie:** advice, formatting, computer skills, proofreading

# INTRODUCTION TO RUTH

"The grass withers and the flowers fall,

but the word of our God endures forever" (Isa. 40:8).

EVERY DETAIL IN THE HOLY BIBLE IS IMPORTANT.

**"Blessed... are those who hear the word of God and obey it"** (Lk. 11:28). **"Man shall not live on bread alone, but on every word that comes from the mouth of God"** (Mt. 4:4). **"Therefore, get rid of all moral filth and the evil that is so prevalent and humbly accept the word planted in you, which can save you. Do not merely listen to the word, and so deceive yourselves. Do what it says"** (Jas. 1:21-22).

**"All Scripture is God-breathed and is useful for teaching, rebuking, correcting, and training in righteousness, so that the servant of God may be thoroughly equipped for every good work"** (2 Ti. 3:16-17). The Bible is the inspired (influenced by the Holy Spirit), inerrant (without error or inaccuracy in its original languages), authoritative (trustworthy, dependable) word of God. Each book of The Holy Bible has its own message. The book of Ruth demonstrates that God can and does save His people. The main character in this book is not Ruth, Naomi, or even Boaz. It is God. He works in every aspect of our lives to accomplish His goals. This story is one of grief, deliverance, courage, mercy, faith, and love. It is the account of an ordinary family who experienced adversity and made some bad choices. In His mercy, God supplied them with a redeemer.

Tragedies and disasters are common in our world today. Life in the days of Ruth and Naomi was no different. The lives of God's people can be joyous and successful, but they can also be difficult and filled with hardships and grief. God can use our trials and tribulations to bring us into a closer relationship with Him. He does not promise us a life of ease, but He does promise to be with us at all times. Our choices, whether good or bad, have consequences. Our decisions not only affect us individually, they can also affect our families, friends, and colleagues. Even when people know what is moral and honorable, they may consciously choose to do what is sinful.

The story of Ruth begins in the town of Bethlehem with the family of Elimelek (also spelled Elimelech). Rather than live in the Promised Land, Elimelek unwisely decided to travel east across the Jordan River and relocate his family in the lawless, pagan land of Moab. At this time, women were ruled by their husbands. Elimelek told his family to go to Moab, so his wife, Naomi, obeyed, taking their two sons with them. Without a doubt, this act disobeyed God's command, **"Do not associate with these nations that remain among you; do not invoke the names of their gods or swear by them. You must not serve them or bow down to them"** (Jos. 23:7). Ignoring God's word, they left His land of promise and traveled to a pagan nation. They experienced hardships they would not have faced had they stayed in Israel. For their disobedience and lack of faith, Elimelek and his sons paid with their lives. **"Good judgment wins favor, but the way of the unfaithful leads to their destruction"** (Pr. 13:15).

God truly loves and cares for His people and is involved in their everyday lives. He is always faithful and blesses His people when they obey Him. **"If you follow My decrees and are careful to obey My commands, I will send you rain in its season, and the ground will yield its crops and the trees their fruit"** (Lev. 26:3-4). The fact Elimelek's family suffered heartbreak and poverty does not mean God ignored them or ceased to love them. He used hardships to teach them important lessons and bring them back into His will. God never abandons His people or stops loving them. Through the discipline of a severe famine, poverty, and death, He brought great blessings to Israel and the world. God's love and providence can be seen throughout the book of Ruth. (Over 150 verses in the Old Testament point to God's love.)

Only two books in the Bible are named for women: Ruth and Esther. Ruth, the Moabite, is not referred to in any other book of the Old Testament. She is named in the New Testament (Mt. 1:5) when citing Jesus' genealogy. Ruth was a young pagan woman who converted and became part of God's covenant people, Israel. She became an ancestor of our Lord and Savior Jesus Christ. Only five women are listed in Christ's family tree (Mt. 1:1-16). The information in this book is in harmony with the books of Judges and 1 and 2 Samuel. Therefore, biblical scholars consider the account accurate.

Pastor Daniel Henderson (former youth pastor, Grace Presbyterian Church, Blairsville, GA) says, "The story of Ruth is one of the greatest short stories ever written. It contains action, suspense, emotion, grief, desolation, defeat, memorable dialogue, virtue, devotion, sacrifice, redemption, victory, and much more."[1] The author uses conversation to help tell the story. More than fifty of the eighty-five verses of this short book contain dialogue.

Psalm 138:8 illustrates the theme of the book of Ruth. **"The LORD will vindicate me; Your love, Lord, endures forever—do not abandon the works of Your hands"** (Ps. 138:8). God is King. He reigns over the entire universe. Planet Earth spins through space according to God's plan. Our Creator is always in control.

He directed His people in ancient Israel and continues to do so today. God plans and provides for our needs, both physical and spiritual. He directed every event in this story. Nothing happened by chance. Everything, whether joyous or tragic, was and is a part of God's divine purpose. Ruth obeyed God, and He blessed her tremendously.

God called Abraham to establish a nation (Ge. 12: 1-3). Approximately one thousand years after Abraham was born, He brought together the family of Ruth and Boaz. They were two honorable, godly people who became ancestors of our Lord and Savior Jesus Christ. (Ruth was the great-grandmother of King David, royal forefather of Christ.)

---

1        Henderson, Daniel. Sermon: "Ruth `1 - God's Kindness on Display." Grace Presbyterian Church (PCA), Blairsville, GA, 12 July 2015.

Inspired by the Holy Spirit, Balaam son of Beor prophesied, **"I see Him, but not now; I behold Him, but not near** [not imminent]. **A star will come out of Jacob; a scepter will rise out of Israel. He will crush the foreheads of Moab, the skulls** [the meaning of the word in the Masoretic Text is uncertain] **of all the people of Sheth"** (Nu. 24:17).

Moabites were the descendants of Abraham's nephew Lot. God destroyed Sodom and Gomorrah because of their terrible sins, but He spared Lot and his family. As they escaped from the city, Lot's wife defied God's orders and looked back. She was turned into a pillar of salt.

Lot and his two daughters first lived in Zoar, but fearing they might be killed, they hid in a cave in the mountains. Since there were no men available to be their husbands and continue their family line, the two daughters got Lot, their father, drunk and slept with him. Their incestuous conduct produced two sons. The older daughter's son, Moab, became the father of the Moabites. The son of the younger daughter, Ben-Ammi, became the father of the Ammonites (Ge. 19).

Jews regarded the Moabites as an inferior race. In Psalm 60:8, David referred to Moab as a "washbasin" or "wash pot." Washbasins were used by slaves to wash dusty, dirty feet. (These words were inspired by God. They point out He is sovereign over Moab and do not infer Moabites were second-rate or worthy of hatred.) Ruth was from Moab, so many Hebrews would have considered her a heathen. However, after observing her love and loyalty to Naomi, the people of Bethlehem accepted her. In the same way, God accepts all sincere believers as members of His family, regardless of their nationality, ethnicity, or prior disloyalty. God's love transforms us.

Moab was a pagan nation (Jdg. 10:6) situated on a high plateau east of the Dead Sea. The Israelites and Moabites had been enemies since the time of Moses (Nu. 21-25). During the reign of King David, Israel and Moab lived in peace (1 Sa. 22:3-4). Hostilities resumed after David's death (2 Ki. 3:5-27; Ezr. 9:1). Moabites were pagan idol worshippers (1 Ki. 11:7, 11:33; 2 Ki. 23:13) who hated Israel. Therefore, God cursed their country (Isa. 15-16; Jer. 48; Eze. 25:8-11; Am. 2:1-3).

God ordered the Israelites not to seek help from the Moabites. When Israel's ancestors needed help, the pagan Moabites placed a curse on God's people and refused to help them. As a result, the Lord cursed them.

God condemned Moab before Naomi, Ruth or Boaz were born. Even though they knew God forbade such acts, the family from "The House of Bread" (Bethlehem) asked for help from the cursed pagans. They ignored God's command.

**"No Ammonite or Moabite or any of their descendants may enter the assembly of the LORD, not even in the tenth generation. For they did not come to meet you with bread and water on your way when you came out of Egypt, and they hired Balaam son of Beor from Pethor in Aram Naharaim** [Northwest Mesopotamia] **to pronounce a curse on you"** (Dt. 23:3-4).

Bethlehem in Judah was approximately 6 miles south of Jerusalem. It was where King David was anointed (1 Sa. 16:1-13), as well as the birthplace of Jesus Christ (Lk. 2:1-20). There was also another city named Bethlehem in the north (Jos. 19:15).

Even though they were close geographically, Moab and Bethlehem differed greatly in both religion and traditions. The people of Bethlehem worshipped the one true God of the Jews, while Moab worshipped idols and false gods.

The Bible does not specify exactly where the family settled. They may have traveled only fifty miles from home. With poorly maintained roads and inadequate transportation, even a relatively short journey would have been grueling.

The story of Ruth is a godly love story in which God acted as the matchmaker. Yahweh is able to coordinate seemingly minor events to achieve His divine purpose. The events in this book took place in Israel during the time of the judges (circa 1375-1050 BC) after Israel, led by Joshua, had entered the Promised Land. This was a time of religious and economic turmoil. The Israelites were in open rebellion against God. They ignored His words when life became rough. They apparently thought they could get away with sinful behavior. God is patient and longsuffering (Ex. 34:6; Nu. 14:18), but there comes a time when He judges and punishes the disobedient. During this time of idolatry and rebellion against God, Ruth, Naomi, and Boaz remained faithful.

The book of Ruth is part of the Hagiographica (Holy Writings) in the Jewish Bible. The unknown author was inspired by the Holy Spirit. Jewish tradition asserts Samuel wrote the book of Ruth, but Biblical records do not list a human author. Because the Jews honored King David and his ancestors, this book was included in their scriptures.

Since the author referred to the time judges ruled, Ruth must have been written after that time. Many biblical scholars believe Ruth was penned during the time Nehemiah lived, circa 445 BC, while others believe it must have been composed much earlier. David is listed in the genealogy at the end of chapter 4, so it could not have been written before David's birth (circa 1011 BC). Solomon, David's son and successor (circa 971-931 BC) was not included in this family tree, so the book probably was not written after David's death. (Exact years for the reigns of David and Solomon are not known. Estimates differ.) Also, the story of Ruth may have been repeated orally for many years before it was written down. Therefore, it is impossible to accurately determine the date it was written. Estimates range from 1,000 BC to 600 BC.

Israel's rainfall was unreliable, so droughts and the famines that followed were common. Wind patterns could bring drought to one area while bringing adequate rain to lands nearby. Grapes and olives were the main food crops in northern Israel, while wheat and barley grew in Judah. The events recorded in this story took place over a period of approximately 11 or 12 years in pre-monarchic Israel (when judges ruled the land before the reign of monarchs or kings), circa 1200-1025 BC. Scholars suggest Ruth may have lived during the time Jair (Yair) was judge (circa. 1126-1105 BC), or during the time of Ehud (the judge who fought the Moabites) or Shamgar (the judge who led the Israelites against the Philistines). It is possible the events occurred during the time Gideon defeated the Midianites with 300 men because that was the only time a famine was recorded during the leadership of the judges. Since the rules of these fifteen judges frequently overlapped, precise dates are unknown.
2

2    Clarke, A., Barnes, A., Benson, J., Exell, J. S., Coffman, J. B., Gill, J., Beza, T., Pett, P., Ellicott, C., Whedon, D., Poole, M., Wesley, J., ... Torrey, R. A. (2017). Verse-by Verse Bible Commentary Ruth1:1. Retrieved January 11, 2017, from https://www.studylight.org/commentary/ruth/1-1. html

The author obviously lived after these events took place and was able to look back on the past. He could see God's influence in everything that happened, even though it was probably not understood at the time. God used hardships as well as blessings to further His plan of redemption for Jews as well as Gentiles.

We are saved through faith, not by our ancestry. God's plan of redemption is for everyone. Salvation is based on obedience and faith, not wealth, education, family, or ethnicity. People of all ages, races, social classes, and nations will be a part of God's eternal kingdom (Rev. 5:9, 7:9).

In English language Bibles, the Septuagint, and the Vulgate, Ruth is the eighth book of the Old Testament, located after Judges in the historical books. In the Jewish Bible, it is part of the Writings and not part of the Deuteronomistic History (a single literary work or group of writings that is believed to have served as source material for Deuteronomy, Joshua, Judges, Samuel, and Kings).

After Joshua's death, there was constant warfare for more than three hundred years. The Jewish people did not have one solitary, strong leader. There was no central government or religious leadership. The twelve tribes had a weak alliance.

According to the book of Judges, this was a chaotic era when people did as they pleased (Jdg. 21:25). Political upheaval was rampant. God's Law and Covenant existed, but people chose to ignore them. Israel behaved like its pagan neighbors rather than as God's chosen people. Instead of obeying God, most people did as they saw fit. There was no human king over Judah because God was their king, but the people disobeyed Him. This was a time of apostasy (defection, rejecting their religious beliefs, often accepting opposing beliefs or ideas). God sent enemies against rebellious Israel. When they asked God for help, He set up judges to lead them. God was always in control.

God blessed those who followed His commandments (Dt. 28:1-14) and punished those who rebelled (Dt. 28:15-25). God wanted His people to obey Him and change their behavior. His warning in the book of Leviticus (Lev. 26:14-22) convinced many people the famine was a punishment sent by God to discipline the disobedient Hebrews who ignored His commands.

Ancient Israel was a farming society. When crops failed, both people and animals faced starvation. Many became sick and died. Numerous famines and prophecies of famines were recorded throughout the Old Testament (Ge. 12:10, 26:1, 41:54-57; Dt. 34:24; 2 Sa. 21:1; Jdg. 6:4-6; 1 Ch. 21:12; 1 Ki. 18:2; 2 Ki. 4:38, 6:25, 25:3; Ps. 105:16; Isa. 51:19; Hag. 1:10-11; Ne. 5:3, and many more). The cause of this particular famine is not known.

Bethlehem in Judah was in both a spiritual and a moral decline. When people ignored God's commands, curses fell upon them. He sent a famine as punishment for their defiance. Drought, hailstorms, excessive rain, floods, insects, plant diseases, and even crop damage by aggressive armies could cause food shortages and lead to starvation. A terrible famine in Judah forced Elimelek, his wife, Naomi, and their sons, Mahlon and Kilion, to leave Bethlehem and travel to Moab to seek food. (Some scholars believe Kilion and Mahlon may be the same men referred to as Joash and Seraph in 1 Chronicles 4:22, but this cannot be verified. Those men also lived in Moab.) God's people exhibited both spiritual and moral famine when they put their faith in man, not in God.

Elimelek thought he knew better than God and did what he believed was in the best interest of his family. He took his family out of a Godfearing town where Jehovah was honored into a pagan land where false gods were worshipped. To look for food and economic opportunity, they went to a territory that was outside God's covenant. God's intention was not to cause Naomi and her family to suffer. Rather, He wanted them to live in the Promised Land with Him and His people. **"'For I know the plans I have for you,' declares the LORD, 'plans to prosper you and not to harm you, plans to give you hope and a future'"** (Jer. 29:11). God's grace and love are more powerful than our disobedience.

God promised to bless and provide for His people. **"Look down from heaven, Your holy dwelling place, and bless Your people Israel and the land You have given us as You promised on oath to our ancestors, a land flowing with milk and honey"** (Dt. 26:15).

As many Israelites did during the time of the judges, Naomi's family did what they thought was right in their own eyes. They chose to leave Bethlehem rather than endure God's punishment. Running away made their lives worse, not better. God expects His people to adhere to certain principles of behavior. Yahweh is always in control, but Elimelek's family wanted a human solution rather than a godly solution to their problems. Notice, Boaz did not leave Bethlehem. He faced the same famine everyone else did, but God caused him to prosper.

The family went their own way and did as they pleased. Did Elimelek believe God would keep His promises? Centuries before, Adam and Eve defied God by eating from the tree of the knowledge of good and evil. Their disobedience brought sin into the world. God punished the couple by banishing them from the Garden of Eden (Ge. 2-3). He punished the disobedient Israelites during the time of judges. Sin brings suffering.

**"For the wages of sin is death, but the gift of God is eternal life in** [or through] **Christ Jesus our Lord"** (Ro. 6:23).

Their journey away from God's land (Israel) and His people was not necessary. Obviously, the people of Bethlehem did not starve to death. Elimelek's family, however, did experience death and grief. They did not repent of their sins and blamed God for everything that went wrong. They believed He was omnipotent (all-powerful), but they did not recognize His love, forgiveness, grace, and mercy. When God gave Moses the Ten Commandments, He declared, **"…The LORD, the LORD, the compassionate and gracious God, slow to anger, abounding in love and faithfulness, maintaining love to thousands, and forgiving wickedness, rebellion and sin"** (Ex. 34:6-7a).

There are other examples of God's elect traveling to other nations for food or refuge. For example, in times of famine, God commanded Abraham to go to Egypt (Ge. 12:10), Isaac to go to Gerar (Ge. 26:1), and Jacob and his family to go to Egypt (Ge. 46:3-4). When Saul tried to murder him, David took his mother and father to Moab to protect them while he waited for God to tell him what to do. Later, Gad the prophet instructed him to go to Judah (1 Sa. 22:3-5). David obeyed. At God's command, Joseph took Jesus and Mary to Egypt to escape the homicidal Herod's order for his soldiers to murder male Jewish babies (Mt. 2:1315). As head of the family, Elimelek was responsible for four people. Perhaps he believed the move to Moab was the only way he could provide for his family. There is one major difference between Elimelek and the men listed above. The men followed God's orders, while Elimelek ignored God and did what he thought was best.

This book describes how problems and obstacles affected an average Hebrew family. Prior to the famine, they had been prosperous and respected, but they disobeyed God and suffered greatly as a result.

Elimelek and his two sons died, leaving three widows behind. Naomi had to bury her beloved Israelite husband and sons in Moab, a cursed foreign land. The three men were dead, and their widows were faced with abject poverty and hopelessness. Naomi saw widowhood as a curse. However, her grief was part of God's divine plan, which sometimes included suffering. (If it didn't, no one would ever suffer.) God allowed Naomi to suffer so that His blueprint for salvation could be fulfilled through her.

C. S. Lewis said, "God whispers to us in our pleasures, speaks in our conscience, but shouts in our pain; it is His megaphone to rouse a deaf world."[3]

Sometimes the pain of one person brings another to God. He does not leave us on our own or give us what we deserve then desert us. Affliction can humble and break us so that we will return to God. He sometimes uses disasters to get our attention. When Naomi lost her beloved husband and sons, God blessed her with a devoted daughter-in-law, and in His time, a redeemer, and a grandson. Through Ruth's descendant, Jesus Christ, God redeemed the world (Jn. 3:16).

Like Abraham, Ruth was a godly person who demonstrated great faith. In obedience to the will of God, she left her home and her family and went to a strange, foreign land. Both Ruth and Abraham trusted God to bless and look after them. God told Abraham that he would bring a great nation into being, and through him, all people would be blessed (Ge. 12:1-3). For 25 years after this promise, Abraham and Sarah remained childless. Even after Abraham sinned with Hagar and fathered a son, Ishmael, God blessed him and Sarah with Isaac, the covenantal son of promise. Despite his unfaithfulness, God fulfilled His covenant with Abraham.

---

3     Lewis, C. S. "God's Megaphone by C.S. Lewis." Tolle Lege. 28 July 2010. Web. 14 Feb. 2017. <https://tollelege.wordpress.com/2010/07/28/gods-megaphone-by-cs-lewis/>. C. S. Lewis, The Problem of Pain (New York: HarperCollins, 1940/1996), 91.

In the ancient world, widows had little importance, respect, or security. A woman's importance and well-being depended on her family. Employment outside the home was practically nonexistent. Her value lay in raising children, tending to her home, and caring for her husband. Sons were more highly valued than daughters, and adult sons would care for their widowed mothers. A childless widow past the age of bearing children was of little value. God lovingly provided for widows through the Mosaic Law. A childless widow faced many hardships. Remarriage to a stable husband offered security. Orpah and Ruth were of childbearing age, so they would have been deemed valuable. Naomi, however, was too old to have another child, so she was of little value and her future looked hopeless. Older widows faced a life of poverty.

Loyalty, love, honor, generosity, and redemption are major themes in this book. Ruth was a virtuous, honorable, hard-working young woman. She was loving and loyal to her mother-in-law, Naomi. Because of this, she earned Boaz's admiration and love (Ru. 2:12). Boaz obeyed God's law and fulfilled his responsibility as the family's kinsman-redeemer. He was very kind to both Ruth and Naomi (Ru. 2:20). Throughout this book, the author demonstrated God was faithful and He loved His covenant people (Ru. 4:14). Because of their faithfulness, God blessed Ruth and Boaz with a son, Obed. As their kinsman-redeemer, Boaz saved both Ruth and Naomi from starvation and the misery faced by poor widows in ancient times. God blessed His people during a time of suffering. What appeared to be good luck or coincidences in Ruth's life was really part of God's plan to save the world. He preordained events from the famine that led Naomi's family to Moab, and in time, to the birth of our Savior, Jesus Christ.

The Hebrew word *hesed* (also spelled *khesed, chesed, checed*) is used 248 times in the Bible, three of which are in the book of Ruth (Ru. 1:8, 2:20, and 3:10). *Hesed* is often translated as kindness or loving-kindness, but also includes the concepts of mercy, grace, covenantal love, devotion, benevolence, commitment, goodness, and sacrifice. *Hesed* is a stubborn love that will not give up in the face of adversity. *Hesed* love expects nothing in return and is not given out of obligation or to obtain some reward. God's unfailing love and unmerited kindness is *hesed*.

There are many examples of *hesed* in this book. Ruth refused to desert Naomi and return to her own people (chapter 1). She worked hard in the fields to provide for her mother-in-law and returned to her every evening rather than socialize with people her own age (chapters 2 and 3). Boaz showed love and compassion for both Ruth and Naomi that was far beyond what was required by law or custom (chapters 2, 3, and 4).

Ruth had been married to Mahlon for ten years but remained childless. In God's time, Ruth married Boaz and became the ancestor of King David and Jesus Christ. Through her, we are all blessed. Both Jews and Gentiles are in Jesus' family tree.

Sometimes God allows disasters to affect His chosen people in order to bring about a greater good. Joni Eareckson Tada was an active, athletic teenager in 1967, until she was tragically paralyzed in a diving accident. Her life seemed to have been totally destroyed, but from quadriplegia, God raised up a mighty warrior who has truly touched the world. Joni, an evangelical Christian, has hosted TV and radio programs, spoken before multitudes, and written more than fifty inspirational books that have been translated into several foreign languages. She founded "Joni and Friends," an organization devoted to helping the disabled. Her family retreats serve thousands of special needs families. As of 2019, another ministry, "Wheels for the World," has provided over 160,000 wheelchairs for the disabled in disadvantaged areas. This faithful woman quotes the Apostle Paul's words to the Romans, **"And we know that in all things God works for the good of those who love Him, who have been called according to His purpose"** (Ro. 8:28). In her weakness, Joni is strong in the Lord. A woman who has no use of her own hands or feet truly serves as Jesus' hands and feet on earth. Through her global organization, Joni ministers to thousands of disabled people and those who love and care for them. [4]

---

4    "Joni Eareckson Tada Story." Life Story Foundation. True inspirational stories of faith and life, 2017. Web. 13 Mar. 2017. <http://www.joniearecksontadastory.com/>.

# RUTH CHAPTER 1

WHO IS THE GOD OF ISRAEL? "IN THE BEGINNING God created the heavens and the earth" (Ge. 1:1). "The eternal God is your refuge, and underneath are the everlasting arms" (Dt. 33:27a). God is omnipresent (always present). We can always trust Him and depend on Him. He has no beginning and no end. He is our creator and our guide. Nothing was, or is, created without Him. He needs nothing, but we depend on Him for everything. Society may change, but God never changes. He is sovereign, and He controls the universe. Our money, education, social standing, and even our thoughts or feelings cannot save us. He will be our refuge if we turn to Him and acknowledge He is Lord of all. God is always on His throne in Heaven.

From the burning bush, God said to Moses, **"I AM WHO I AM. This is what you are to say to the Israelites: 'I AM has sent me to you... The LORD, the God of your fathers—the God of Abraham, the God of Isaac, and the God of Jacob—has sent me to you.' This is My name forever, the name you shall call Me from generation to generation"** (Ex. 3:14-15). God is eternal (unending, everlasting). The God of ancient Israel is the same God we worship and serve today.

People may choose to allow outside influences to lead them astray. They may run away from their problems to protect themselves or their families rather than depend on God. Elimelek and his family chose to move to Moab because they did not trust God to provide for them. God sometimes allows misfortunes so His people will turn back to Him.

According to Rev. Mike Moreau (Pastor, Central Presbyterian Church, Kingston, SC), leaving the Promised Land was contrary to God's will of precept (dealing with right and wrong), but not His will of decree (what He ordains to take place, part of His sovereign plan).

## RUTH 1:1-5

**1 In the days when the judges ruled** [or judged]**, there was a famine in the land. So a man from Bethlehem in Judah, together with his wife and two sons, went to live for a while in the country of Moab. 2 The man's name was Elimelek, his wife's name was Naomi, and the names of his two sons were Mahlon and Kilion. They were Ephrathites from Bethlehem, Judah. And they went to Moab and lived there.**

**3 Now Elimelek, Naomi's husband, died, and she was left with her two sons. 4 They married Moabite women, one named Orpah and the other Ruth. After they had lived there about ten years, 5 both Mahlon and Kilion also died, and Naomi was left without her two sons and her husband.**

The world in which Elimelek and his family lived was falling apart. Moral guidelines had eroded. Views of good and evil had changed, and sinful behavior was tolerated. Many no longer trusted in God's sovereignty. The time of the judges was a period of sinfulness, apostasy (abandoning one's faith), moral decay, social turmoil, lack of self-control, and false religions (Jdg. 17:6). A faithful remnant remained loyal to Yahweh, and He remained loyal and loving to His people.

Sometimes His faithful people suffered pain and hardships in their lives. This does not mean God deserted His people or no longer loved them. God always knows what is best. His ways are not our ways. In His own good time, according to His divine plan, He will work everything out for the good of those who love Him (Ro. 8:28).

In Biblical times, famines were common. As a result, many agricultural and fertility deities such as Asherah, Baal, or Anat were worshipped in the Levant, a region west of the Mediterranean Sea. (Today, Jordan, Israel, Lebanon, Syria, and Palestine make up the Levant.)[5] The extent of the famine documented in the book of Ruth is not known, but it is apparent many people faced starvation.

Naomi and her family were from Bethlehem-Judah, a town about five miles south of Jerusalem. (Bethlehem means "house of bread," and Judah means "praise.") Bethlehem grew barley, wheat, grapes, and almonds. Normally a diversification of crops would ensure a town's survival during times of agricultural shortages, but evidently that was not the case during this famine.

The author stated (in verse 2) they were Ephrathites from Bethlehem. This means they were people from the area of Ephrath (also spelled Ephratah or Ephrathah), the ancient name of Bethlehem (Ge. 35:16). The word *Ephrathite* could refer to any resident of Bethlehem, but sometimes was used to signify a person was a member of an old, established family rather than a newcomer.

The prophet Micah prophesied the Messiah would be born in Bethlehem Ephrath (Mic. 5:2). The use of the two-word name was to distinguish the city of David from another town with a similar name, Bethlehem in Zebulun. David's father was referred to as an Ephrathite named Jesse (1 Sa. 17:12), and Jesse of Bethlehem (1 Sa. 16:1).

Moab was a land located east of the Jordan River and the Dead Sea with an average yearly rainfall of approximately sixteen inches. Moab often escaped famines that affected its neighbors. Rather than risk starvation in Bethlehem, the family went to Moab searching for food. (The exact location in which they settled was not revealed. If they had lived in a city, they would have been forced to interact with pagans. It is possible they may have chosen to live in rural areas where they would not be defiled by the Moabites' idolatry.)

In verse one, the author stated they went to Moab "for a while." The family apparently thought this was temporary rather than a permanent move. They only planned to remain in Moab until the famine ended

---

5        "Levant." The Free Dictionary by Farlex. Collins English Dictionary – Complete and Unabridged, 12th Edition 2014 © HarperCollins Publishers, 2014. Web. 17 Jan. 2017. <http://www.thefreedictionary.com/Levant>.

and then return to their home. By verse two, the author indicated they lived there (NIV, WYC, ICB). Other translations of the Bible use terms that show more permanent residence, such as: continued there (KJ21, ASV), stayed there (AMP, ERV), settled there (CEB, CJB, NLT, MSG), or sojourned there (ESV, NASB). Their plans obviously changed. A temporary visit turned into a decade-long stay.

The Bible tells us nothing of the genealogy of either Naomi or Elimelek. We know they were devout Hebrews. Some researchers propose Elimelek may have been the brother of Salmon, prince of Judah, the husband of Rahab and father of Boaz. If that is true, Elimelek would have been Boaz's uncle.

Sin always has consequences. The sons of Elimelek and Naomi married Moabite women who were outside God's covenant. Mahlon married Ruth, while Kilion married Orpah. Scholars believe the names of the family members hold significance in the story. The name Elimelek meant "my God is king." This implied he had a strong faith in the God of Israel. Many theologians feel he should have trusted God's provision and not looked for refuge in a pagan land. Naomi's name signified "fair," "sweet," "pleasant," "sweet one," or "pleasantness of Jehovah."

However, Mahlon's name indicated "infirmity" or "sickly," and Kilion's denoted "pining," "wasting away," "frail," or "consumption." If the sons' names were accurate, they may have been continually sick. Possibly Elimelek moved his family because he believed his sons would die of starvation if they remained in Bethlehem. Chronically ill children frequently died young. Were these self-fulfilling prophecies? (For example, a child who is constantly told he or she is stupid or worthless often grows up believing and behaving as if that is correct.) Children with names indicating infirmity may live as if an early death is a foregone conclusion.

The names of the daughters-in-law are also important. Orpah meant "stiff-necked," "stubborn," "fawn," or "hind" (female deer over three years of age), while the name Ruth meant "friend," "friendship," or "beauty." (Both designations come from the Hebrew language. Their meaning in the language of Moab is unknown.)

When Elimelek died, possibly soon after the family reached Moab, Naomi became a widow. She lost her husband's support and protection.

Women at that time had few opportunities for employment. They depended on their husbands or sons for everything. Their responsibilities were in the home, not in outside occupations. A widow with no sons sometimes had to beg, or even sell herself into slavery or prostitution to avoid starvation. The rights and safeguards widows have today were unknown in the ancient world.

Yahweh loved and cared for the poor, orphans, and widows (Ps. 68:5, 146:9; Jer. 49:11). Because of His love and compassion, He gave instructions for their care and protection (Dt. 14:28-29, 24:17-20, 26:12-13).

Based on the customs of her day, Naomi likely married in her mid-teens, and may have become the mother of two sons by the age of twenty. Her sons probably married in their early twenties. At the time Naomi returned to Bethlehem, she may have been in her late forties, but it is also possible she could have been considerably older. Ruth and Orpah, her daughters-in-law, were likely in their mid to late twenties. The author does not specify how old these women were, but their ages were an important element in this story. Naomi was almost certainly not old by twenty-first century standards, but she was beyond the age of childbearing. Evidently, she was no longer able to labor in the fields, which suggests old age or disability. Orpah and Ruth, however, were young enough to become mothers, which was of great importance in ancient Israel.

Elimelek's death was recorded in verse 3, and the sons' marriages were recorded in verse 4, therefore most biblical scholars believe they were married after Elimelek died. God warned His people they would face severe punishment for disobeying Him (Lev. 26:14-46). Was Elimelek's death due to his move to Moab instead of trusting God to provide for his family? When the family moved from Bethlehem (meaning "house of bread") to Moab (meaning "waste" or "nothingness"), they were no longer in God's will. If this famine was a punishment for sin, as many believe, Elimelek should have prayed, repented, and attempted to lead his friends and family back to God. Instead, he left God's Promised Land and went to a pagan land of idols and false gods. Disaster soon followed. From terrible tragedy came generous blessings from God. If the family had not moved to Moab, Ruth would not have married Mahlon, become a member of Naomi's family, and eventually, an ancestor of Christ. Everything was all part of God's plan. The deaths of Elimelek, Mahlon, and Kilion brought Naomi and Ruth back to God's covenant land and people. The incidents in this story were not just flukes that worked out satisfactorily for Naomi and Ruth. God foreordained (determined beforehand) everything that led to the birth of His beloved Son Jesus Christ.

Loving fathers and mothers do not ignore or neglect their children. They guide and discipline them. Would concerned parents condone activities that might hurt their children or others? God does whatever is needed to cause His elect to return to Him. He will not let us run away or hide forever. He will discipline us, and if we refuse to repent and do His will, He may allow us to fail or even perish. We will reap what we sow (Gal. 6:9). There is always a price to pay for disobeying God. In the short term, sin may bring pleasure, but it eventually leads to loss, disappointment, and death (Ro. 6:21; Pr. 13:15). Elimelek's family left Bethlehem intending to save themselves, but instead, three deaths occurred.

Naomi's sons may have died from an accident, disease, constant poor health, or even murder. The Bible does not say. Many biblical scholars believe they died at approximately the same time. Some people have stated the marriages of Naomi's two sons to Moabite women were prohibited by the Law of Moses (Dt. 23:3, 7:3-4; Ezr. 9:2; Ne. 13:23), and their deaths were a consequence of their sins, but that is not accurate. That prohibition was given later. Marriages of Israelites to Moabites were not forbidden, as were marriages to Hittites, Girgashites, Amorites, Canaanites, Perizzites, Hivites, and Jebusites (Dt. 7:1-3). While marriages between Moabites and Hebrews were not actually banned, they were not condoned either. Most Israelites regarded Moabites as inferior or lower class.

When Naomi's family met Ruth, she may have been a Gentile pagan who worshipped idols. At some point, she converted to the Hebrew religion and worshipped Yahweh. As a result, a Gentile woman became a respected member of a Jewish family. Her ancestry was unimportant.

She came to faith in God and later became an ancestor of Jesus Christ. It is not known if Orpah converted to Judaism. Since she returned to her family in Moab, even if she had converted, she probably returned to pagan idol worship.

John Gill, Matthew Poole, Joseph Benson, and John Wesley all believe Ruth and Orpah may have been Jewish proselytes (converts to Judaism) at the time of their marriages, while others believe their conversions came after marriage.[6] The sons' marriages may have been tolerated since they were living in a foreign land.

Some historians believe the total time Naomi lived in Moab was ten years, but John Gill and various others believe verse four implies that they lived in Moab for ten years following the sons' marriages to Ruth and Orpah. Therefore, she may have resided in Moab for eleven or twelve years. [7]

God cautions His people, **"Do not be yoked together with unbelievers. For what do righteousness and wickedness have in common? Or what fellowship can light have with darkness?"** (2 Co. 6:14). This quote comes from the Apostle Paul in the New Testament. However, **"All Scripture is God-breathed and is useful for teaching, rebuking, correcting and training in righteousness, so that the servant of God may be thoroughly equipped for every good work"** (2 Ti. 3:16-17). New Testament concepts can apply to Old Testament behaviors. God knows an unbelieving spouse can lure a believer away from Him and into sinful behavior. This is not a condemnation of other nationalities, races, or ethnic groups. It is an admonition to abstain from marriage with non-believers. After Mahlon's death, Ruth did not return to her pagan gods. Rather, she sought help from Almighty God.

---

6        Clarke, A., Barnes, A., Benson, J., Exell, J. S., Coffman, J. B., Gill, J., Beza, T., Pett, P., Ellicott, C., Whedon, D., Poole, M., Wesley, J., ... Torrey, R. A. (2017). Verse-by Verse Bible Commentary Ruth 1:4. Retrieved January 11, 2017, from https://www.studylight.org/commentary/ruth/1.4.html

7        Clarke, A., Barnes, A., Benson, J., Exell, J. S., Coffman, J. B., Gill, J., Beza, T., Pett, P., Ellicott, C., Whedon, D., Poole, M., Wesley, J., ... Torrey, R. A. (2017). Verse-by Verse Bible Commentary Ruth 1:4. Retrieved January 11, 2017, from https://www.studylight.org/commentary/ruth/1.4.html

Some have theorized Ruth and Orpah were sisters, or that Ruth (and perhaps Orpah) was the daughter of Eglon, king of Moab. There is no proof for either story. Naomi referred to Orpah as Ruth's sister-in-law, rather than her sister (Ru. 1:15). Furthermore, if Ruth had been a king's daughter, it is unlikely the family would have had to endure the miseries of poverty. This legend may have been invented to give Ruth a better pedigree.[8] By God's grace, Ruth and Boaz became ancestors of Jesus! No family tree could be better than that!

## RUTH 1:6-7

**6 When Naomi heard in Moab that the LORD had come to the aid of His people by providing food for them, she and her daughters-in-law prepared to return home from there. 7 With her two daughters-in-law she left the place where she had been living and set out on the road that would take them back to the land of Judah.**

The people of Bethlehem repented, and God blessed them with food. Naomi believed God had brought about the famine to punish the people of Bethlehem for their unfaithfulness (Jdg. 6:1-6). Like the Prodigal Son (Lk. 15:17), she realized she needed to go home. As a widow, she could make her own decisions. Her change of heart led to a change of location. Some historians believe this famine began during Gideon's time and ended seven years later when he defeated the Midianites (Jdg. 7).

The Midianite invaders frequently stole most of Bethlehem's crops and destroyed everything they could not haul with them (Jdg. 6:3-6). This often caused severe food shortages. Communication was very poor, so it is possible the famine may have ended months before the good news reached Moab.

---

8    Clarke, A., Barnes, A., Benson, J., Exell, J. S., Coffman, J. B., Gill, J., Beza, T., Pett, P., Ellicott, C., Whedon, D., Poole, M., Wesley, J., … Torrey, R. A. (2017). Verse-by Verse Bible Commentary Ruth 1:4. Retrieved January 11, 2017, from https://www.studylight.org/commentary/ruth/1. 4. html

## RUTH 1:8-9a

**8 Then Naomi said to her two daughters-in-law, "Go back, each of you, to your mother's home. May the L**ORD** show you kindness *(hesed)*, as you have shown kindness *(hesed)* to your dead husbands and to me. 9a May the L**ORD** grant that each of you will find rest in the home of another husband."**

Yahweh was the sacred covenant name of the God of Israel. The ancient Hebrew written language did not use vowels. Using our alphabet, this word would be written YHWH. The Hebrews considered His name to be so holy they would not say it aloud. In time, the pronunciation was forgotten. English language Bibles usually use the word LORD (all capital letters) when translating YHWH. Naomi used God's sacred name, Yahweh, to bless her daughter-in-law, Ruth, rather than using a more generic name, God (Ru. 1:8).

Naomi decided to return to Bethlehem where people worshipped Yahweh. She had stayed far too long in a land where idols and false gods were honored. In addition, her friends and family were in Bethlehem. It was time for her to go home.

Ruth and Orpah went with their beloved mother-in-law on the first part of her trek to Bethlehem. This could have been viewed as good manners. Naomi may have thought they would walk with her part of the way, turn back at Moab's border, and then rejoin their own people. The older woman sorrowfully told her cherished daughters-in-law goodbye. She planned to travel the rest of the way alone. All three cried at the thought of parting forever.

When Naomi realized both young women planned to go to Bethlehem with her, she tried to dissuade them. Moab was Israel's enemy, so Moabites would probably receive a hostile reception in Bethlehem. Naomi had been a stranger in a foreign land, so she understood the hardships her daughters-in-law would face in Israel. It would be nearly impossible for two alien women to find husbands. Most devout Hebrew men would not want to marry poverty-stricken Moabite widows when proper Jewish ladies were available. Her much-loved daughters-in-law would likely be outcasts and remain single. Naomi believed it would be best for them to return to their homeland, marry Moabite husbands, and have Moabite babies.

She told Ruth and Orpah to return to their mother's house. (Naomi's instruction did not imply their fathers had died or deserted their families. Men and women frequently lived in separate residences. Daughters lived with their mothers.) This was her way of releasing them to remarry. Her advice made perfect sense in human terms.

Naomi did not pray for herself. Instead, she asked God to bless the two young widows. She believed God loves all races, ethnicities, and social classes, and that God's kingdom was not limited to Jews. All believers were grafted into the family of God. Asking for His blessings on Ruth and Orpah was evidence of her faith. **"Finding rest in the house of another husband"** (Ru. 1:9a) was a euphemism asking God to bless them with devoted husbands who would keep them safe and provide for their needs. In ancient Israel, women could only expect peace and security if they were married. This blessing for Ruth and Orpah meant they were no longer obliged to look after her. The older woman was more interested in their well-being than she was in her own. She had lost her husband and two beloved sons, but she was willing to send her daughters-in-law back to their parents so they could live safer and more stable lives. Naomi had lived for at least a decade in Moab, a pagan land, but her faith in God could still be seen.

## RUTH 1:9b-13

**9b Then she kissed them goodbye and they wept aloud 10 and said to her, "We will go back with you to your people." 11 But Naomi said, "Return home, my daughters. Why would you come with me? Am I going to have any more sons, who could become your husbands? 12 Return home, my daughters; I am too old to have another husband. Even if I thought there was still hope for me—even if I had a husband tonight and then gave birth to sons— 13 would you wait until they grew up? Would you remain unmarried for them? No, my daughters. It is more bitter for me than for you, because the LORD's hand has turned against me!"**

Believing she might never see either Ruth or Orpah again, Naomi sadly kissed them goodbye. Notice the love Naomi demonstrated for

Ruth and Orpah. They were her daughters-in-law, but she called them her daughters. They were not merely the widows of her deceased sons. She claimed them as her own children. It was also obvious both young women loved Naomi and wanted to go with her.

Naomi demonstrated selfless love for Ruth and Orpah. She believed God was against her, so she faced an uncertain future. As a destitute, childless widow, all she could offer them was her love, and love could not pay for shelter or food. Naomi was unable to provide them with more sons to marry, so she instructed them to go back to their own people and gods where they would have a better life and find appropriate husbands.

God was concerned with the welfare of the poor and lonely. Thanks to His provision, widows in Israel did have one advantage the widows in many other areas did not. Three thousand years ago, levirate marriages were the customary way to keep families from dying out. These marriages protected childless widows and could produce children to carry on the family name. (The Latin word *'levir'* means brother-in-law.) Hebrew widows were barred from marrying outsiders. They had to marry close relatives of their deceased husbands. Naomi never mentioned such a possibility, so Elimelek must not have had additional sons (with another wife) or a brother who could fulfill his family duty to his nephews' widows. (Levirate marriage is only mentioned two other times in the Bible: Ge. 38 and Dt. 25:5-10.)

Naomi could not provide for herself, much less for her sons' widows. Since they were young, it was very important for them to remarry and hopefully have children. This was a matter of security rather than romance. If a widow had no children from her first marriage, the brother of the deceased husband was required to marry his widow and raise children in his name. In verse 12, Naomi stated that she was **"too old to have another husband."** Second marriages for women beyond the age of childbearing were uncommon. Naomi had no other sons for Orpah and Ruth to marry, and she was too old to have more children. If she could have given birth to more sons, her daughters-in-law would certainly not want to wait until those sons were old enough to marry them! By that time, the young women would also have been too old to have children. God could provide what Naomi could not.

In verse 13, Naomi informed them, **"…the Lord's hand has turned against me!"** She believed God was punishing her, and if they stayed with her, they would suffer as well. Believing they had no hope to remarry or have children in Bethlehem, she lovingly instructed them to leave her. God had other plans. He would provide a righteous man to marry Ruth and preserve Elimelek's family line.

In ancient times, it was very important for a woman to have a husband and children. Naomi had neither. She faced a life of loneliness and poverty. When she left Bethlehem, she had been a happily married woman with two sons, but when she returned, she was a destitute, childless widow filled with despair. She seemed unable or unwilling to acknowledge any grief or pain other than her own. Orpah and Ruth had not lost children as she had, but they had lost their husbands and faced the same hardships she did.

**"The Lord's hand"** (verse 13) was a familiar idiom for God's deeds. Naomi assumed God had deserted her. The family's journey away from God had cost them everything. All her hopes and dreams were gone. Yahweh had taken her husband and both children. Ancient people wanted to be buried in their homeland, but the people she loved most were now interred in Moab, a detested pagan land.

## RUTH 1:14-18

**14 At this they wept aloud again. Then Orpah kissed her mother-in-law goodbye, but Ruth clung to her. 15 "Look," said Naomi, "your sister-in-law is going back to her people and her gods. Go back with her." 16 But Ruth replied, "Don't urge me to leave you or to turn back from you. Where you go I will go, and where you stay I will stay. Your people will be my people and your God my God. 17 Where you die I will die, and there I will be buried. May the Lord deal with me, be it ever so severely, if even death separates you and me." 18 When Naomi realized that Ruth was determined to go with her, she stopped urging her.**

Ancient cities had their own deities related to their location or geography, such as a god of the mountain or a god of the river. Moab's chief god was called Chemosh (Nu. 21:29; 1 Kings 11:7). His name meant "destroyer," "subdue," or "fish god." Archaeological evidence verifies the Moabites offered human sacrifices to this god (2 Ki. 3:26-27). The Moabites believed Chemosh would bring his obedient servants victory in battle, but if they disobeyed or displeased him, he would cause their enemies to defeat them. They also worshipped Baal of Peor (Nu. 25:35), another false god whose worship included nudity.

The ancient Moabites worshipped Chemosh and Baal of Peor rather than Yahweh as the Jews did. Naomi surely wanted her daughters-in-law to worship her God, but she apparently felt their physical security was more important than their souls. On the surface, Naomi's instruction to Ruth and Orpah to return to their gods, not just to return to their people, might sound wise and generous. However, such an act would have condemned the young women. Naomi was a devout Jew. She knew Chemosh and Baal were false gods who could offer nothing but eternal damnation. She was surely familiar with God's command, **"I am the LORD your God, who brought you out of Egypt, out of the land of slavery. You shall have no other gods before** [or besides] **Me. You shall not make for yourself an image in the form of anything in Heaven above or on the earth beneath or in the waters below. You shall not bow down to them or worship them; for I, the LORD your God, am a jealous God, punishing the children for the sin of the parents to the third and fourth generation of those who hate Me, but showing love to a thousand generations of those who love Me and keep My commandments.** (Ex. 20:2-6). God further said, **"Do not bow down before their gods or worship them or follow their practices. You must demolish them and break their sacred stones** [or obelisks] **to pieces"** (Ex. 23:24). At first, both Ruth and Orpah affirmed their desire to travel to Bethlehem with their mother-in-law. Remember, the three women had been family for ten years and loved each other dearly. The Biblical scholar, John Wesley, suggested Naomi's command was actually a test to prove their sincerity rather than a real effort to send them back to their homes and gods. [9]

Orpah's promise to go with her mother-in-law on a difficult journey to Bethlehem seemed genuine, but it was brief. She loved both Naomi

---

9        Clarke, A., Barnes, A., Benson, J., Exell, J. S., Coffman, J. B., Gill, J., Beza, T., Pett P., Ellicott, C., Whedon, D., Poole, M., Wesley, J., ... Torrey, R. A. (2017). Verse-by-Verse Bible Commentary Ruth1:15. Retrieved January 11, 2017, from https://www/commentary/ruth/1-15. html

and Ruth, but her pagan gods, people, and country drew her back. Motivated by love, Naomi convinced her to return to her people where she could remarry and have a good life. Orpah chose to leave her new family and return to her homeland. (During her marriage to Kilion, Orpah might have outwardly converted, but it could not have been a true conversion since she willingly returned to her pagan gods and idols.)

Orpah was not evil or selfish. Remember, her husband's name, Kilion, meant "consumption" or "wasting." She may have taken care of a sickly husband throughout her ten-year marriage. The birth of children was a necessity as well as a blessing for a married couple, but Orpah and Kilion had remained childless. Now she was a lonely widow facing a life of poverty. (Many Moabites believed their gods were real, but thought their powers were limited to Moab. Different gods ruled in other lands. They incorrectly assumed Yahweh was only powerful in Israel.) After Naomi spoke a second time, Orpah turned back. She cared for Naomi, but not enough to leave the security of Moab. She obeyed Naomi's command, but Ruth showed more love by disobeying. Orpah left Naomi to search for happiness in her own land with her own people and gods, but Ruth loved Naomi far too much to leave her. The author does not suggest either Ruth or Naomi criticized Orpah for her decision.

True love involves faithfulness. Ruth loved her impoverished mother-in-law and promised to keep the family together, no matter what it cost her personally. She willingly gave up her own family, homeland, and freedom to take care of Naomi. She rejected the pagan gods of Moab and worshiped the one true God. She was willing to live in a foreign land with unfamiliar customs even though she realized the Jews were unlikely to accept her. This was not a short-term plan she could walk away from if things became difficult. She made a binding promise to Naomi in the name of God.

Just as God's love is selfless and sacrificial (Jn. 15:13), Naomi and Ruth's profound love for each other was unselfish and self-sacrificing. Naomi was willing to face the unknown alone rather than keep Ruth from having a happy, secure life. Ruth would not desert Naomi, which sounded foolish by worldly standards. Naomi could not offer her anything: no husband, no house, and no food. Starvation was always a possibility. Ruth loved Naomi and wanted to live with her, surrounded by God's people. Even though she was willing to leave Moab behind, she did not expect a happy life in Bethlehem. She was willing to go to a land where men had all the power and poor childless widows had few rights or choices. She made an oath (vow, pledge) to bind herself to Naomi and invoked God's judgment upon herself if she ever deserted her. She even refused to leave her mother-in-law when the older woman died (Ru. 1:17).

Ruth's conversion to faith in Yahweh took tremendous courage. She deserted the Moabite gods Chemosh and Baal of Peor to serve the true God. In Ruth's day, when people made promises or oaths, they usually swore by the name of their god or gods. Ruth made her oath in the name of Yahweh, the God of Israel, not in the name of Chemosh or any other pagan god. Surely Ruth's conversion to faith in Yahweh brought Naomi great joy and reassurance. She could be certain her beloved daughter-in-law's soul was secure.

Many years after the events in this story took place, James, the half-brother of Jesus said, **"But someone will say, 'You have faith; I have deeds.' Show me your faith without deeds, and I will show you my faith by my deeds"** (Jas 2:18). James' words applied to Ruth, just as they pertain to believers today.

In verses 16 and 17, Ruth spoke in covenantal, biblical language (words that were used in scripture). Ruth's choice of words, common at that time, made the Lord a witness to her pledge (1 Sa. 14:44; 1 Ki. 19:2, 20:10; 2 Ki. 6:31). Evidently Ruth received religious instruction. The pagan Moabite may have been brought to saving faith and learned covenantal vocabulary from her late husband or her devoted mother-in-law. Did Naomi tell Ruth that God had delivered the Israelites from the Egyptians and led them across the Red Sea and through the desert? Did Mahlon explain sacrifices and worship? We will never know, but someone taught Ruth about God, as commanded in Deuteronomy 11:18-19.

Love and affection for another human being, no matter how wonderful he or she may be, is not enough to draw a person to faith in God. Surely Naomi shared her faith in Yahweh with Ruth, but only the Holy Spirit could turn her away from the pagan gods of Moab to faith in the true God. Ruth willingly abandoned her pagan ways and swore her loyalty to Naomi, her people, and her God.

There is no way of knowing which scriptures Naomi or Mahlon may have shared with Ruth. The following verses could have been used to instruct the young woman and lead her to faith in Yahweh.

**"I will take you as My own people, and I will be your God. Then you will know that I am the LORD your God, who brought you out from under the yoke of the Egyptians"** (Ex. 6:7).

**"I will walk among you and be your God, and you will be My People"** (Lev. 26:12).

**"Tell them that this is what the LORD, the God of Israel, says: 'Cursed is the one who does not obey the terms of this covenant— the terms I commanded your ancestors when I brought them out of Egypt, out of the iron-smelting furnace ... Obey Me and do everything I command you, and you will be My people, and I will be your God'"** (Jer. 11:3-4).

**"So you will be My people, and I will be your God"** (Jer. 30:22).

**"Then you will live in the land I gave your ancestors; you will be My people, and I will be your God"** (Eze. 36:28).

Truly, God is involved in the lives of His people. **"The righteous person may have many troubles, but the LORD delivers him from them all"** (Ps. 34:19). Scripture does not promise believers will have trouble-free lives. However, He is faithful and will be with us every step of the way. He can turn tears into joy and tragedies into blessings.

The book of Ruth is one of the most well-known examples of faithfulness and devotion found anywhere in either religious or secular literature. Ruth kept her promise to Naomi, which brought many blessings to both women.

Love changed Ruth's life. Since she had married Naomi's son, she had become familiar with the customs and religion of the Hebrews. Even though the Bible does not specifically say she converted to Judaism, scripture tells us that Ruth declared, **"...Your people will be my people and your God my God"** (Ru. 1:16). Ruth's promise to Naomi was actually a covenant with God. She claimed both Israel and Israel's God. Clearly Ruth did convert.

In verse 17, Ruth stated, **"Where you die I will die, and there I will be buried..."** Ruth wanted to be buried in the same place as

Naomi. There are two theories for this statement. First, Ruth could have meant she wished to be buried beside Naomi in the family plot, which is common today. Second, she may have wanted to be buried in the same grave or tomb as the older woman, which was not unusual in those days. Spouses, siblings, or even close friends were sometimes buried together (2 Sa. 19:37) because they hoped to rise together on Judgment Day.

Finally, Ruth said, **"May the LORD deal with me, be it ever so severely, if even death separates you and me"** (Ru. 1:17). In Old Testament times, when people took oaths, they often called down curses upon themselves if they broke their promises. Ruth pledged her oath in the name of the Lord. She invoked a formal curse upon herself if she broke her word to Naomi. The loyal young woman would not change her mind. Nor would she desert her mother-in-law or her God. Naomi saw how sincere Ruth was and ceased trying to discourage her.

The author did not report Naomi expressed any affection or appreciation following Ruth's loving, selfless declaration. He merely stated Naomi **"stopped urging her"** (Ru. 1:18). Was it possible the older woman was so bitter and grief-stricken she could not understand Ruth's desire to go with her to Bethlehem?

## RUTH 1-19-21

**19 So the two women went on until they came to Bethlehem. When they arrived in Bethlehem, the whole town was stirred because of them, and the women exclaimed, "Can this be Naomi?"**

**20 "Don't call me Naomi** [which means pleasant]**," she told them. "Call me Mara** [which means bitter], **because the Almighty** [Hebrew Shaddai] **has made my life very bitter. 21 I went away full, but the LORD has brought me back empty. Why call me Naomi? The LORD has afflicted** [or has testified against] **me; the Almighty has brought misfortune upon me."**

Ruth willingly accompanied Naomi to Bethlehem, even though she understood such an act could hurt her chance to find a good husband and the security marriage offered. Their journey was about 50 to 75 miles. (The exact route is unknown.) First, they went downhill 4,500 feet from Moab to the Jordan Valley. After crossing the river, they had to climb uphill 3,750 feet through the Judean hills before reaching Bethlehem. This would have been a tiring trek for Ruth, but it was far more difficult for the older Naomi. Their journey may have taken from seven to fourteen days. The younger woman could probably have made the trip in less time, but considering the stamina of the elder woman, she may have walked more slowly and taken frequent rests.

The residents were shocked to see Naomi when the two women arrived in Bethlehem. It is unlikely she had traveled to her hometown during her decade in Moab. Her friends and family may not have been informed of the deaths of her husband and sons. They may not have known if Naomi was still alive. Long ago, when people moved from one area to another, they were often never seen or heard from again.

When Naomi's family left, the residents of Bethlehem may have only numbered a few hundred. The population could have decreased through starvation or emigration (leaving one's own country to settle in another) due to the famine.

Before the famine, Naomi was a contented woman with a good husband and two much loved sons. Within a few years, she experienced hardships (the famine and living in a pagan land), bereavement (the loss of her husband and sons), and desertion (Orpah left and returned to her people). She believed God had turned against her and no longer cared about her or her family.

When she returned more than a decade later, she was a destitute, childless, and sorrowful widow. Her grief and poverty affected her attitude. She still believed in God, but she was no longer hopeful. God had humbled her. She was overwhelmed and thought her name no longer fit. Her joyful life was now empty. Her husband and sons were dead, and her hopes and dreams were gone. She thought the God she had deserted when she left Bethlehem had now deserted her. She blamed Him for all her problems.

Based on the reactions of the Bethlehemites, Naomi and Elimelek must have been well known and respected. The women asked, **"Can this be Naomi?"** (Verse 19). Had she changed so much she was unrecognizable? (The men may have been working in the fields so were not involved in the conversation.) They were not sure if this poor woman could actually be Naomi. Both women must have been tired and dirty. Their clothes may have been torn. Frequently people who have experienced grief or suffering develop wrinkles or white hair and appear much older than their chronological age.

Naomi did not say God was evil or unfair, just that He had treated her harshly. She understood God was a powerful king, but she no longer acknowledged He was either loving or merciful. Her husband and children had died, and her daughter-in-law, Orpah, had left her. (Ruth, her devoted daughter-in-law, gave up everything to be with her. Had she forgotten? If Naomi praised her in any way, the author did not report it.)

Naomi did not know how she would survive. She blamed God for her terrible situation. Grief controlled her life, and she became self-absorbed. Naomi means "pleasant" or "cheerful." She felt her name was no longer accurate and asked to be called Mara (bitter), but there is no evidence this was done. Mara (Marah) was the bitter water the Israelites encountered in the desert (Ex. 15:23). In verses 20-21, she told the women to call her Mara **"because the Almighty has made my life very bitter. I went away full, but the LORD has brought me back empty. Why call me Naomi? The LORD has afflicted** (testified against, a term frequently used when a person witnessed in court) **me; the Almighty has brought misfortune upon me."**

Notice, she used the name "the Almighty" as well as "the LORD." "Almighty" showed she believed He ruled the world (Ge. 17:1, 28:3, 35:11), and "LORD" is His covenant name (Ex. 5:2, 7:17, 10:2, etc.). The Almighty caused her hardships in Moab, but the LORD testified against her. Because she and her family had left His covenant land, they had suffered. She believed God no longer cared about her. When faced with great hardships, people sometimes run away, blame others, or blame God. Naomi tried to escape from her problems (Ru. 1:1-5). Then she blamed God for her suffering (Ru. 1:19-22).

Despite what she thought, Naomi was really not empty. God never ignores or deserts His people. He used Ruth to bring her both security and joy. Her loving daughter-in-law promised never to leave her.

Naomi knew life in Bethlehem would be tough, but at least starvation was no longer a threat. When she left her hometown, there was famine. When she returned, there was plenty of food from an abundant barley harvest, but she felt empty due to the loss of her husband and sons. It is easy to understand why she wanted to change her name.

Pastor Daniel Henderson suggests there are two possible meanings for Naomi's comment. First, she left with her husband and sons (full), but she came home without them (empty). She was now filled with grief, sorrow, and desperation. Second, when Naomi and her family left Bethlehem to travel to Moab, they were full of themselves. They were determined to succeed on their own terms, not God's. Now she was coming home as the prodigal daughter, empty, broken, humble, and repentant. God had emptied her of everything but her need for Him.[10]

## RUTH 1:22

**22 So Naomi returned from Moab accompanied by Ruth the Moabite, her daughter-in-law, arriving in Bethlehem as the barley harvest was beginning.**

After the rains during October and November, ancient farmers plowed their fields and planted the grain. Their crops grew during both the winter rains and spring rains. Wheat and barley were usually planted together, but they were not harvested at the same time. Barley matured in late March or early April. Devout Hebrews offered part of this crop to God as a first fruit (first agricultural crop) offering. God had told Moses, **"Speak to the Israelites and say to them: 'When you enter the land I am going to give you and you reap its harvest, bring to the priest a sheaf of the first grain you harvest'"** (Lev. 23:10). When the barley was ready for harvest, the people celebrated. They believed a good barley harvest meant they would have a good wheat harvest in June.

Harvesting grain required many workers. First, the grain was cut with sickles (Dt. 16:9; Joel 3:13). The stalks (stems) were then fastened into bundles or sheaves (Ps. 126:6). Poor people could then enter the fields to glean (gather or collect) anything that was left (Lev. 23:22). The

---

10      Henderson, Daniel. Sermon: "Ruth -God's Kindness on Display." Grace Presbyterian Church (PCA), Blairsville, GA, 12 July 2015.

sheaves were taken to the threshing floor. (Sometimes a roof was built over the floor to shield the grain from rain. The sides were left open to allow the wind to flow freely.) The grain was removed from the stalks. Several methods were used for this process. The stalks may be dropped on the floor where oxen (Dt. 25:4; Hos. 10:11), carts (Isa. 28:28), or other heavy objects were dragged or driven across the stems to separate the grain from the straw. Workers with winnowing forks tossed the grain into the air (Jer. 15:7). The wind blew away the seed coverings and other lightweight waste (chaff). The heavy grain fell to the floor where it was sifted to remove any debris left behind. The grain was collected into sacks for sale or storage. Grain might also be stored in silos. Finally, women ground the grain into flour using millstones.

The word "return" was used seven times in Ruth chapter 1 in the King James Version of the Bible. (Other translations differ slightly.) Returning infers repentance. Naomi returned to Bethlehem and the Hebrew people, and most importantly, she returned to her God. The God she had blamed for all her problems was once again acknowledged as her provider. As the apostle Paul told believers in Rome, **"And we know that in all things God works for the good of those who love Him, who have been called according to His purpose"** (Ro. 8:28). Even though those words were written more than a millennium after her death, they applied to Naomi just as they do to us today.

Chapter one started with the despair of a famine but ended with the optimism of a bountiful harvest. This was not simple luck. There are no coincidences in the Bible. God provided what Naomi and Ruth needed, just as He provides for us today. He used a Gentile from an enemy nation to bring blessings to Naomi, and in time, to Israel and the entire world. Our God is a compassionate and generous God.

God drew them to Israel, the land of His covenant blessing. Naomi and Ruth hiked to Bethlehem, the House of Bread, when plenty of food was available. He sent rain to the land to provide His people with an abundant harvest. The grief and spiritual famine in Naomi's life was ending as well.

God changes our thoughts and desires, and He helps us do what we cannot do by ourselves. We may not always see what He is doing, but He is always there. When Ruth promised she would stay with Naomi, she could not foresee the future. The idea of scavenging for food in a foreign land among unfamiliar people must have been frightening. Rather than fear of the unknown, Ruth was guided by her love for Naomi and her God.

God was, and is, always faithful to us, even when we are not faithful to Him. He wants us to love and obey Him. He blessed Ruth and Naomi, and in so doing, He blessed the entire world through His Son, Jesus Christ.

# RUTH CHAPTER 2

NAOMI'S LIFE WAS FILLED WITH HARDSHIPS. When faced with starvation, her family left the Promised Land to search for food in Moab, Israel's enemy. Her husband and both her sons died in that pagan land. Orpah, one of her daughters-in-law, left the older woman and returned to her family and her false gods. Naomi faced poverty and an uncertain future, but all was not lost. God was and is always in control, and Naomi and her family were an integral part of His divine plan.

Ruth, her faithful daughter-in-law, loved her dearly. She promised to remain with her mother-in-law and worship Yahweh, the God of Israel. The two widows left Moab and hiked to Bethlehem. The life of a widow in the ancient world was difficult. The life of a hated Moabite widow in Israel was even more challenging.

## RUTH 2:1

**Now Naomi had a relative on her husband's side, a man of standing from the clan of Elimelek, whose name was Boaz.**

A family or clan was a social group originating from a shared ancestor. It was responsible for both the physical and financial survival of its members during hard times.

Boaz was a prosperous, well-respected landowner and farmer. Many Bethlehemites worked for him. He was from the same clan as Elimelek, although their exact relationship was never explained. Naomi probably knew Boaz from her earlier life in Bethlehem (verse 1). Scholars do not know if Naomi tried to contact him or any of her own relatives when she returned to Israel. No communication is mentioned in scripture.

Boaz's name means "in him is strength," "lively," or "quick." The author states Boaz was a mighty man of wealth (KJ21, ASV), powerful and rich (DRA), a man of outstanding character (GW), or a man of standing (NIV). He was surely a godly man who was honest, kind, and generous. He prayed for his workers and treated them fairly. As a result, they admired and respected him. He treated everyone with respect, even those who were often scorned by others, such as strangers, widows, and the destitute. God often uses honorable men and women to be his hands and feet on earth. While many Israelites ignored God, Boaz always tried to do His will. He displayed great thoughtfulness to Ruth and Naomi, as well as to his laborers.

When Elimelek's family fled to Moab to escape starvation from the famine, Boaz remained in the Promised Land. Elimelek and his two sons suffered and died, while Boaz prospered. When Ruth met him, he owned property in Bethlehem and employed many workers.

Some theologians theorize Boaz and Ibzan, one of the judges of Israel, could have been the same man. Ibzan led Israel for seven years and had thirty sons and thirty daughters (Jdg. 12:8-9). There is no Biblical verification for this hypothesis.

By tradition, Boaz is said to be the nephew of Elimelek, but this is not scripturally verified. He had a somewhat disreputable bloodline. His mother, Rahab, had been a Canaanite prostitute (Jos. 6:17) before her marriage to Salmon. (According to Father David Neuhaus, Rahab's name meant "wide as a road." He suggests this may have been a crude reference to her profession.[11]

This theory seems unlikely. What parents would name their baby such an unsavory name? Carl Hagensick states her name meant "pride,"

---

11      Neuhaus, David M., SJ. "Jesus: Who Do You Think You Are?" *Thinking Faith*. Web. 13 Feb. 2017. <http://www.thinkingfaith.org/articles/ jesus-who-do-you-think-you-are-2-rahab-ruth-and-boaz>.

which might have been more reasonable in a pagan society.)[12] There is no biblical record of this marriage. Possibly because of her sinful reputation, Matthew was the only biblical author to record Rahab was Boaz's mother, and therefore, Ruth's mother-in-law (Mt. 1:5).

Jericho was a wicked city, so God ordered Joshua to destroy the city and kill all its inhabitants. **"But you must destroy it and everything in it, to show that it now belongs to the LORD. The woman Rahab helped the spies we sent, so protect her and the others who are inside her house. But kill everyone else in the town"** (Jos. 6:17 CEV).

Rahab rescued two Hebrew spies sent to Jericho by Joshua (Jos. 2). In return for her help, she asked the men to spare both her life and the lives of her family. She was willing to risk her life to protect the Hebrew spies. Her courage saved both her living family (Jos. 6:23, 6:25; Heb. 11:31) and her descendants. Due to her bravery, her reputation improved (Jas. 2:25). Rahab, the prostitute from Canaan, was the first Jewish convert in the Promised Land. She was not condemned by her past. A sinful heathen became a worshipper of the true God, Yahweh.

Some scholars, both Jewish and Christian, have attempted to prove that Rahab, the mother of Boaz, was not the same as Rahab the harlot. The idea that a prostitute could marry into a prominent family and eventually become the ancestor of the Messiah was repugnant. However, no Biblical evidence supports that theory. ["Rahab" was also a symbolic name for Egypt (Ps. 87:4, 89:10; Isa. 51:9) and should not be confused with the woman from Jericho.]

In ancient times, some prostitutes were also innkeepers. Most researchers believe Rahab was such a person (Jos. 2:1, 6:17). Many travelers visited her inn, so she could have overheard plans to attack Jericho and nearby areas. She may also have heard stories about the plagues God sent to Egypt and how He led the Israelites through the Red Sea and drowned their enemies. Later, He kept them alive by feeding them mana in the desert (Ex. 7-16). Details of these miracles convinced

---

12      Hagensick, Carl. "Faith Hanging On A Thread." The Herald of Christ's Kingdom, 03 Jan. 2003. Web. 14 Feb. 2017. <http://www.heraldmag.org/literature/bio_7.htm>.

many pagans the Israelites worshipped a very powerful God. She told the Hebrew spies, **"When we heard this, we lost heart, and everyone's courage failed because of you, for the Lord your God is God in heaven above and on earth below"** (Jos. 2:11 CSB).

Christian author and preacher Max Lucado suggests Boaz might have been a bachelor because of his mother's former profession. Most good Hebrew fathers would not have allowed their daughters to marry the son of a prostitute.[13] Pastor and author John MacArthur proposes he could have been either single (never married) or a widower.[14] Scripture is not clear. However, the Bible does verify a Gentile woman of ill repute and a Moabite proselyte to Judaism were members of Jesus' family tree. Our Lord obviously does not care about pedigree or social status and nor should we. He cares for the condition of the heart.

The names of the two Hebrew spies are unknown, but many biblical scholars think Salmon, the father of Boaz (1 Ch. 2:11; Mt. 1:5) was one of those men. He may have been the same man as Salma (1 Ch. 2:51, 2:54).

## RUTH 2:2-3

**2 And Ruth the Moabite said to Naomi, "Let me go to the fields and pick up the leftover grain behind anyone in whose eyes I find favor." Naomi said to her, "Go ahead, my daughter." 3 So she went out, entered a field and began to glean behind the harvesters. As it turned out, she was working in a field belonging to Boaz, who was from the clan of Elimelek.**

God is in control of every incident. He blessed Naomi, Ruth, and Boaz according to His plan. When the two women returned to Bethlehem, it was during the barley harvest. The famine had ended and food was plentiful. God directed Ruth to Boaz's land because he was the relative who could help them.

---

13      Lucado, Max. Books of Ruth and Esther. World Publishing, 1996. 9.
14      MacArthur, John. "Ruth." The MacArthur Study Bible (NASB). Nashville, TN: Thomas Nelson, 2013. 363.

In Ruth's day, many people lived in towns or villages for safety. Agricultural fields usually lay outside the city walls. Piles of stones were used to designate plot boundaries. Few fields were surrounded by walls or fences. Ruth may have crossed land belonging to other families before entering Boaz's field.

Ruth did not know Boaz was a kinsman of her late father-in-law. Nor did she wander into his field by coincidence. She was providentially led by God. This was all a part of His plan. Nothing was left to chance. God used Boaz to bestow His blessings on the two widows. He initiated a way for Ruth and Boaz to eventually marry and become ancestors of the Messiah.

The author did not indicate Naomi instructed Ruth to glean. The young woman took the initiative to find food for herself and her mother-in-law. The Lord provided for poor widows. Mosaic Law (Lev. 19:9, 23:22; Dt. 24:19) stated landowners must not harvest all the crops from their fields. (Harvesters cut the grain with flint sickles. They were required to leave some behind to be gathered or gleaned by the widows, the destitute, or strangers.) God used gleaning laws to provide for those who could not afford to buy food. Those blessed with plenty were to share with those in need. By God's decree, nobody would starve. God used Boaz to bring His grace to two impoverished widows.

**"When you reap the harvest of your land, do not reap to the very edges of your field or gather the gleanings of your harvest. Do not go over your vineyard a second time or pick up the grapes that have fallen. Leave them for the poor and the foreigner. I am the LORD your God"** (Lev. 19:9-10).

**"When you reap the harvest of your land, do not reap to the very edges of your field or gather the gleanings of your harvest. Leave them for the poor and for the foreigner residing among you. I am the LORD your God"** (Lev. 23:22).

**When you are harvesting in your field and you overlook a sheaf, do not go back to get it. Leave it for the foreigner, the fatherless and the widow, so that the LORD your God may bless you in all the work of your hands. When you beat the olives from your trees, do not go over the branches a second time. Leave what remains for the foreigner, the fatherless and the widow. When you harvest the grapes**

**in your vineyard, do not go over the vines again. Leave what remains for the foreigner, the fatherless and the widow. Remember that you were slaves in Egypt. That is why I command you to do this** (Dt. 24:19-22).

Gleaning was a right, not a favor given by a wealthy landlord. Mosaic Law required landowners to allow the poor to glean (to gather what the harvesters left behind) in their fields. In this way, the able-bodied poor worked to fulfil their needs rather than receive charity.

Ruth believed God would make it possible for her to glean the grain left by the harvesters. As a foreign woman, she risked being attacked by the male harvesters. Courageously, Ruth told Naomi she would **"pick up the leftover grain behind anyone in whose eyes I find favor"** (Ru. 2:2). She requested permission to glean from Boaz's manager before entering the field rather than demand her right to glean. Even though gleaning was allowed by law, some landowners or managers refused such requests. Ruth was a hard-working young woman who always submitted to her mother-in-law. She asked Naomi's consent to glean in the fields rather than announce, "I will go glean." Naomi agreed. Gleaners worked hard. They rose early and toiled all day with only brief rest periods. They usually worked until nightfall.

Ruth demonstrated her loyalty and love for Naomi with her hard work; Naomi showed her devotion to Ruth by her words. Ruth was really Naomi's daughter-in-law, but she called her daughter (Ru. 2:2).

This was a barley harvest. However, some translations refer to gleaning among the ears of corn (KJ21, BRG, DARBY, WYC, and YLT). The word corn was often used as a generic term for any type of grain. Therefore, rye, barley, oats, and wheat could all have been called corn.

## RUTH 2:4

**Just then Boaz arrived from Bethlehem and greeted the harvesters, "The LORD be with you!"**

**"The LORD bless you!" they answered.**

Boaz was a great man, not because he was rich and owned land, but because of his godly character. Led by the Holy Spirit, he brought God's blessings to both Ruth and Naomi. [Some people believe the Holy Spirit entered the world on Pentecost (Ac. 2), but this is incorrect. The Holy Spirit existed from the beginning, just as God the Father and Jesus the Son did.] God's love, grace, and provision can be seen throughout this story.

The author states Boaz **"arrived from Bethlehem"** (Ru. 2:4). Since his home was in Bethlehem, it was necessary for him to walk from town to his field to talk with his employees and check on his crops. Even though Boaz was a rich and powerful man, he cared about his workers. He did not just happen to visit the field when Ruth was gleaning. God preordained the encounter.

Boaz was a thoughtful employer and a man of God. He greeted his harvesters using the Lord's name, and they replied in the same way. Blessing one another was not unusual (Ps. 128:5-8), but this greeting was more than just a friendly hello. God was very important in this employer/ employee relationship. The greetings, "The Lord be with you" and "The Lord bless you" were common among the Hebrews. Some people have suggested they were familiar greetings without religious significance, just as people today might say, "God bless you" when a person sneezes. However, since Boaz obeyed God and always tried to do His will, it is obvious these were not just empty words. A person's relationship with God can be seen in the way he or she treats other people. Boaz depended on God, and it showed.

## RUTH 2:5-7

**5 Boaz asked the overseer of his harvesters, "Who does that young woman belong to?"**

**6 The overseer replied, "She is the Moabite who came back from Moab with Naomi. 7 She said, 'Please let me glean and gather among the sheaves behind the harvesters.' She came into the field and has remained here from morning till now, except for a short rest in the shelter."**

The overseer (manager) supervised Boaz's property. He provided the reapers with food and water, directed their work, and paid their wages. He also supervised the gleaners.

Only Ruth worked in the fields while Naomi remained home. Why did Naomi not glean with Ruth? She was able to walk from Moab to Bethlehem, so she was not an invalid. However, gleaning grain took far more effort than walking. Gleaning involved hours of bending and stooping in the hot sun. After gathering and binding the grain into bundles (sheaves), gleaners brought the heavy sheaves to the threshing floor where they had to beat and winnow (remove the chaff from) the grain. Gleaning was not a job for the feeble. The medicines or joint replacement surgeries we take for granted today were unimaginable in Ruth's day. Since there was no indication that Naomi was lazy or just expected Ruth to take care of her, it may be assumed that she was no longer physically able to perform such hard work.

Even if she was too old to work, Naomi could have gone with Ruth for companionship, but she did not. Two women together would have been safer than a single woman working alone in the field. Boaz understood that Ruth was in danger, so Naomi should have seen the risks as well. Boaz's first words to Ruth showed he was concerned for her safety. There were no warnings from Naomi, or if any were given, the author did not record them. Was she only interested in herself, not in Ruth's safety? Naomi's indifference may have indicated she believed God was in control and would protect Ruth without any help from her. God used Boaz to make certain Ruth was not mistreated or bullied.

Boaz was very interested in Ruth. Her clothing or accent may have revealed she was not an Israelite. In verse 5, he asked, **"Who does that young woman belong to?"** Three millennia ago, husbands, fathers, sons, or brothers protected the women in their families. Boaz's question simply showed his concern for Ruth and did not imply he thought she was a slave. To some, a woman working alone without a companion or protector might be seen as unimportant or someone without a family. Such a person might be mistreated.

Israel has a hot, dry climate. Agricultural workers went to the fields early in the day because morning temperatures were cooler. Since afternoon was the hottest part of the day, they usually rested after lunch. They resumed their work when temperatures began to cool and worked until dark.

Ruth diligently worked all day **"except for a short rest in the shelter"** (Ru. 2:6). The shelter could have been a tent, small farmhouse, or temporary hut constructed beside the field. The temperature in the shelter was usually cooler than in the field.

Ruth desired to find food and take care of her mother-in-law. She was not trying to find herself a rich husband. Boaz was checking on his crop and his workers, not looking for a wife. Ruth could have gleaned in any field, but God guided her to Boaz's field. Boaz was far more generous than the Law required. He blessed Ruth and Naomi with food, and in His time, God blessed Boaz with a family.

## RUTH 2:8-9

**8 So Boaz said to Ruth, "My daughter, listen to me. Don't go and glean in another field and don't go away from here. Stay here with the women who work for me. 9 Watch the field where the men are harvesting, and follow along after the women. I have told the men not to lay a hand on you. And whenever you are thirsty, go and get a drink from the water jars the men have filled."**

The Law did not require landowners to provide food, water, or protection for their workers. Father John Massie (my father, an Episcopal/Anglican priest) suggested since Boaz was the son of Rahab, a Gentile prostitute from Jericho, he may have been more tolerant of strangers than his neighbors were. Boaz was impressed with Ruth's modesty, hard work, and loyalty to Naomi. She faithfully did what was necessary to provide for herself and the older woman. Not all rich men would have been moved by a poor widow's love and devotion to her mother-in-law. He told his male employees not to harm her in any way. Often workers abused foreign women. (Some field hands treated unprotected women improperly.) Boaz knew this, so he instructed Ruth to stay in his field, gleaning with his female workers where he could ensure her safety. (There was a division of labor among the harvesters. Men usually worked with men and women worked with women. Fields were not separated by fences or barricades, so Ruth could have inadvertently wandered into an area where Boaz could not protect her.) He even directed her to drink from his water jars when she was thirsty. (The water containers were likely guarded so that only those entitled could obtain a drink.) Not only was he concerned with her physical safety, he protected her honor as well.

At their first meeting, Ruth did not know Boaz was a relative. She was a hardworking woman who was very thankful for her good fortune. Boaz's interest in Ruth changed in just a few verses. At first, he referred to her as a "young woman" (Ru. 2:5) and asked who she was, but after he learned a little about her, he called her "my daughter" (Ru. 2:8), just as Naomi did (Ru. 2:2). This showed he considered her to be part of his family and was willing to protect her. Boaz may have been considerably older than Ruth. It is doubtful he would have called her "daughter" if they were close to the same age. This implies he thought of her as someone who needed his protection rather than as a prospective wife. When Ruth left Moab with Naomi, she thought she would never remarry or have children. She likely viewed Boaz as her protector, not as a potential husband.

In Israel's dry climate, water was scarce. During the workday, jars of water were provided for the hot, thirsty workers. It was usually a woman's job to bring water for the workers, but in Boaz's field, the young men did this task. Ruth the Moabite could have been required to bring the water to the Israelites (Dt. 29:10-11; Jos. 9:21-27), but Boaz provided it for her. Leaving the field to search for water would have taken time and exposed Ruth to danger. Boaz's generous offer to share his drinking water displayed his concern for her safety. (Water jars excavated in this area were porous. Tiny droplets of water seeped through the pores and collected on the outside of the clay jars. When this water evaporated, the water inside the jars cooled.)

## RUTH 2:10-13

**10 At this, she bowed down with her face to the ground. She asked him, "Why have I found such favor in your eyes that you notice me—a foreigner?"**

**11 Boaz replied, "I've been told all about what you have done for your mother-in-law since the death of your husband—how you left**

your father and mother and your homeland and came to live with a people you did not know before. 12 May the LORD repay you for what you have done. May you be richly rewarded by the LORD, the God of Israel, under whose wings you have come to take refuge."

13 "May I continue to find favor in your eyes, my lord," she said. "You have put me at ease by speaking kindly to your servant—though I do not have the standing of one of your servants."

In Ruth's day, greetings often included more than a simple "hello." Hand kissing, hugging, kneeling, and even lying on one's face before a higher-class person were customary. Ruth respectfully prostrated herself before Boaz and thanked him for his thoughtfulness. Prostration (lying face down on the ground) could show either respect for a person or devotion to God. A person of lower rank often lay before a person of higher rank to show deference or subservience. Since Moabites were the Jews' enemies, she considered herself unworthy to receive his generosity.

Boaz loved Yahweh, and it showed in the way he lived his life and treated the people around him. He respected the poor and obeyed God's gleaning laws. He provided abundantly for Ruth and Naomi.

Boaz had never met Ruth, but he learned a great deal about her from listening to other people. He knew she was a virtuous widow who showed great loyalty and devotion to Naomi. She had left her home in Moab, her family, and her pagan gods to care for her mother-in-law. He could see she was a righteous woman and praised her for the love and kindness she had given Naomi. Boaz asked God to repay her for all she had done for her mother-in-law. Ruth had faith in God and did what was right in His eyes. She carried out her promises to Naomi, and God lavishly blessed her.

The phrase **"under whose wings you have come to take refuge"** (Ru. 2:12) refers to the fact young birds seek shelter under their mother's wings when they encounter danger (Ex. 19:4; Dt. 32:10-11; Ps. 17:8, 36:7, 91:4). During a rainstorm, young chicks frequently huddle under their mother's wings to stay warm and dry. Boaz was a righteous believer who knew Ruth had requested God's protection. This passage implies Ruth had become a convert to the Jewish religion.

Ruth's great-grandson David wrote, **"Have mercy on me, my God, have mercy on me, for in You I take refuge. I will take refuge in the shadow of Your wings…"** (Ps. 57:1). Ruth had true faith in Yahweh. She sought refuge under His wings, and He showed her His love, protection, and mercy.

Jesus said, **"For all those who exalt themselves will be humbled, and those who humble themselves will be exalted"** (Lk. 14:11). Ruth was filled with gratitude. She humbly and respectfully bowed before the wealthy Boaz and addressed him as "my lord" (lower case l). She told him she was inferior to his servants and acknowledged she was a foreigner, but Boaz did not care. His kindness to an immigrant amazed her. She may have suffered prejudice and scorn from other Israelites, but certainly not from Boaz. If she was familiar with Moses' words, **"No Ammonite or Moabite or any of their descendants may enter the assembly of the LORD, not even in the tenth generation"** (Dt. 23:3), she must have been concerned. Boaz did not judge her for her poverty or her ethnicity. He saw her as a godly woman, not a detested Moabite. He was considerate and told Ruth he admired her for the devotion and consideration she had shown Naomi.

Even in times of apostasy (abandoning religious faith), God takes care of His faithful people (Ps. 17:8, 36:7, 63:7). Through Boaz, Ruth received the Lord's mercy. Yahweh used Boaz to answer his own prayers (Ru. 2:12).

## RUTH 2:14-18

**14 At mealtime Boaz said to her, "Come over here. Have some bread and dip it in the wine vinegar."**

**When she sat down with the harvesters, he offered her some roasted grain. She ate all she wanted and had some left over. 15 As she got up to glean, Boaz gave orders to his men, "Let her gather among the sheaves and don't reprimand her. 16 Even pull out some stalks for her from the bundles and leave them for her to pick up, and don't rebuke her."**

**17 So Ruth gleaned in the field until evening. Then she threshed the barley she had gathered, and it amounted to about an ephah. 18 She carried it back to town, and her mother-in-law saw how much she had gathered. Ruth also brought out and gave her what she had left over after she had eaten enough.**

Boaz's kindness towards an immigrant was unusual. A Moabite had no legal rights in Israel, and gleaners did not usually sit with the reapers. Boaz invited Ruth to join him and share his food. He showed great respect for the young woman and provided her with plenty of food. After they finished eating, he sent more home for Naomi. Boaz served Ruth, rather than requiring her to serve him.

Breakfast and lunch were small meals. Heavy work after a large meal was unadvisable. The large evening meal, usually vegetable stew and bread was eaten after the work was completed. They frequently dipped their bread in vinegar-based dressing or sauce. The roasted grain was probably fresh barley that had been cooked over a fire. Poor people were allowed to collect the leftovers after the reapers had harvested the best grain, but Boaz instructed his workers to let Ruth glean where they were working. He even told his men, **"Let her gather among the sheaves and don't reprimand her. Even pull out some stalks for her from the bundles and leave them for her to pick up, and don't rebuke her"** (Ru. 2:15-16).

Boaz was a compassionate man who honored the Law of Moses. He could have ordered his men to give Ruth sacks of grain, but he understood her desire to work for what she took. She was diligent and hardworking and did not want charity. He told his workers to be deliberately careless and drop extra grain for her to collect. In that way, Ruth would feel she had earned the grain rather than received a handout. His generosity guaranteed both Ruth and Naomi would have enough food for several months.

As Boaz requested, his harvesters dropped part of the grain. Ruth worked diligently and gathered a large amount (*ephah*) of barley. Merriam Webster dictionary defines an *ephah* as "an ancient Hebrew unit of dry measure equal to… a little over a bushel."[15] That would be more than

---

15       "Ephah." Biblehub. com. 2017. Accessed November 21, 2017. http:// biblehub.com/ topical/e/ephah. htm.

seven imperial gallons or nine US gallons. Such a tremendous amount of grain would be impossible for one woman to carry. Charles Ryrie suggests that the measure may have been closer to half a bushel,[16] while Robert Deffinbaugh proposes that she collected about thirty pounds of grain.[17] MacGregor, in *The Interpreter's Bible*, states that Ruth gathered "about two-thirds of a bushel."[18] (The *ephah* was a homemade vessel, so its size could vary.) Boaz did not send anyone with Ruth to help carry her heavy load, so apparently this *ephah* was an amount she could carry. Before Ruth went home, she threshed (beat) and winnowed the grain, making her load lighter and easier to carry.

After harvesting the grain, the workers bound the barley stalks into sheaves (bundles) and carried them to the open-air threshing floor. Ruth threshed (separated the seed from a harvested plant by striking) the grain she had gleaned. She probably beat the barley with a stick to separate the grain from the chaff (husks or seed coverings and any other debris separated from the grain during the threshing process). Finally, she winnowed her grain (threw everything up in the air to let the wind blow the unwanted chaff away). Sometimes the workers gathered the chaff and burned it in their fires.

Boaz's generous treatment of Ruth was unusual and surpassed what the Law required (Lev. 19:9; Dt. 24:19). It would have been more lucrative for Boaz to order his workers to harvest all the grain rather than leave some for the poor to glean, but man's way was not God's way. Boaz obeyed God.

## RUTH 2:19-20

**19 Her mother-in-law asked her, "Where did you glean today? Where did you work? Blessed be the man who took notice of you!"**

16      Ryrie, C. C., Th. D., Ph. D. (1986). "Ruth." The Ryrie Study Bible (KJV). Chicago, IL: Moody Press.423.

17      Deffinbaugh, Robert L. "2. Can eHarmony Beat This? (Ruth 2)." Bible.org. N. 24 Jan. 2010. Web. 14 Feb. 2017. <https://bible.org/seriespage/2-can-eharmony-beat-ruth-2>

18      MacGregor, G. "RuthText, Exegesis and Exposition." The Interpreter's Bible Vol. II. New York: Abingdon Press, 1954. 843.

**Then Ruth told her mother-in-law about the one at whose place she had been working. "The name of the man I worked with today is Boaz," she said.**

**20 "The Lord bless him!" Naomi said to her daughter-in-law. "He has not stopped showing his kindness *(hesed)* to the living and the dead." She added, "That man is our close relative; he is one of our guardian-redeemers** [The Hebrew word for guardian-redeemer is a legal term for one who has the obligation to redeem a relative in serious difficulty" (see Lev. 25:25-55)].

When Ruth finished gleaning, she went home to Naomi. She brought both the grain she had gleaned and the food left over from her meal. The faithful young woman could have chosen to socialize with the young men and women who worked for Boaz, but her loyalty to her mother-in-law was more important. She returned home after work. She only left Naomi to acquire food.

When she reached home, she showed Naomi all the grain she had gleaned. Then she prepared the older woman's supper. She told Naomi everything that had transpired that day. Naomi must have been astounded by the amount of grain she had obtained. She could tell Ruth had worked on the land of a kind and generous person.

Ruth did not mention Boaz's name until verse 19, after she had completed the rest of her story. When Naomi learned of Boaz's kindness, she immediately asked God to bless him. Strangely, she did not praise her hard-working daughter-in-law. The people living in Bethlehem observed Ruth's faithfulness and devotion to Naomi, but the older woman appeared to be indifferent.

Ancient Israelites followed God's command to take care of their families. The Hebrew word *"goel"* (also spelled *go'el*) is translated "redeemer" in English. The word redeem means to buy a thing back and return it to its owner who was forced to sell it. (For example, if you sell your horse to another person, then later buy your animal back from its new owner, you have redeemed your horse.) The ASV uses the term "near kinsman," the NIV uses the expression "guardian-redeemer," and the OJB, TLV, and VOICE indicate he was a "kinsman-redeemer." The AMP and CEV describe Boaz as their "close relative," the ERV states he was their "protector," and the HCSB calls him their "family redeemer."

These different translations may sound confusing, but all these terms mean the same thing. The redeemer was required, by covenant, to protect the honor and the belongings of his family. He was obliged to take care of family members who had been affected by death or hardship. *Goelim* (plural of *goel*) sometimes avenged the deaths of relatives who were killed by others (Nu. 35:12, 35:16-21; Dt. 19:6, 19:12), and he could collect debts owed to the deceased (Nu. 5:8). He was further required to redeem family land (Lev. 25:25-28; Jer. 32:6-9), and people who had been sold into slavery (Lev. 25:47-55). Israel did not have policemen, so kinsman-redeemers sometimes executed those who had murdered family members (Nu. 35:16-21), and assisted relatives involved in lawsuits (Pr. 23:11).

If a destitute Israelite had to sell his land, his redeemer could buy it back to preserve family ownership. God provided a way for impoverished family members to avoid becoming slaves. Even though a kinsman was not forced to marry a relative's widow, Israelites usually honored this duty (Dt. 25:5-10).

In verse 20, Naomi stated Boaz **"has not stopped showing his kindness to the living and the dead."** (She and Ruth were the living, and her husband and sons were the dead.) Boaz had shown mercy to the widows of his relative, Elimelek, and his son, Mahlon. Remember, Orpah, the wife of Kilion, had returned to her own people (Ru. 1:14). Elimelek owned land in Bethlehem. When he died, land ownership passed to his sons Mahlon and Kilion, but they had also died. While they were living in Moab, someone else must have managed their property. Unless Naomi could find a kinsman to redeem the land, it might be lost to a non-relative. God never neglects anyone. He provided for widows and orphans whose providers had died or were unable to care for them. A kinsman-redeemer's duty was to buy family land that might be sold due to poverty or death. He must also redeem property that had already been sold. God set up this plan so that property ownership would remain with the original family (Lev. 25:25; Jer. 32: 7-10).

Naomi's faith had been greatly tested. At last she understood God had not forsaken her. He had graciously blessed her through both Boaz and her daughter-in-law, Ruth. The young woman's arrival in Boaz's field was through the providence of God, not coincidence or good luck.

## RUTH 2:21-23

**21 Then Ruth the Moabite said, "He even said to me, 'Stay with my workers until they finish harvesting all my grain.'"**

**22 Naomi said to Ruth her daughter-in-law, "It will be good for you, my daughter, to go with the women who work for him, because in someone else's field you might be harmed."**

**23 So Ruth stayed close to the women of Boaz to glean until the barley and wheat harvests were finished. And she lived with her mother-in-law.**

Boaz invited Ruth to glean in his fields during both the barley and wheat harvests. His thoughtfulness guaranteed the two widows would not go hungry. The barley harvest began after the Feast of Unleavened Bread in late March or early April and concluded in early to mid-May. The wheat harvest continued until late May or early June, ending with the Feast of Weeks (*Shavout*). Thanks to God's provision and Boaz's generosity, Ruth gleaned enough grain during both harvests to provide food for several months.

When Ruth told Naomi what had happened, she emphasized Boaz's kindness and generosity, but she did not mention his praise for her. She never boasted or repeated the compliments she received.

Boaz warned the hard-working young woman to stay close to his employees where she could glean in safety. Understanding the dangers she faced, Naomi encouraged Ruth to obey Boaz's instructions. It also would have been ungrateful to glean on another's property after Boaz had been so generous. Naomi wanted to encourage Boaz to think of Ruth as more than a poor gleaner.

Boaz's generosity was really God's providence, not just his duty to two destitute widows. The God under whose wings she had taken shelter (Ru. 2:12) kept her safe as He fed her physically and spiritually.

Ruth worked diligently in Boaz's field. She faithfully honored the promise she had made to Naomi. Rather than seek romance with any of the young men, she returned home to care for her mother-in-law. The young woman repeatedly put the needs of others ahead of her own.

# RUTH CHAPTER 3

IN THE UNITED STATES, WIDOWS MAY APPLY FOR Benefits from their late husband's Social Security, and widows with children receive support payments until their children reach age eighteen or finish high school. No such safeguards existed in Ruth's day. However, God provided for His people through His gleaning laws, laws of redemption, and years of Jubilee.

**Consecrate the fiftieth year and proclaim liberty throughout the land to all its inhabitants. It shall be a jubilee for you; each of you is to return to your family property and to your own clan... In this Year of Jubilee everyone is to return to their own property. If you sell land to any of your own people or buy land from them, do not take advantage of each other... but fear your God. I am the LORD your God. Follow My decrees and be careful to obey My laws, and you will live safely in the land... The land must not be sold permanently, because the land is Mine and you reside in My land as foreigners and strangers. Throughout the land that you hold as a possession, you must provide for the redemption of the land. If one of your fellow Israelites becomes poor and sells some of their property, their nearest relative is to come and redeem what they have sold. If, however, there is no one to redeem it for them but later on they prosper and acquire sufficient means to redeem it themselves, they are to determine the value for the years since they sold it and refund the balance to the one to whom they sold it; they can then go back to their own property.**

**But if they do not acquire the means to repay, what was sold will remain in the possession of the buyer until the Year of Jubilee. It will be returned in the Jubilee, and they can then go back to their property.** (Lev. 25:10-28).

Being destitute, Naomi and Ruth needed the money for their basic needs. There was really no option. Naomi had to sell her family's land. No matter who bought the land, it would be returned to Naomi or her heirs in the year of Jubilee (Lev. 25:10). Ancient Israelites did not think they owned any part of the Promised Land because God was the only property-owner. The Canaanites and other people who did not live according to His law were driven out. God's people, the Israelites, were then able to occupy the land. Yahweh gave the land to the tribes and clans of Israel. God is omniscient (all knowing). He knew poverty, hardships, disabilities, or death could force people to sell their land. God's Law, given to Moses, provided a way for the property to be given back to its original owner in the year of Jubilee. Every fifty years, by God's decree, Jubilee was observed. Captives and slaves were set free, and debts were forgiven. God loved and provided for His people.

## RUTH 3:1-5

**1 One day Ruth's mother-in-law Naomi said to her, "My daughter, I must find a home** [Hebrew- find rest] **for you, where you will be well provided for. 2 Now Boaz, with whose women you have worked, is a relative of ours. Tonight he will be winnowing barley on the threshing floor. 3 Wash, put on perfume, and get dressed in your best clothes. Then go down to the threshing floor, but don't let him know you are there until he has finished eating and drinking. 4 When he lies down, note the place where he is lying. Then go and uncover his feet and lie down. He will tell you what to do."**

**5 "I will do whatever you say," Ruth answered. 6 So she went down to the threshing floor and did everything her mother-in-law told her to do.**

In the first two chapters, Naomi was bitter and felt God had treated her harshly. She had said, **"Call me Mara"** (Ru. 1:20). In chapter three, there was a change in her attitude. She was no longer self-absorbed, thinking only of her own problems. Instead, the older woman began to think about the needs of her loyal daughter-in-law, and plan for her future. The events in chapter three took place several months after Ruth and Naomi arrived in Bethlehem. The wheat and barley crops had been harvested, and the two women had plenty of grain. However, Ruth had no husband to provide for her. Naomi told Ruth that Boaz was their relative. As their kinsman, he had specific responsibilities. She wanted what was best for Ruth and knew she would be safe and secure if she remarried. Naomi believed Boaz would be a suitable husband.

Behavior that seems peculiar or inappropriate in twenty-first century America was considered proper three thousand years ago in Israel. It was appropriate for Ruth to appeal to Boaz for help since he was the *goel* (kinsman-redeemer) of Elimelek's family. If Boaz married Ruth, she would be protected, and Elimelek's name would be preserved. Just as it is today, maintaining the family was very important to God.

Workers carried the grain to the threshing and winnowing floor, a large, flat area of bedrock or compacted clay worn smooth by many years of hard work. It was located in eastern Bethlehem. For small harvests, workers beat the grain with sticks. For larger harvests, animals often walked on the crop to separate the grain from the chaff (seed coverings, stems, twigs, leaves). Sometimes animals dragged a wagon or threshing sledge (wide, heavy timber) over the grain. After the grain was threshed, it was winnowed to separate the grain from the chaff. Winnowing was usually done by several people. They threw the heap of grain and chaff into the air with a pitchfork. The heavy grain fell to the ground and the Mediterranean winds blew the lighter chaff away. They repeated this process several times until most of the chaff was removed. The remaining grain was sifted to get rid of heavier waste, such as pebbles or lumps of earth. Winnowing was usually done after sunset to take advantage of breezes.

The "rest" (Ru. 3:1) Naomi wanted for Ruth was a secure home and a good marriage. She loved Ruth very much and wanted to find her a suitable husband. In Ruth's day, marriages were usually arranged by the woman's parents (Ge. 24:3, 34:4; Jdg. 14:2). If Ruth's parents were still alive, they lived in Moab, so Naomi felt it was her responsibility to provide for her beloved daughter-in-law. God guided the events, but He expected the two women to do their parts.

Naomi conceived a plan to find a loving, godly husband for Ruth. A marriage to a kinsman would preserve Elimelek's family line and provide the young woman with a secure future. The older woman would benefit as well. Ruth was a foreigner, so she probably did not understand many of the Hebrew's customs. Naomi's instructions were very detailed. If Ruth was going to propose marriage to Boaz, she needed to know where to go, what to wear, what to say, and how to behave.

Ruth may have worn clothes that indicated she was still in mourning for her late husband. This is speculation since the author did not specify the length of time since Mahlon's death. (Widows customarily wore dark colored clothing for a period of time after their husband's death to signify they were grieving. Men understood this meant a widow was not available for dating or marriage.) If Ruth had been wearing mourning clothes, she needed to change into garments that showed she was no longer in mourning and was interested in remarriage.

Naomi told Ruth to wear her best clothes and perfume (some translations say to anoint herself with oil) to show Boaz she was interested in him. Naomi told Ruth how to attract a good husband, but never mentioned it was important to trust in God. Since Naomi knew that Boaz was their relative, it is possible she knew there was a closer family member who could assume Boaz's place as kinsman-redeemer.

Naomi's plot could have ruined the reputations of two highly regarded people. Threshing floors were sometimes used for immoral behavior (Hos. 9:1), especially when alcohol was consumed. However, Naomi knew both Ruth and Boaz were honorable and believed nothing improper would take place.

Boaz may have been closer to Naomi's age than to Ruth's. (John MacArthur suggests that he might have been 45 to 55 years old.)[19]

Naomi understood Ruth would need to take the first step. She gave her daughter-in-law detailed instructions to prepare for her meeting with Boaz. She was to go to the threshing floor and stay out of sight until Boaz

---

19     MacArthur, John. "Ruth." The MacArthur Study Bible (NASB). Nashville, TN: Thomas Nelson, 2013. 363.

went to sleep (verse 3). Then she would uncover his feet and lie down (verse 4). This ancient custom was one way a moral, unmarried woman could propose to a single man. Nothing sinful or indecent should be inferred.

## RUTH 3: 6-9

**6 So she went down to the threshing floor and did everything her mother-in-law told her to do. 7 When Boaz had finished eating and drinking and was in good spirits, he went over to lie down at the far end of the grain pile. Ruth approached quietly, uncovered his feet and lay down. 8 In the middle of the night something startled the man; he turned—and there was a woman lying at his feet!**

**9 "Who are you?" he asked.**

**"I am your servant Ruth," she said. "Spread the corner of your garment over me, since you are a guardian-redeemer of our family."**

People rejoiced after a good harvest. Jews thanked Jehovah. Pagans thanked various agricultural and harvest gods.

In verse 7, the author states Boaz's **"heart was merry."** After a famine that had lasted several years, Bethlehem had an abundant harvest. Boaz was in good spirits and thanked God for His many blessings. Some have assumed this verse implies he was drunk. Boaz undoubtedly did consume some wine, since it was a part of Jewish feasting, but since he was described as a righteous and upright man, suggesting he was intoxicated is probably inaccurate.

Boaz was a wealthy man, so he certainly owned a house. Since breezes were used to winnow the grain, the threshing floor was open to the air. Robbers or hungry animals could have stolen or destroyed the freshly harvested grain if it had been left unguarded. Boaz probably slept on the threshing floor to protect his crops.

John Gill suggests there could have been another reason for Boaz's presence on the threshing floor. The harvest celebration must have lasted far into the night. His house was in the town, not close to the fields. He may have decided it was too late to go home and opted to sleep with his grain. He would be where he was needed for work the next day.[20] However, since Naomi was aware of Boaz's plan to sleep on the threshing floor, this theory seems questionable. It is far more likely that he was there simply to prevent theft.

Ruth respected her mother-in-law, trusted her judgment, and obeyed her directions. She was a young, poor, foreign-born laborer, while Boaz was a rich landowner and a citizen of Bethlehem. It was unusual but not unheard of for a younger woman to propose to an older man. Ruth did as her mother-in-law instructed, even though she risked shame and humiliation if Boaz rejected her.

**"How can a young person stay on the path of purity? By living according to Your word"** (Ps. 119:9).

Much has been said about Ruth uncovering Boaz's feet (Ru. 3:4). In some translations of the Bible, the term "feet" is a euphemism for a person's private area (Isa. 7:20; Eze. 16:25), but most of the time the word was used as it is today, for the part of the body on which we stand or walk. In addition, "uncover" sometimes referred to sexual activity (Lev. 18 and 20; Dt. 22:30, 27:20; Eze. 16:35-39). God prohibited such behavior outside marriage (Lev. 19:29, 20:10; Ex. 20:14). Both Ruth and Boaz were moral, honorable people, so implying Ruth did anything more than remove the blanket or cloak from his feet would be wrong. This was an acceptable way for Ruth to show Boaz she was willing to become his wife.

Ruth did not lie beside Boaz, which would imply she was his equal. Instead, she lay at his feet, which showed her submission. Servants often lay at their master's feet so they could be available if needed. As his kinsman's widow, Ruth did not make demands. She came as Boaz's humble servant to claim her right to a levirate marriage.

The author does not indicate what startled Boaz. Possibly Ruth bumped against his foot, and he realized that he was not alone. Editors

---

20      Clarke, A., Barnes, A., Benson, J., Exell, J. S., Coffman, J. B., Gill, J., Beza, T., Pett, P., Ellicott, C., Whedon, D., Poole, M., Wesley, J., ... Torrey, R. A. (2017). Verse-by-Verse Bible Commentary Ruth3:7. Retrieved January 11, 2017, from https://www/commentary/ruth/3-7. html

of The Lutheran Study Bible hypothesize that the cool night air might have disturbed him when his feet were uncovered. Boaz probably wore an outer garment called a *kanaph* which was also used as a blanket or covering to keep him warm at night.[21]

As a widow, Ruth was an unmarried young woman. She could have married any of the handsome younger men, but she obeyed Naomi and followed the Israelites' tradition. She chose not to remarry outside the family. Ruth surely could have found an honorable husband closer to her own age, but preserving Naomi's family was more important.

The Hebrew language shows differences not seen in English. Ruth called herself Boaz's servant. She used the word *ama*, which disclosed she was a relative of Boaz, rather than *shipha* (2 Sa. 17:17), which meant she was a member of the servant class. This distinction was significant.

## RUTH 3:10-13

**10 "The Lord bless you, my daughter," he replied. "This kindness (*hesed*) is greater than that which you showed earlier: You have not run after the younger men, whether rich or poor. 11 And now, my daughter, don't be afraid. I will do for you all you ask. All the people of my town know that you are a woman of noble character. 12 Although it is true that I am a guardian-redeemer of our family, there is another who is more closely related than I. 13 Stay here for the night, and in the morning if he wants to do his duty as your guardian-redeemer, good; let him redeem you. But if he is not willing, as surely as the Lord lives I will do it. Lie here until morning."**

Ruth and Boaz had met during the harvest, but they had not dated. During courtship, a person is usually on his or her best behavior to impress the other individual. Boaz and Ruth had been part of a large group and had interacted with other people. Boaz could observe Ruth's character as she gathered the grain and cared for her mother-in-law. Ruth witnessed Boaz's dealings with his employees and the other gleaners.

Ruth referred to herself as Boaz's "servant" (Ru. 3:9), but he fondly called her "daughter" (Ru. 3:10-11). The wealthy, influential Jewish man

21    Englebrecht, E. A. (Ed.). (2009). "Ruth." The Lutheran Study Bible. St. Louis, MO: Concordia Publishing House. 427.

spoke with respect and kindness to a foreigner. He was impressed with her love for Naomi and wanted to protect and care for her. The term "daughter" did not indicate he thought of her as a child. Rather, it was a term of endearment that indicated he was willing to be her redeemer.

All the citizens of Bethlehem knew Ruth was **"a woman of noble character"** (Ru. 3:11). She had earned Boaz's respect. He told her not to be afraid. He promised to do as she asked, if the closer kinsman agreed. Boaz trusted God. Notice, he did not comment on Ruth's beauty, nice clothes, or good-smelling perfume (or oil). Possessions and beauty will not ensure happy marriages. Righteousness, love, and loyalty attracted Boaz to the young widow.

In verse 10, Boaz stated, **"This kindness** (hesed) **is greater than that which you showed earlier..."** By this, he meant she had shown love to her husband, and after he died, to Naomi. She willingly left Moab to follow her mother-in-law to a foreign country with unfamiliar customs. She worked hard to support both herself and the older woman. The kindness she showed to Boaz (her desire to be his wife) was even greater than the kindness she had shown to Naomi. Even though she could have attracted a younger and possibly better-looking suitor, she was willing to marry an older man to preserve the family and provide her childless deceased husband (and Naomi) with descendants.

Boaz was obviously attracted to Ruth, but he did not volunteer to act as her kinsman-redeemer until she asked for his help. Since he was older than Ruth, perhaps closer to Naomi's age, he may have thought she would find him unattractive. (The author did not describe either Boaz's or Ruth's physical appearance since that was not important to the story.) Surely Boaz was flattered Ruth had chosen him.

Boaz prayed for Jehovah to bless the virtuous young woman. He was attracted by her integrity and godly character. Instead of thinking of herself, her main concerns were Naomi's needs, redeeming the land, and providing the family with an heir. Ruth showed she was loyal to God and her family. Boaz trusted God and saw His influence in everything Ruth did.

In verse 11, Boaz reassured Ruth, **"don't be afraid. I will do for you all you ask."** Ruth had suffered many hardships. Her husband and brother-in-law had died. (Most experts believe her father-in-law died before her marriage to Mahlon.) She had left her home, religion, and family behind in Moab. Her sister-in-law had abandoned her and Naomi. She was a childless widow, living in a foreign land with her destitute mother-in-law, gleaning for food.

In Ruth 2:12, Boaz said, **"May you be richly rewarded by the LORD, the God of Israel, under whose wings you have come to take refuge."** Ruth's request (Ru. 3:9) for Boaz to spread the corner of his garment over her was a euphemism for marriage or a request for protection and assistance. (The Hebrew word for "skirt" is also translated "wing." Just as a mother bird protects her chicks from danger by hiding them under her wings, God protects His children under His wings.) This was her way of letting him know her time of mourning for her late husband was over and she was now available for marriage. Boaz understood her words were a request for protection as well as a marriage proposal.

The act of a man spreading his garment over a single woman indicated he was willing to marry her. God used the same terminology when referring to His care for Israel. **"I spread the corner of My garment over you... I gave you My solemn oath and entered into a covenant with you," declares the Sovereign LORD, "and you became Mine"** (Eze. 16:8). Even in the twenty-first century, some Jewish grooms place a cotton or silk shawl around their brides as a symbol of their protection.

**Boaz asked, "Who are you?" She said, "I am Ruth, your servant girl. Spread your cover** [or the corner of your garment; or your wings] **over me** [a request for the provision and protection of marriage]**, because you are a relative** [guardian; kinsman-redeemer] **who is supposed to take care of me."** (Ru. 3:9 EXB). This custom is not mentioned elsewhere in the Bible, however, Boaz obviously understood Ruth was proposing marriage and did not view her action as promiscuous or inappropriate.

Marriage to a Moabite was not forbidden (Ex. 34:11-16; Dt. 7:1-3). Further, Ruth had become a devout convert to Judaism (Ru. 1:16), and was no longer a worshipper of Chemosh, the pagan god of Moab.

Boaz did not act like a rich man doing his poor servant a favor. Rather, he said Ruth was doing him a great kindness. Ruth demonstrated she was devoted to her family and loyal to her deceased husband and her beloved mother-in-law. This was certainly not a destitute widow's selfish desire for a good life. She wanted what was best for her family. Boaz was willing to redeem the land and wanted to marry Ruth and provide an heir for her late husband. Both Ruth and Boaz exhibited godly behavior. Neither compromised their moral beliefs. This conversation was actually a business meeting where they discussed legal issues rather than a romantic date.

When Boaz called Ruth a **"woman of noble character"** (Ru. 3:11), he showed he did not think of her as his servant. She was a godly woman worthy of marriage to a righteous man. The apostle Paul said love **"always protects, always trusts, always hopes, always perseveres"** (1 Co. 13:7). Covering her with his garment symbolized his guardianship, protection, and provision. Boaz was a righteous man, and he believed that Ruth was righteous as well. He responded appropriately. By making this oath, Boaz called down God's punishment upon himself if he broke his promise to Ruth (Ru. 3:13).

Boaz was a man of integrity who lived according to God's word. He stated he was Ruth's guardian-redeemer and was willing to marry her, however, there was a closer relative who must be consulted first. Boaz was willing to risk losing Ruth rather than do anything that was against God's will. He wanted to make sure that Ruth was properly cared for, even if it meant another man would marry her. Since there was a closer relative, Boaz was not obligated to become Ruth's redeemer. He was motivated by love rather than duty. He felt obliged to offer Naomi's land to this man first. If the man did not want to act as redeemer, Boaz was willing.

Ruth showed her love and trust for Naomi by obeying her. She believed in Naomi's God and adopted her country (Ru. 1:16) and customs. Offering to become Boaz's wife took great courage. Boaz must have been shocked. His comment, **"if he wants to do his duty as your guardian-redeemer, good; let him redeem you. But if he is not willing, as surely as the LORD lives I will do it"** (Ru. 3:13). did not mean he was not willing to marry Ruth. It was necessary to first offer the opportunity to become the redeemer to the closer relative. The phrase **"as surely as the LORD lives I will do it"** indicated Boaz meant what he said. By making this oath (see Jer. 4:2), he promised to take Ruth as his wife and redeem the inheritance if the other man refused. Today in twenty-first century America, we expect a declaration of love before a person contemplates marriage, but ancient marriages were often legal unions in which love and devotion were rarely considered. Boaz simply promised to perform his duties as goel if the nearer kinsman refused.

Naomi may not have personally known the closer kinsman, but she probably knew of his existence. She might not have believed he was able or willing to become the *goel*. Since Ruth wanted to have children for her late husband, a married kinsman might have been unwilling to do anything that endangered his own children's inheritance or property rights. Boaz strictly obeyed the Law of Moses. He tried to do everything according to God's plan rather than follow his own desires. Whether he or the relative married the young widow, she would soon have a new husband to care for her and Naomi. The identity of the closer relative was not given. John MacArthur suggests he might have been Boaz's older brother or possibly the brother or cousin of Elimelek.[22]

## RUTH 3:14-18

**14 So she lay at his feet until morning, but got up before anyone could be recognized; and he said, "No one must know that a woman came to the threshing floor."**

**15 He also said, "Bring me the shawl you are wearing and hold it out." When she did so, he poured into it six measures of barley and placed the bundle on her. Then he** [many Hebrew manuscripts, Vulgate, and Syriac state "she"] **went back to town.**

**16 When Ruth came to her mother-in-law, Naomi asked, "How did it go, my daughter?"**

**Then she told her everything Boaz had done for her 17 and added, "He gave me these six measures of barley, saying, 'Don't go back to your mother-in-law empty-handed.'"**

**18 Then Naomi said, "Wait, my daughter, until you find out what happens. For the man will not rest until the matter is settled today."**

---

22      MacArthur, John. "Ruth." The MacArthur Study Bible (NASB). Nashville, TN: Thomas Nelson, 2013. 365.

Ruth did not wish to dishonor Boaz's reputation. She discreetly went to the threshing floor after dark to propose to him. She did not want a respectable man to face scorn or humiliation if he was not willing or able to be her redeemer.

Boaz was honorable and discreet. He wanted to protect Ruth's good reputation as well as his own. Sometimes prostitutes visited the threshing floor at night. He did not want Ruth's visit to be misconstrued as immoral behavior. However, it was very dangerous for a young, single woman to travel alone at night. To protect both her reputation and her physical safety, he told her not to leave until dawn. In the early morning light, she would be able to see well enough to walk home, but it would still be dark enough other people would be unlikely to recognize her.

Boaz was a thoughtful and generous man. He knew Naomi and Ruth needed food, so he gave her a large amount of grain to carry home in her shawl. (The exact quantity, six measures, is unclear.) Her shawl was made of a durable, rough material that was strong enough to carry a heavy load. People had previously seen Ruth carrying grain in her shawl (also translated apron, veil, mantle, or cloak). Since she used her shawl to carry the grain, her head would have been uncovered. Anyone who recognized her would assume she had been out early to obtain food for herself and Naomi. God protected two righteous people from false accusations. After providing Ruth with grain, Boaz left for Bethlehem to search for the nearer kinsman.

Did Boaz know Naomi was behind this marriage proposal? Notice, in verse 17, he said, **"Don't go back to your mother-in-law empty-handed."** This could have been his way of letting Naomi know her plan had worked, and Ruth would be provided for.

Boaz was interested in Ruth's reputation and provided both women with food. The author did not record Boaz saying, "Don't go back to your mother-in-law empty-handed." Ruth told Naomi he uttered those words. This does not imply Ruth invented the dialogue to impress Naomi. It would be impossible for the author to record every word that was said. When the older woman returned to Bethlehem, she declared, **"I went away full, but the LORD has brought me back empty"** (Ru. 1:21). Boaz made sure that was no longer the case.

In verse 17, Naomi asked, **"How did it go, my daughter?"** Some versions of the Bible translate this passage as, **"Who art thou, my daughter?"** (KJ21, ASV, BRG, etc.). It was common for an older woman to address a younger woman in this way even if they were not related. Since she addressed Ruth as "my daughter," she obviously knew she was talking to a woman. Perhaps in the early light Naomi was unable to recognize her daughter-in-law. In an age before glasses or cataract surgery, it is possible Naomi's vision was clouded. It could have been necessary to confirm her visitor's identity. As soon as she realized Ruth had returned, Naomi was anxious to hear everything that had happened.

Daniel Whedon, Charles Ellicott, and Peter Pett suggest Naomi's greeting may have been her way to determine Ruth's status rather than her identity. Was she now engaged to the wealthy Boaz, or was she returning home as she had left, a destitute widow?[23]

Naomi knew Boaz was an honorable man, so she told Ruth to be patient. She knew he would make sure Ruth's future was secure. The author recorded no further dialogue for either woman. The mission God gave Naomi was completed. Her beloved daughter-in-law would be cared for. The story continued with words spoken by other individuals. Ruth may have thought Boaz's gift of grain was to provide for her present needs, but Naomi likely interpreted his acts differently. If Boaz had been unhappy with Ruth's request, it is unlikely he would have given her so much grain. It was reasonable for Naomi to interpret his generosity as a promise to marry Ruth. In the words of her great-grandson, David, **"Cast your cares on the LORD and He will sustain you; He will never let the righteous be shaken"** (Ps. 55:22).

The book of Ruth tells how an ancient family went from tragedy to triumph and received God's love, protection, and provision. Ruth did not enter Boaz's field looking for a husband. Leaving Moab made finding another husband improbable if not impossible, or so she thought. She

---

23      Clarke, A., Barnes, A., Benson, J., Exell, J. S., Coffman, J. B., Gill, J., Beza, T., Pett, P., Ellicott, C., Whedon, D., Poole, M., Wesley, J., ... Torrey, R. A. (2017). Verse-by-Verse Bible Commentary Ruth3:16. Retrieved January 11, 2017, from https://www/commentary/ruth/3-16. html

was a poor widow trying to provide enough food for herself and her mother-in-law. God brought Ruth and Boaz together while they were serving Him as well as others. God prompted Boaz to love and protect Ruth because of the care and devotion she showed Naomi.

Paul's words to the Romans certainly apply to this situation. **"And we know that in all things God works for the good of those who love Him, who have been called according to His purpose"** (Ro. 8:28).

People with similar interests and moral beliefs are naturally drawn together. Boaz and Ruth were both virtuous, kind, considerate, and generous people who loved their Lord. They never discussed their rights or what they deserved, only their responsibilities. Ruth had the right to glean in the fields, but she asked permission. She did not have to take care of Naomi. She willingly chose to take on that task, just as Boaz willingly accepted the responsibilities of a redeemer. Is it any wonder they fell in love? This was truly a match made in Heaven.

The Hebrews believed they were God's chosen people, and everyone else, particularly the despised Moabites, was not. Boaz's men informed him Ruth was from Moab (Ru. 2:7), but he was more interested in her righteous reputation than her citizenship. He knew she was honorable and loyal, and he wanted to marry her (Ru. 3:11).

For a Moabite, this approval was a true blessing from God. Ruth was no longer thought of as an inferior immigrant or an outsider. Her old Moabite identity was gone forever. She was now a child of God! What was true for Ruth thirty centuries ago applies to believers today, regardless of language, nationality, or ethnicity.

# RUTH CHAPTER 4

**M**EANWHILE BOAZ WENT UP TO THE TOWN GATE **AND sat down there just as the guardian-redeemer he had mentioned came along. Boaz said, "Come over here, my friend, and sit down." So he went over and sat down.**

Chapter four described what Boaz said and did. No dialogue was recorded for either Ruth or Naomi. Boaz was a skillful negotiator who presented the facts to the nearer family member in such a way that he was not willing to act as Naomi and Ruth's kinsman-redeemer. Boaz, however, was willing to risk everything he owned to be their redeemer and ensure Elimelek's name would never be forgotten.

Boaz was an ethical man. He was not willing to marry Ruth until he discussed the situation with the nearer kinsman. That was the honorable thing to do. It was necessary to offer the nearer kinsman the opportunity to fulfill his family obligations if he was willing or able to do so. The morning after Ruth's visit to the threshing floor, Boaz headed to the city gate to search for the close relative. Wisely, he planned to meet with the man during the day when witnesses were present. Boaz could provide Mahlon, the son of Naomi and Elimelek, with an heir. This would keep land ownership in the family and make certain their names would continue.

Did the closer relative know Naomi, now a poverty-stricken widow, had returned to Bethlehem? Possibly. He may have decided to ignore situation to avoid unwanted family responsibilities. The honorable Boaz could not allow the widows' hard times to continue any longer.

Since Boaz was not Elimelek's son, he did not have to marry Ruth or provide Mahlon with an heir. This child would inherit Elimelek's property, not the new husband, so marrying Ruth would be a financial burden. In addition, becoming the redeemer would include supporting Naomi. Boaz was willing and financially able to take on these obligations. He loved the two women enough to ensure they would never face homelessness or starvation again.

The author stated Boaz went up to the gate. The threshing floor was not located below the gate. Threshing floors were usually built on hills that were higher than nearby land so buildings would not block the breezes necessary for winnowing the grain. City gates were usually hubs of business, trade, and legal activity. The author may have used the phrase "up to the gate" to indicate the area's importance.

In ancient Israel, most cities were built on hills. They were surrounded by walls for protection. Agricultural fields and the water supply needed for the crops were located outside the walls. Since towns were not built with forums (meeting places) or town squares appropriate for conducting business, the city gate served as both a social and commercial center where fields and land were sold (Ge. 23:10-18), crops were marketed (2 Ki. 7:1), worship was held (2 Ki. 23:8), legal proceedings took place (Ne. 8:1-2), ceremonies, speeches, and prophecy were given (1 Ki. 22:10; Ne. 8:1-2), court cases were decided (Dt. 21:19), and even executions took place (Dt. 17:5), much as courthouses, municipal buildings, churches, or meeting halls are today. Sometimes open-air shelters were built near the gate to protect people from the sun or rain. People often passed through the gate several times a day as they conducted their business. This was the perfect place to find the other relative.

The nearer kinsman did not just happen to walk by while Boaz waited by the gate. His arrival at just the right time was according to God's divine plan for the family. Boaz's greeting to the relative, "Ho, such a one!" (KJ21, ASV, BRG, and others) certainly sounds odd. Other translations render this as "friend" (AMP, ESV, NIV, NLT, RSV, and others), "Sir" (CEB), "Such-and-such" (CJB), or even "John Doe" (NLT). The New Jewish Publication Society refers to this man as "Mr. So-and-So." The DRA says Boaz "called him by name," but does not specify what that name was. This does not imply Boaz did not know the kinsman's name. The author may not have known his name, but it is more likely he chose to conceal it since the man refused to raise children in Mahlon's name. This omission was probably done deliberately to show his name was not important. He refused to preserve Mahlon's name, so his name was excluded to ensure he would not be remembered. The name of Boaz has endured for many centuries, but the unwilling relative will forever be anonymous.

If the family's land still belonged to Naomi, she needed to sell it to support herself and her daughter-in-law. A widow was not able to sell her late husband's property. She needed a man to represent her. The *goelim* (kinsman redeemers) had the first opportunity to buy the land.

Some translations of the Bible state that Boaz referred to Elimelek as "our brother" (KJV, KJ21, ASV, BRG, etc.), while others indicate that Boaz called him "our relative" (ASV, ERV, NIV, ESV, MSG, etc.). This was a common way to refer to a member of the same clan. The author does not imply Boaz was really Elimelek's sibling. Therefore, Boaz was not legally required to redeem the land or marry Ruth.

### RUTH 4:2-5

**2 Boaz took ten of the elders of the town and said, "Sit here," and they did so. 3 Then he said to the guardian-redeemer, "Naomi, who has come back from Moab, is selling the piece of land that belonged to our relative Elimelek. 4 I thought I should bring the matter to your attention and suggest that you buy it in the presence of these seated here and in the presence of the elders of my people. If you will redeem it, do so. But if you will not, tell me, so I will know. For no one has the right to do it except you, and I am next in line."**

**"I will redeem it," he said.**

**Then Boaz said, "On the day you buy the land from Naomi, you also acquire Ruth the Moabite, the dead man's widow, in order to maintain the name of the dead with his property."**

Elders governed ancient cities (Dt. 19:12; Jdg. 8:14). The author does not reveal how many elders served in Bethlehem. Since Boaz took "ten of the elders of the town," there must have been more than ten men performing that duty. Apparently a quorum of ten men was needed to conduct legal business. (The Merriam-Webster Dictionary states that a quorum is "the smallest number of people who must be present at a meeting in order for decisions to be made. ")[24] These men supervised the town's business (1 Ki. 12:6-8; Jer. 26:17-19). They acted as the town's council, and sometimes represented the people before Yahweh (Lev. 4:13-15). They also decided issues affecting levirate marriages and the duties of kinsman-redeemers (Dt. 25:5-10). To avoid the appearance of favoritism, non-family members served as witnesses in legal transactions. In case anyone ever questioned what was said or done at this meeting, Boaz wanted these elders to be his witnesses.

A family's land could not be permanently sold. When the family moved from Bethlehem to Moab, Elimelek may have sold the rights to his harvest while retaining actual ownership of the land. As a result, Naomi was destitute. She still owned the family's property, but not the crops produced on that land. Naomi asked Boaz to redeem it for the family. Due to poverty, she could not redeem it herself. She probably wanted Boaz to redeem the harvest rights (lease), not the land itself, until the year of Jubilee. (All property was returned to its original owner in the year of Jubilee.) Hebrews believed God, not they, owned the property.

Elimelek's land now belonged to his widow, Naomi. Had her sons lived, they would have inherited their father's land. Since they were dead, the property passed to their mother, and then to their widows. (Women inherited land only if there were no male heirs.) Orpah was not part of this discussion because she had returned to her family in Moab.

Israelites were not allowed to transfer land from one tribe to another. Land ownership was required to remain in the original tribe. **"No inheritance in Israel is to pass from one tribe to another, for every Israelite shall keep the tribal inheritance of their ancestors"** (Nu. 36:7).

---

24      "Quorum." Merriam-Webster, Incorporated, 2017. Web. 23 Feb. 2017. <https://www.merriam-webster. com/dictionary/quorum.

According to God's Law, if an impoverished Israelite were forced to sell his land, the next of kin could redeem the property by paying fair market value (price the property would sell for on the open market) until the year of Jubilee (Lev. 25:23-28).

Boaz had a deep and personal relationship with Yahweh. He endeavored to obey the Law of God, and placed a high priority on faithfulness, reverence, devotion, and godly behavior. He did far more than extend hospitality to strangers. As the kinsman-redeemer, he foreshadowed (indicated a future event) the redeeming work of our savior and redeemer, Jesus Christ. Because of his actions, Ruth became an ancestor of the Messiah and a member of the household of God (Eph. 2:19). Boaz paid the price to redeem and restore Ruth and Naomi, just as Jesus paid the price to redeem and restore His people (1 Cor. 6:20).

Naomi was past the age of having more children. If she had not had a daughter-in-law (Ruth), the levirate law would not have been relevant. Ruth was Mahlon's widow. When Naomi died, the land would pass to her. The kinsman could not redeem the land without marrying Ruth and raising children in Mahlon's name.

Maintaining the name of the dead was very important in ancient Israel. If a man had no sons, his name could be preserved through his daughters. They would inherit his property (Nu. 27:1-11). This marriage obligation only applied to widows within the man's tribe (Nu. 36).

## RUTH 4:6-8

**6 At this, the guardian-redeemer said, "Then I cannot redeem it because I might endanger my own estate. You redeem it yourself. I cannot do it." 7 (Now in earlier times in Israel, for the redemption and transfer of property to become final, one party took off his sandal and gave it to the other. This was the method of legalizing transactions in Israel.)**

**8 So the guardian-redeemer said to Boaz, "Buy it yourself." And he removed his sandal.**

At first the relative agreed to redeem the land. Then Boaz explained the kinsman would also have to marry Mahlon's widow, Ruth. This close relative was interested in redeeming the land but did not want to marry a

Moabite widow or support her mother-in-law. The writer did not explain how the man's marriage to Ruth would endanger his estate. Perhaps the cost of redemption was too high. It is also possible he already had a wife and children, although none was mentioned. The purpose of a levirate marriage was to preserve the name of the dead person, so the inheritance would continue through the line of Elimelek and Mahlon rather than through the line of the redeemer.

Boaz skillfully explained this situation. Naomi was too old to have more children, but Ruth was young. If she bore a child, the land would continue in Elimelek's line, not the redeemer's. He would have to support Naomi, Ruth, and any future children born of their marriage in addition to any children he already had. The cost was too large, so he gave up his right to become the family's redeemer. Boaz was anxious to act as the kinsman-redeemer, although he was not legally required to do so. He wanted to redeem Elimelek's property and provide for his widow and daughter-in-law. He maintained their family name, which is still remembered throughout the world, not just in ancient Israel. The relative was far more concerned with protecting his own inheritance.

Daniel Whedon suggests an alternative possibility for the kinsman's refusal. Notice Boaz wisely referred to Ruth as "the Moabite" (Ru. 4:5). It is likely many people in Bethlehem believed Kilion and Mahlon's deaths were God's punishment for marrying Moabite wives. Redeeming the land meant the relative also had to marry Mahlon's Moabite widow. He may have rejected Boaz's offer due to fear of his own death.[25]

Albert Barnes put forward a third potential reason for the kinsman's refusal. Was he a poor man? The price for the land as well as the cost of supporting both Naomi and Ruth may have been too great for him to pay. He simply could not afford to become the redeemer, even if he wanted to. This was not a problem for the wealthy Boaz.[26]

As Boaz had wished, the relative gave up his right to act as Ruth and Naomi's redeemer in the sandal ceremony. (The ceremony was

---

25    Clarke, A., Barnes, A., Benson, J., Exell, J. S., Coffman, J. B., Gill, J., Beza, T., Pett, P., Ellicott, C., Whedon, D., Poole, M., Wesley, J., … Torrey, R. A. (2017). Verse-by-Verse Bible Commentary Ruth 4:6. Retrieved January 11, 2017, from https://www/commentary/ruth/4-6. html

26    Ibid

explained in Dt. 25:5-9. Notice, in verse 7, the author explained this was the custom in former times. Apparently, the sandal (or shoe) ceremony was no longer observed when the book was written. It is also possible this explanation was added later.) No legal document was required. By taking off his sandal, the relative showed he gave up his right to be kinsman-redeemer. Boaz gladly took his place. This refusal was not viewed as a disgrace. The right of redemption was simply reassigned from the unnamed relative to Boaz. Taking the relative's sandal indicated Boaz was willing to act as redeemer. This ceremony was legally binding. (J. B. Coffman believes Boaz returned the sandal to the kinsman when the ceremony was completed.)

Before written contracts, public sandal ceremonies were used to indicate the parties involved agreed to the transaction (Am. 2:6, 8:6). Peter Pett suggests, "This custom may be connected with the fact that it was the shoe which trod on the land denoting the owner's possession. "[27] Boaz obtained Elimelek's estate from Naomi and married her daughter-in-law, Ruth. Since Boaz was not Mahlon's brother, the obligations of a levirate marriage did not apply to him. He willingly chose to marry Ruth and take care of Naomi.

## RUTH 4:9-12

**Then Boaz announced to the elders and all the people, "Today you are witnesses that I have bought from Naomi all the property of Elimelek, Kilion and Mahlon. 10 I have also acquired Ruth the Moabite, Mahlon's widow, as my wife, in order to maintain the name of the dead with his property, so that his name will not disappear from among his family or from his hometown. Today you are witnesses!"**

**11 Then the elders and all the people at the gate said, "We are witnesses. May the LORD make the woman who is coming into your home like Rachel and Leah, who together built up the family**

---

27    Clarke, A., Barnes, A., Benson, J., Exell, J. S., Coffman, J. B., Gill, J., Beza, T., Pett, P., Ellicott, C., Whedon, D., Poole, M., Wesley, J., ... Torrey, R. A. (2017). Verse-by-Verse Bible Commentary Ruth 4:7. Retrieved January 11, 2017, from https://www/commentary/ruth/4-7. html

**of Israel. May you have standing in Ephrathah and be famous in Bethlehem. 12 Through the offspring the LORD gives you by this young woman, may your family be like that of Perez, whom Tamar bore to Judah."**

Boaz was delighted. Since the relative was not willing or able to be the kinsman-redeemer, Boaz was free to marry Ruth. Financially, this was not a wise move. Naomi's land would go to their son, not to Boaz, and supporting two widows was expensive. Boaz showed genuine biblical kindness. **"Freely you have received; freely give"** (Mt. 10:8).

The witnesses proclaimed blessings on Ruth and their future children. First, they prayed Ruth would be like Rachel and Leah, wives of Jacob. (His name was changed to Israel.) The twelve tribes of Israel came from Rachel (Jacob's favorite wife), Leah (also his wife), and two handmaids: Zilpah and Bilhah (Ge. 46:8-27). In ancient Israel, children born to handmaids were listed as the wives' offspring, so the elders did not feel it was necessary to mention Zilpah and Bilhah. Behavior considered immoral today was acceptable in Jacob's day. The phrase **"built up the family of Israel"** (verse 11) meant they had many children for Jacob.

Thirty-five percent of the babies born in Ruth's day died before their fifth birthday, so large families were common and necessary. Most women had many children. The witnesses hoped Ruth and Boaz would as well. God answered their prayers. The righteous couple had many descendants and became ancestors of Jesus Christ. (Scripture records only one child, Obed, born to Ruth and Boaz.)

Second, the elders prayed they would be respected and honored in Bethlehem. Ephrathah was an ancient name for Bethlehem (Ge. 35:16, 35:19, 48:7).

Their third prayer was for their family to be like Perez, also spelled Pharez. Boaz was a member of the prominent clan of Perez, the son of Judah (Ge. 38:26-29), and an ancestor of King David (Ru. 4:18-26) and Jesus Christ (Mt. 1:1-16).

Tamar, the Canaanite, was a Gentile like Ruth. She was the widow of Er, Judah's oldest son. The second brother, Onan, refused to have a child with Tamar in the name of his deceased brother, Er. By God's judgment, Onan died for his sin. The third son, Shelah, refused to give her a levirate marriage. Tamar tricked her father-in-law, Judah, by pretending to be a prostitute. She had twin sons with him. Perez, the older twin, was the forefather of the Bethlehem Ephrathites (Ge. 38:1-30; 1 Ch. 2:3-5). Judah, not knowing her true identity, unintentionally fulfilled the levirate requirement to his son's widow. Ancient Hebrews did not consider this incest, and the twins were not illegitimate. Both Tamar and Ruth are listed in the genealogy of Jesus (Mt. 1:3, 1:5). Through them, Judah became an ancestor of Jesus Christ, the Messiah of the world.

Pastor Mike Moreau explains, "What God considers immoral never changes. In Old Testament times, God often permitted what was contrary to His moral law to accomplish His objectives. I believe one husband and one wife was God's original plan."

The family line of the relative who rejected Ruth has been lost forever. **"Good people are remembered long after they are gone, but the wicked are soon forgotten"** (Pr. 10:7 CEV). The man who would not risk damaging his inheritance remains forever nameless.

To redeem Naomi's land, Boaz married Ruth and provided an heir. This was part of God's divine plan. Since Ruth and Mahlon had not been able to have children, Boaz did not know if Ruth would be able to have his child. However, he believed God would work things out according to His plan. The elders asked God to give Boaz a family like Perez, an ancestor of the tribe of Judah. God answered that prayer and gave a baby to the childless Ruth.

Boaz trusted God and did what was right in His eyes. As a result, God blessed His faithful servant. Boaz became the great-grandfather of King David, and an ancestor of the Messiah who came to save the elect of the human race.

## RUTH 4:13-15

**13 So Boaz took Ruth and she became his wife. When he made love to her, the LORD enabled her to conceive, and she gave birth to a son. 14 The women said to Naomi: "Praise be to the LORD, who this day has not left you without a guardian-redeemer. May he become famous throughout Israel! 15 He will renew your life and sustain you in your old age. For your daughter-in-law, who loves you and who is better to you than seven sons, has given him birth."**

Boaz married Ruth. According to Adam Clarke, "The Law of Moses had prohibited the Moabites, even to the tenth generation, from entering into the congregation of the Lord, but most Jews believed this law did not apply to women. Even if it did, Ruth might have been exempt since she was already a member of Naomi's family through marriage to her son. She had left her own country (Moab), people, and gods, and had become a convert (proselyte) to Yahweh, the God of Israel." It is doubtful an unconverted Moabite woman would have been allowed into the congregation.[28]

God loves His people and rewards those who obey Him. He used Naomi to bless Ruth. The older woman endured hardships and grief, but she did not lose her faith in God. The women of Bethlehem declared Ruth's love was a greater blessing to her **"than seven sons"** (Ru. 4:15). This was a significant tribute. Seven was regarded as a number of completeness or perfection. Seven sons would have been a great blessing and a perfect family. Sons were more desirable than daughters because they were providers and protectors. Some viewed daughters as expensive burdens. Ruth was loyal to Naomi and blessed her in many ways. She became the wife of a wealthy man and the mother of a son who became Naomi's heir. She did more for Naomi than seven sons could have done. Because she dearly loved her mother-in-law, Ruth gave up her country, family, and religion. She went to a new land and believed in their God. Ruth's son, Obed, gave Naomi a male heir. Property was passed down the male line, so the family's inheritance was preserved.

God rescued Ruth from the hardships of a destitute widow and blessed her with a godly husband and a healthy son.

Notice, in verse 13, the writer said the Lord, **"enabled her to conceive."** Ruth had been unable to have a child during her ten-year marriage to Mahlon. This pregnancy was a blessing from God, the giver

---

28      Clarke, A., Barnes, A., Benson, J., Exell, J. S., Coffman, J. B., Gill, J., Beza, T., Pett, P., Ellicott, C., Whedon, D., Poole, M., Wesley, J., … Torrey, R. A. (2017). Verse-by-Verse Bible Commentary Ruth 4:14. Retrieved January 11, 2017, from https://www/commentary/ruth/4-14. html

of life. Yahweh gladly received a faithful Moabite proselyte into His covenant people. He commanded His faithful followers to do the same. **"The foreigner residing among you must be treated as your native-born. Love them as yourself, for you were foreigners in Egypt. I am the LORD your God"** (Lev. 19:34).

In verse 14, the women said on "this day," the day of Obed's birth, the Lord gave Naomi a grandson who became her redeemer. (Boaz became the redeemer of both Ruth and Naomi, but upon his death, the duty fell to Obed.) John Gill suggests the women mentioned in this verse may have been friends and neighbors who helped with Obed's birth.[29]

**"In their hearts humans plan their course, but the LORD establishes their steps"** (Pr. 16:9).

Praise God! First, He blessed Naomi with a loving and loyal daughter-in-law who gave up her homeland, family, and gods to take care of her. Now, the childless widow was blessed with a grandson to love. Even though Obed was Boaz's biological son, he was considered to be Naomi's grandson. He would be responsible for her care upon his father's death or disability. The woman who had grieved for her husband and sons was now filled with joy and hope for the future.

Experts do not agree to whom the women referred when they said, **"May he become famous throughout Israel!"** (Ru. 4:14). Many believe they meant God, because He blessed Naomi and sent Obed as a forefather of Jesus. Some feel they referred to Boaz, because of his kindness and faithfulness. Finally, others imagine they spoke of Obed. He would take care of Naomi in her old age. As the head of her family, he would inherit the family's land. He would be the forefather of both King David and Jesus Christ.

In verse 15, the author wrote Obed, not Boaz, would sustain Naomi in her old age. Remember, Boaz was older than Ruth. He could have been as old as Naomi. Since men often have shorter lifespans than women, he might have died or been unable to care for her when she was no longer capable of caring for herself.

---

29    Clarke, A., Barnes, A., Benson, J., Exell, J. S., Coffman, J. B., Gill, J., Beza, T., Pett, P., Ellicott, C., Whedon, D., Poole, M., Wesley, J., … Torrey, R. A. (2017). Verse-by-Verse Bible Commentary Ruth 4:14. Retrieved January 11, 2017, from https://www/commentary/ruth/4-14. html

## RUTH 4:16-17

**16 Then Naomi took the child in her arms and cared for him. 17 The women living there said, "Naomi has a son!" And they named him Obed. He was the father of Jesse, the father of David.**

Nothing is beyond the love and abilities of God. Sometimes He allows trials so we will depend on Him. He showed love and kindness to both the living (Ruth and Naomi), and the dead (Mahlon and Elimelek). He provided Naomi with a devoted daughter-in-law and an heir to carry on the family name so Mahlon and Elimelek would not be forgotten. (Kilion's widow, Orpah, had left the family.) He ended the famine and brought the two poverty-stricken widows back to Bethlehem. Through Boaz, He gave them food, security, and a home. Boaz and Ruth had a son, Obed, who was an ancestor of King David and our Lord Jesus Christ. **"Know therefore that the LORD your God is God; He is the faithful God, keeping His covenant of love to a thousand generations of those who love Him and keep His commandments"** (Dt. 7: 9).

God never makes mistakes. He has a purpose for everyone and everything. There are no coincidences with God. My friend, Ethel Herin, often referred to such events as "God-incidences." Had there been no famine, Naomi, her husband, and sons would never have left Israel and moved to Moab. Had the family not moved to Moab, they would never have met Ruth. Had Mahlon lived, Ruth would never have married Boaz and given birth to Obed. God has a purpose for everything that happens, whether good or bad. His time is not our time, but His way is always right. Through God's grace, a pagan Moabite became a child of God and an ancestor of our Messiah.

**"There is a time for everything, and a season for every activity under the heavens: a time to be born and a time to die, a time to plant and a time to uproot, a time to kill and a time to heal, a time to tear down and a time to build, a time to weep and a time to laugh, a time to mourn and a time to dance, a time to scatter stones and a time to gather them, a time to embrace and a time to refrain from**

embracing, a time to search and a time to give up, a time to keep and a time to throw away, a time to tear and a time to mend, a time to be silent and a time to speak, a time to love and a time to hate, a time for war and a time for peace" (Ecc. 3:1-8).

Some traditions believe Boaz was a childless widower at the time he met Ruth. Scripture neither verifies nor contradicts this idea.

In verse 16, the NIV states Naomi cared for Obed, but many translations assert she became his nurse (ASV, KJ21, ASV, AMP, ESV, and others). This did not imply the older woman served as his wet nurse (a woman who breast-feeds a child not her own). She simply loved and took care of him, as any loving grandmother would. (His biological paternal grandmother was Rahab, mother of Boaz. No mention is made of Ruth's Moabite family.) This story is far more than the story of a happy grandmother doting on her new grandson. Obed's birth led to the nativity of our Messiah, Jesus Christ.

In verse 17, the neighbor women said, **"Naomi has a son!"** They were not incorrect. In the ancient Hebrew language, the word for son could mean either "male child of" or "male descendant of," which could lead to confusion.

Verse 17 also states that they, the women living there, named the baby Obed because he would care for Naomi in her old age. (Obed is a diminutive form of the name Obadiah which means a "servant of the Lord" or "worshipper of God." Obed means "one who serves" or "servant.") He is the only child in the Bible said to be named by anyone other than his parents. This does not mean the women actually chose Obed's name. They may have suggested a suitable name, but only his father and mother had the right to choose his name. Baby Obed grew up to serve the God of Israel and take care of his family's needs, particularly those of Ruth and Naomi.

**"He settles the childless woman in her home as a happy mother of children. Praise the LORD"** (Ps. 113:9).

When Naomi left Moab and returned to Bethlehem, she felt bitter and empty. Now she was joyful and hopeful. Her arms and her heart were now filled with a cherished grandson. God gave her the strength and grace to overcome her grief and hope for a joyous future. Just as his parents and grandmother did before him, Obed trusted, obeyed, and served God.

Ruth was truly a godly woman, as described in Proverbs 31. "**A wife of noble character who can find? She is worth far more than rubies. Her husband has full confidence in her and lacks nothing of value. She brings him good, not harm, all the days of her life... She opens her arms to the poor and extends her hands to the needy... Her husband is respected at the city gate, where he takes his seat among the elders of the land... She is clothed with strength and dignity; she can laugh at the days to come. She speaks with wisdom, and faithful instruction is on her tongue. She watches over the affairs of her household and does not eat the bread of idleness. Her children arise and call her blessed; her husband also, and he praises her: "Many women do noble things, but you surpass them all. Charm is deceptive, and beauty is fleeting; but a woman who fears the LORD is to be praised. Honor her for all that her hands have done, and let her works bring her praise at the city gate**" (Pr. 31:10-31).

Prayer and blessings were very important in the book of Ruth. Day or night, God is always ready to listen to His people.

Naomi prayed for Orpah and Ruth: "**May the LORD grant that each of you will find rest in the home of another husband**" (Ru. 1:9).

Boaz prayed for Ruth: "**May the LORD repay you for what you have done. May you be richly rewarded by the LORD, the God of Israel, under whose wings you have come to take refuge**" (Ru. 2:12).

Naomi prayed for Boaz: "**The LORD bless him!**" Naomi said to her **daughter-in-law. "He has not stopped showing his kindness to the living and the dead." She added, "That man is our close relative; he is one of our guardian-redeemers**" (Ru. 2:20).

Boaz again prayed for Ruth: "**The LORD bless you, my daughter... This kindness is greater than that which you showed earlier: You have not run after the younger men, whether rich or poor**" (Ru. 3:10).

Then the elders and all the people at the gate said, "**We are witnesses. May the LORD make the woman who is coming into** your home like Rachel and Leah, who together built up the family of Israel. May you have standing in Ephrathah and be famous in Bethlehem. Through the offspring the LORD gives you by this young woman, may your family be like that of Perez, whom Tamar bore to Judah" (Ru. 4:11-12).

The women said to Naomi: "Praise be to the LORD, who this day has not left you without a guardian-redeemer. May he become famous throughout Israel!" (Ru. 4:14).

## RUTH 4:18-22

18 This, then, is the family line of Perez: Perez was the father of Hezron, 19 Hezron the father of Ram, Ram the father of Amminadab, 20 Amminadab the father of Nahshon [brother-in-law of Aaron and tribal leader in Israel (Ex. 6:23; 1 Ch. 2:10), leader of Judah during the Exodus (Nu. 1:7, 2:3, 7:12, 10:14)], Nahshon the father of Salmon, [Some Hebrew manuscripts call him Salma.] 21 Salmon the father of Boaz, Boaz the father of Obed, 22 Obed the father of Jesse, and Jesse the father of David.

The family tree in the book of Ruth extends as far as King David. From his line, Jesus the Messiah would be born. The time span shown in this genealogical list is approximately 845 years, from Perez (circa 1885 BC) to David (circa 1040 BC). Only ten generations are shown, so many scholars assume this is probably a compressed genealogy. However, with God, all things are possible (Mt. 19:26; Mk. 10:27). Remember, Shem, Ham, and Japheth were born after Noah was 500 years old (Ge. 5:32). When Isaac was born, Sarah was 90 and Abraham was 100 (Ge. 17:17). Every generation was probably not included. Less well-known names could have been left out, while prominent names were included. By showing Perez was an ancestor of David, the family tree can be traced back to Judah (Ge. 49:8-10), Jacob (Ge. 28:10-14), Isaac (Ge. 26:24), and Abraham (Ge. 12:1-2). David was not listed as King David, which implies the book was written after David's birth, but before he became king.

In a levirate marriage, a brother of Ruth's late husband, Mahlon, would have been required to marry her. Mahlon's only brother, Kilion, was also dead, so the marriage of Ruth and Boaz was not a true levirate marriage. Had this been the case, Obed would have been listed as the son of Mahlon, but he was not. He was always considered to be the son of Boaz, the second husband of Ruth.

Some scholars believe the genealogy listed in the book of Ruth was not in the original text. They speculate it could have been added at a later time. Albert Barnes suggests it may have come from a family book belonging to the house of Pharez.[30] The pedigree in First Chronicles is similar to the one listed in Ruth 4:18-22, however, there are some differences in spelling. (See Chapter 5)

Salmon (Salma, Salmah) may have been one of the spies sent to Jericho who was protected by Rahab (Jos. 2). This theory cannot be biblically verified. Boaz's mother Rahab and the harlot Rahab may not have been the same woman. Without last names or corroborating details, it is often impossible to make positive identification.

Prophecy established the Messiah would come from the line of Judah. **"Judah will hold the royal scepter, and his descendants will always rule. Nations will bring him tribute and bow in obedience before him"** (Ge. 49:10 GNT).

Nothing happens by chance. Yahweh is always faithful. He instituted His plan to redeem the world through His Son Jesus Christ before He created the world. God uses ordinary people to do amazing things. He supplied a kinsman-redeemer for a destitute Moabite widow, and she became an ancestor of Jesus Christ (Mt. 1:1-17; Lk. 3:23-38).

God does not demand racial and ethnic purity. Remember, Jesus had a Canaanite and a Moabite in His family tree. The books of Matthew and Luke provide the genealogy of Jesus, showing He descended from Boaz and Ruth. Without Ruth, a poor woman from a pagan nation, Jesus would not have been born.

Most genealogies are patriarchal. That means fathers and grandfathers are listed, but mothers and grandmothers are usually ignored. Matthew

---

30      Clarke, A., Barnes, A., Benson, J., Exell, J. S., Coffman, J. B., Gill, J., Beza, T., Pett, P., Ellicott, C., Whedon, D., Poole, M., Wesley, J., … Torrey, R. A. (2017). Verse-by-Verse Bible Commentary Ruth 4:18. Retrieved January 11, 2017, from https://www/commentary/ruth/4-18. html

included Rahab and Ruth (Mt. 1:5), but Luke did not (Luke 3:32). Mark and John do not record any part of Jesus' ancestry. Some names are well-known, but others are unfamiliar. God can use anyone in His divine plan. (See Chapter 5 for Jesus' family tree as recorded by Matthew, Luke, and Ezra in First Chronicles.)

The book of Ruth was filled with doubt, uncertainty, setbacks, and hard times, but there was also a great deal of hope too. The lives of God's righteous people are rarely without troubles. The book of Ruth began with famine and death (Naomi's husband and sons) and ended with the joyous birth of Obed. There were many difficulties along the way. With the move from Moab to Bethlehem, the tone changed from despair to hope and from death to life. Both Ruth and Naomi had hope for the future. Ruth entered Bethlehem as a despised foreigner, but she became a beloved daughter of the King. For ten years, she had been unable to conceive, then God blessed her and Boaz with a son. She became an ancestor of the Messiah who came to save the world (Jn. 3:16). God changed the lives of two grieving widows and brought them joy. The lesson this book teaches is as valid in the twenty-first century as it was thousands of years ago. We must trust God even in times of grief or suffering. He has a plan for our lives that He will reveal in His own time. Pray and study the word of God rather than depend on the advice of friends. No matter how good it may sound, not all guidance is godly.

**"For it is not those who hear the law who are righteous in God's sight, but it is those who obey the law who will be declared righteous"** (Romans 2:13). Boaz and Ruth were not righteous because they kept the Law better than other people. They were righteous because they were faithful to God. Yahweh provided a righteous remnant who endeavored to do His will. Ruth and Boaz had a godly marriage and became the parents of a son, Obed, who became Jesus' ancestor.

More than 900 years before the birth of Christ, Solomon, the son of King David wrote: **"My son, pay attention to what I say. Remember my commands. Listen to wisdom, and do your best to understand. Ask for good judgment. Cry out for understanding. Look for wisdom like silver. Search for it like hidden treasure. If you do this, you will understand what it means to respect the LORD, and you will come to know God** (Pr. 2:1-5 ESV).

The author never complimented Naomi, but he showed great respect for both Ruth and Boaz. The people of Bethlehem praised God for His blessings, but never praised Naomi. Perhaps they felt she did what was right in her own eyes rather than depend on the mercy and providence of God.

Ruth was a caring woman who showed great love and respect for Naomi. Her loving deeds did more to demonstrate God's love than words could have ever expressed. She was hardworking (Ru. 2:2, 2:7), polite (Ru. 2:10), appreciative (Ru. 2:13), considerate (Ru. 2:14), and most important, she loved God (Ru. 1:16). When she entered Bethlehem as a Moabite (Ru. 2:10) she was less important than a servant (Ruth 2:13), but by God's providence and grace, she married Boaz (Ru. 4:13) and became Obed's mother (Ru. 4:17). Love overcame fear, hopelessness, poverty, grief, bitterness, and loneliness.

Pagan gods were believed to be capricious and undependable, but Yahweh was and is a covenant-keeping God. He is our security in times of trouble. The path Ruth and Naomi traveled was often treacherous, but God was with them each step of the way. We can depend on Him every hour of every day. His care is constant. We can rest because God never rests.

This story began in sorrow but ended with great joy. The lessons we can learn from the book of Ruth are important today. Obviously, we do not have to worry about levirate marriages or sandal ceremonies, but we still face many of the problems they did in Ruth's day. Trials and temptations, famines, poverty, death, and childlessness are just as real in the twenty-first century as they were hundreds of years ago. We may even be tempted to follow the practices of godless people because they are easy or fun. God still uses adversities to train and shape us according to His will so that we will bring glory to His name. Nothing can separate us from the love of God. He is worthy of our trust and praise.

Ruth and Boaz entered into their marriage covenant to serve God, not each other. Had Ruth chosen a younger husband, she might have had fun, but she would not have fulfilled the will of God. Nor would she have been the ancestor of our Lord.

**"If God is for us, who can be against us?"** (Ro. 8:31b). God does not promise us pain-free lives. We may not understand the hardships that befall us, but we must trust God and believe He will never desert His people. The apostle Paul wrote, **"I am sure that God Who began the good work in you will keep on working in you until the day Jesus Christ comes again"** (Php. 1:6 NLV). Even the most faithful believers face misfortunes. Do we trust God, or do we do what is right in our own eyes and take the easy way out? Trusting in ourselves and our opinions can lead to disaster. Only Jesus can save us and give us eternal life with Him in Heaven,

The "Field of Boaz" lies east of Beit Sahour, a Palestinian town south of Bethlehem. According to tradition, this is where Ruth gleaned grain (Ru. 2). The "Shepherds' Field" lies nearby. It is believed to be the field where the angel announced Jesus' birth to the shepherds (Lk. 2:8-11), eleven centuries after the events in this book took place.

Everything recorded in the book of Ruth pointed to the birth of Jesus Christ, our redeemer. He willingly paid the price for our salvation.

**"For you know that it was not with perishable things such as silver or gold that you were redeemed from the empty way of life handed down to you from your ancestors, but with the precious blood of Christ, a lamb without blemish or defect"** (1 Pe. 1:18-19).

**"For even the Son of Man did not come to be served, but to serve, and to give his life as a ransom for many"** (Mk. 10:45).

**"...the Father knows Me and I know the Father—and I lay down My life for the sheep"** (Jn. 10:15).

# Chapter 5: Final Thoughts

G ENEALOGY OF JESUS SOME PEOPLE FIND IT DIFFICULT TO COMPARE THE genealogies recorded by Matthew and Luke. From Abraham to David, the records are alike. However, from David to Jesus, they differ. Matthew recorded only 27 names, while Luke listed 42. Some believe this discrepancy is due to the fact many people were known by several names or even nicknames. For example, the Apostle Peter was also known as Simon (Mt. 10:2; Lk. 6:16), Simon Bar (son of) Jonah (Mt. 16:17), Simon Peter (Mt. 16:16), and Cephas (Jn. 1:42).

Others believe this apparent discrepancy is due to the fact Luke listed Mary's genealogy, while Matthew recorded Joseph's. (Joseph was Mary's husband, but not Jesus' father. Jesus was the Son of God.) Early church historians accepted these genealogical records as accurate. No one attempted to prove Jesus was not the Messiah because He was not David's descendant. Matthew lists four women (Tamar, Rahab, Ruth, and Mary) in Jesus' pedigree. Only Mary was an Israelite. The other three ladies were Gentiles.

# FROM THE GOSPEL OF LUKE, CHAPTER 3

**23** Now Jesus himself was about thirty years old when he began his ministry. He was the son, so it was thought, of Joseph, the son of Heli,

**24** the son of Matthat, the son of Levi, the son of Melki, the son of Jannai, the son of Joseph,

**25** the son of Mattathias, the son of Amos, the son of Nahum, the son of Esli, the son of Naggai,

**26** the son of Maath, the son of Mattathias, the son of Semein, the son of Josek, the son of Joda,

**27** the son of Joanan, the son of Rhesa, the son of Zerubbabel, the son of Shealtiel, the son of Neri,

**28** the son of Melki, the son of Addi, the son of Cosam, the son of Elmadam, the son of Er,

**29** the son of Joshua, the son of Eliezer, the son of Jorim, the son of Matthat, the son of Levi,

**30** the son of Simeon, the son of Judah, the son of Joseph, the son of Jonam, the son of Eliakim,

**31** the son of Melea, the son of Menna, the son of Mattatha, the son of Nathan, the son of David,

**32** the son of Jesse, the son of Obed, the son of Boaz, the son of Salmon [Some early manuscripts Sala], the son of Nahshon,

**33** the son of Amminadab, the son of Ram [Some manuscripts state "Amminadab, the son of Admin, the son of Arni;" other manuscripts vary widely.], the son of Hezron, the son of Perez, the son of Judah,

**34** the son of Jacob, the son of Isaac, the son of Abraham, the son of Terah, the son of Nahor,

**35** the son of Serug, the son of Reu, the son of Peleg, the son of Eber, the son of Shelah, **36** the son of Cainan, the son of Arphaxad, the son of Shem, the son of Noah, the son of Lamech,

**36** the son of Methuselah, the son of Enoch, the son of Jared, the son of Mahalalel, the son of Kenan,

**37** the son of Enosh, the son of Seth, the son of Adam, the son of God (Lk. 3: 23-38).

# FROM THE GOSPEL OF MATTHEW, CHAPTER 1

**This is the genealogy** [or is an account of the origin] **of Jesus the Messiah** [or Jesus Christ: Messiah (Hebrew) and Christ (Greek), both mean Anointed One] **the son of David, the son of Abraham:**

**Abraham was the father of Isaac, Isaac the father of Jacob, Jacob the father of Judah and his brothers,**

**Judah the father of Perez and Zerah, whose mother was Tamar, Perez the father of Hezron, Hezron the father of Ram,**

**Ram the father of Amminadab, Amminadab the father of Nahshon, Nahshon the father of Salmon,**

**Salmon the father of Boaz, whose mother was Rahab, Boaz the father of Obed, whose mother was Ruth, Obed the father of Jesse,**

**and Jesse the father of King David. David was the father of Solomon, whose mother had been Uriah's wife,**

**Solomon the father of Rehoboam, Rehoboam the father of Abijah, Abijah the father of Asa** [Greek-Asaph],

**Asa the father of Jehoshaphat, Jehoshaphat the father of Jehoram, Jehoram the father of Uzziah,**

**Uzziah the father of Jotham, Jotham the father of Ahaz, Ahaz the father of Hezekiah,**

**Hezekiah the father of Manasseh, Manasseh the father of Amon** [Greek-Amos], **Amon the father of Josiah,**

**and Josiah the father of Jeconiah** [Jehoiachin] **and his brothers at the time of the exile to Babylon.**

**After the exile to Babylon:**

**Jeconiah was the father of Shealtiel, Shealtiel the father of Zerubbabel,**

**Zerubbabel the father of Abihud, Abihud the father of Eliakim, Eliakim the father of Azor,**

Azor the father of Zadok, Zadok the father of Akim, Akim the father of Elihud,

Elihud the father of Eleazar, Eleazar the father of Matthan, Matthan the father of Jacob,

and Jacob the father of Joseph, the husband of Mary, and Mary was the mother of Jesus who is called the Messiah. (Notice Joseph is listed as the husband of Mary, not the father of Jesus.)

Thus, there were fourteen generations in all from Abraham to David, fourteen from David to the exile to Babylon, and fourteen from the exile to the Messiah (Mt. 1: 1-17).

# FROM THE BOOK OF FIRST CHRONICLES, CHAPTER 2

The genealogy recorded in First Chronicles is similar to Ruth 4:18-22, although there are differences in spelling.

**Judah's daughter-in-law Tamar bore Perez and Zerah to Judah.**

**He had five sons in all.**

**The sons of Perez: Hezron and Hamul.**

**The sons of Zerah: Zimri, Ethan, Heman, Kalkol and Darda** [Dara in some Hebrew manuscripts]—**five in all.**

**The son of Karmi: Achar,** [Achar means trouble; Achar is called Achan in Joshua. ] **who brought trouble on Israel by violating the ban on taking devoted things** [The Hebrew term refers to the irrevocable giving over of things or persons to the Lord, often by totally destroying them].

**The son of Ethan: Azariah.**

**The sons born to Hezron were: Jerahmeel, Ram and Caleb** [Hebrew Kelubai, a variant of Caleb].

**From Ram Son of Hezron**

**Ram was the father of Amminadab, and Amminadab the father of Nahshon, the leader of the people of Judah.**

**Nahshon was the father of Salmon,** [Septuagint (see also Ru. 4:21); Hebrew Salma] **Salmon the father of Boaz,**

**Boaz the father of Obed and Obed the father of Jesse.**

**Jesse was the father of Eliab his firstborn; the second son was Abinadab, the third Shimea, 14 the fourth Nethanel, the fifth Raddai, 15 the sixth Ozem and the seventh David** (1 Ch. 2:4-15).

# DIG DEEPER- DISCUSSION QUESTIONS

## INTRODUCTION

1. Who do you believe is the main character in the Book of Ruth? Explain your answer.
2. Do you believe the fact Elimelek and his family suffered hardships indicated God no longer cared for His people? Explain your answer.
3. What evidence do you see that shows God was at work in the people's lives?
4. Does God show favoritism based on race, ethnicity, social class, gender, or prior religious beliefs? Explain your answer.
5. How was the religion of the Moabites different from the religion of the Jews?
6. Why did Elimelek's family move to Moab?
7. What hardships were faced by widows in ancient Moab and Israel?
8. Describe the term "*hesed*."

## CHAPTER 1

1. Describe the behavior of the Hebrews during the time of the judges.

2. Why were fertility gods and agricultural gods worshipped in the Levant?

3. In what ways were the names of the family members significant in this story?

4. Why were widows without sons especially poverty-stricken? How did God show his care for widows?

5. Why does God warn believers not to be yoked together with unbelievers? Is this a condemnation of other nationalities or ethnic groups?

6. Why did Naomi decide to return to Bethlehem?

7. Why did Naomi tell Ruth and Orpah to return to their homeland and their gods?

8. What was a levirate marriage? How did this protect ancient families?

9. How were Ruth's actions different from Orpah's? Do you believe Orpah was a cruel or uncaring person?

10. Explain how Ruth's words revealed she believed in God?

11. Why did Naomi instruct the Bethlehemites to call her Mara?

## CHAPTER 2

1. Who was Boaz's mother? Why was her life and the lives of her family spared when Joshua and the Hebrews attacked her city (Jericho)?

2. Why do you believe Ruth gleaned in Boaz's field rather than in another landowner's field?

3. How did Mosaic law provide for poor widows?

4. How did Boaz demonstrate he truly was a man of God?

5. What was "gleaning?" Was this a safe job for a woman?

6. In what ways did Boaz show his concern for Ruth?

7. What was a guardian-redeemer? What were his duties?

## CHAPTER 3

1. What was the "Year of Jubilee"? How did this show God's love and care for His people?
2. What unusual instructions did Naomi give Ruth? How did this show a change in Naomi's attitude?
3. What "rest" did Naomi desire for Ruth? Why was this important?
4. Why did Ruth uncover Boaz's feet? Was this considered inappropriate?
5. Why did Boaz not immediately agree to marry Ruth? What did this reveal about his character?

## CHAPTER 4

1. What was the importance of a city gate in ancient Israel?
2. Why do you believe the author did not reveal the nearer-kinsman's name?
3. Why did Boaz include Ruth's ethnicity when negotiating with the unnamed man?
4. What was the purpose of the sandal ceremony?
5. Why might Obed's birth be considered a miracle from God?
6. Give examples of ways God answers prayers. You may use illustrations from this story as well as instances in your own life.
7. Why was listing Boaz's genealogy important?
8. Why is it often difficult to authenticate the identities of certain people mentioned in the Bible?

# RESOURCES

Adams, Mark. "Ruth When Life Is Not Fair (Ruth 1:1-17)." Lecture, Redland Baptist Church, Rockville, Maryland. May 21, 2000. Accessed April 24, 2018. http://www.redlandbaptist.org/sermon/ ruth-when-life-is-not-fair/.

"Apostasy." Vocabulary. com, Web. 31 Jan. 2017. https://www. vocabulary. com/dictionary/apostasy.

Barker, William. "Boaz." Everyone in the Bible. Westwood: Fleming H, Revel, 1966. 65-66.

Barker, William. "Elimelech." Everyone in the Bible. Westwood: Fleming H, Revel, 1966. 93.

Barker, William. "Naomi." Everyone in the Bible. Westwood: Fleming H, Revel, 1966. 254.

Barker, William. "Orpah." Everyone in the Bible. Westwood: Fleming H, Revel, 1966. 270.

Barker, William. "Rahab." Everyone in the Bible. Westwood: Fleming H, Revel, 1966. 294-295.

Barker, William. "Ruth." Everyone in the Bible. Westwood: Fleming H, Revel, 1966. 301.

Barker, William. "Salmon." Everyone in the Bible. Westwood: Fleming H, Revel, 1966. 304.

Barton, George A. "Ruth, Book of." Jewish Encyclopedia. com, 1906. Web. 28 Jan. 2016. http://www. jewishencyclopedia. com/ articles/12947-ruth-book-of. Biblegateway. https://www. biblegateway. com/passage/

Braimer, Stephen J. "Kinsman Redeemer." Baker's Evangelical Dictionary of Biblical Theology. 1996. Web. 27 Jan. 2016. http:// www. biblestudytools. com/dictionaries/bakers-evangelical-dictionary/kinsman-redeemer. html.

Burton, Judd H. "Chemosh Lord of the Moabites." About, Inc., 30 Aug. 2016. Web. 25 Jan. 2017. http://ancienthistory. about. com/od/ cgodsandgoddesses/a/chemosh. htm.

Carr, Alan. "Ruth: Pursued by Grace 1Three Tombstones in a Washpot. (Ruth 1:1-7)." Sermons and Outlines. 2003. Accessed April 24, 2018. http://www.sermonnotebook.org/old testament/Ruth 1_1-7.htm.

Carr, Alan. "Ruth: Pursued by Grace 2-Three Widows in a Washpot (Ruth 1:6-18)." Sermons and Outlines. 2003. Accessed April 30, 2018. http:// www.sermonnotebook.org/old testament/Ruth 1_6-18.htm.

Carr, Alan. "Pursued by Grace 3Coming Home The Hard Way (Ruth 1:19-22)." Sermons and Outlines. 2003. Accessed April 30, 2018. http:// www.sermonnotebook.org/old testament/Ruth 1_19-22.htm.

Carr, Alan. "Pursued by Grace 4Searching for Grace (Ruth 2:1-3)." Sermons and Outlines. 2003. Accessed April 30, 2018. http://www. sermonnotebook.org/old testament/Ruth 4_13-22.htm.

Carr, Alan. "Pursued by Grace 5In the Field of Grace (Ruth 2:4-17)." Sermons and Outlines. 2003. Accessed April 30, 2018. http://www. sermonnotebook.org/old testament/Ruth 2_4-17.htm.

Carr, Alan. "Pursued by Grace 6Good News From the Field of Grace (Ruth 2:17-21)." Sermons and Outlines. 2003. Accessed April 30, 2018. http://www. sermonnotebook. org/old testament/Ruth 2_17-21.htm.

Carr, Alan. "Pursued by Grace 7Abiding in the Field of Grace (Ruth 2:21-23)." Sermons and Outlines. 2003. Accessed April 30, 2018. http:// www.sermonnotebook.org/old testament/Ruth 2_21-23.htm.

Carr, Alan. "Pursued by Grace 8Looking For a Little Rest (Ruth 3:1-2)." Sermons and Outlines. 2003. Accessed April 30, 2018. http://www. sermonnotebook.org/old testament/Ruth 3_1-2.htm.

Carr, Alan. "Pursued by Grace 9Getting Ready to Meet the Master (Ruth 3:3)." Sermons and Outlines. 2003. Accessed April 30, 2018. http://www.sermonnotebook.org/old testament/Ruth 3_3.htm.

Carr, Alan. "Pursued by Grace 10Looking For a Place at His Feet (Ruth 3:1-11)." Sermons and Outlines. 2003. Accessed April 30, 2018. http://www.sermonnotebook.org/old testament/Ruth 3_1-11.htm.

Carr, Alan. "Pursued by Grace 11Redeemed, Redeemed, By Love Divine (Ruth 3:9-4:12)." Sermons and Outlines. 2003. Accessed April 30, 2018. http://www. sermonnotebook. org/old testament/Ruth 3_9-4_12.htm.

Carr, Alan. "Pursued by Grace 12Somebody Pinch Me Please (Ruth 4:13-22)." Sermons and Outlines. 2003. Accessed April 30, 2018. http://www.sermonnotebook.org/old testament/Ruth 4_13-22.htm.

"Chaff." Merriam Webster, Web. 27 Jan. 2017. https://www.merriam-webster. com/dictionary/chaff.

"Chemosh." New World Encyclopedia, 13 May 2013. Web. 25 Jan. 2017. http://www. newworldencyclopedia. org/entry/Chemosh.

Churchyard, G. (2002, March). There is a Redeemer. Retrieved January 12, 2017. http://www. easyenglish. info/bible-commentary/ruth-law. htm.

Clarke, A., Barnes, A., Benson, J., Exell, J. S., Coffman, J. B., Gill, J., Beza, T., Pett, P., Ellicott, C., Whedon, D., Poole, M., Wesley, J., … Torrey, R. A. (2017). Verse-by-Verse Bible Commentary Ruth. Retrieved January 11, 2017, from https://www. studylight. org/commentary/ruth. html

Coogan, Michael D., ed. "Ruth." The New Oxford Annotated Bible with the Apocrypha: Revised Standard Version, containing the second edition of the New Testament and an expanded edition of the Apocrypha. 3rd ed. New York, NY: Oxford U Press, 2001. 391-397.

"Deuteronomist." Encyclopædia Britannica. 20 July 1998. Web. 10 Mar. 2017. https://www.britannica. com/topic/Deuteronomist.

Deffinbaugh, Robert L. "1. Return to Bethlehem (Ruth 1)." Bible. org. 10 Jan. 2010. Web. 17 Feb. 2017. https://bible.org/seriespage/1-return-bethlehem-ruth-1.

Deffinbaugh, Robert L. "2. Can eHarmony Beat This? (Ruth 2)." Bible. org. N. 24 Jan. 2010. Web. 14 Feb. 2017. https://bible.org/seriespage/2-can-eharmony-beat-ruth-2

Deffinbaugh, Robert L. "Cutting Corners: Naomi's Under Cover Operation (Ruth 3)." Bible.org. 31 Jan. 2010. Web. 20 Feb. 2017. https://bible.org/ seriespage/3-cutting-corners-naomi-s-under-cover-operation-ruth-3.

Deffinbaugh, Robert L. "4. Redeemed (Ruth 4)." Bible.org. 2010. Web. 20 Feb. 2017. https://bible.org/seriespage/4-redeemed-ruth-4.

"Emigration." English Oxford Living Dictionaries. Oxford University Press, 2017. Web. 24 Jan. 2017. https://en.oxforddictionaries.com/definition/emigration.

Englebrecht, E. A. (Ed.). (2009). "Ruth." The Lutheran Study Bible. St. Louis, MO: Concordia Publishing House. 422-430.

"Ephah." Biblehub.com. 2017. Accessed November 21, 2017. http://biblehub. com/topical/e/ephah.html

"Ephah." Merriam Webster, Web. 27 Jan. 2017. https://www.merriam-webster. com/dictionary/ephah.

"Ephratah." WebBible Encyclopedia, Web. 26 Jan. 2017. http://www. christiananswers. net/dictionary/ephratah.html.

"5 Essential Lessons from the Book of Ruth You Need to Know." Bible Study Tools. July 13, 2015. Accessed April 24, 2018. https://www. biblestudytools. com/bible-study/explore-the-bible/5-essential-lessons-you-need-to-know-from-the-book-of-ruth. html.

Evans, Tony, ed. "Faith Through Trials." *Explore the Bible*, Winter 201617, 121-140.

Life Way. com

"Frequently Asked Questions About The Jubilee Of Mercy: What is a jubilee year?" United States Conference of Catholic Bishops, 2017. Web. 17 Feb. 2017. http://www.usccb.org/beliefs-and-teachings/ how-we-teach/new-evangelization/jubilee-of-mercy/frequentlyasked-questions-about-the-jubilee-of-mercy. cfm.

Gifford, Jerry. "Facing the Hidden Dangers that Threaten the Home–Ruth." Life Way. First Baptist Church of Franklin, KY, Web. 12 Feb. 2015. http://www.lifeway.com/Article/ sermon-ruth-facing-hidden-dangers-home-family-marriage.

Gifford, Jerry. "The Burden and Bitterness of a Barren Life– Ruth 1." Life Way. First Baptist Church of Franklin, KY, Web. 12 Feb. 2017. http://www.lifeway.com/Article/ sermon-ruth-burden-bitterness-barenness-joy-fulfillment.

Gifford, Jerry. "Holding the Family Together when Your World Is Falling Apart–Ruth 1." Life Way. First Baptist Church of Franklin, KY, Web. 14 Feb. 2017. http://www.lifeway.com/Article/ sermon-ruth-holding-family-together.

Gifford, Jerry. "Why Do Some WalkAway?–Ruth 1." Life Way. First Baptist Church of Franklin, KY, Web. 13 Feb. 2017. http://www. lifeway.com/ Article/sermon-ruth-facing-hidden-dangers-home-family-marriage.

Gifford, Jerry. "Virtuous Realities, Part 1–Ruth 1, 2." Life Way. First Baptist Church of Franklin, KY, Web. 16 Feb. 2017. http://www. lifeway. com/Article/sermon-ruth-virtue-relationships-1.

Gifford, Jerry. "Virtuous Realities, Part 2–Ruth 2." Life Way. First Baptist Church of Franklin, KY, Web. 16 Feb. 2017. http://www. lifeway. com/ Article/sermon-ruth-virtue-relationships-2.

Gifford, Jerry. "Love Is In The Air Ruth 3." Life Way. First Baptist Church of Franklin, KY, Web. 15 Feb. 2015. http://www.lifeway. com/ Article/sermon-ruth-build-relationships-love-marriage.

Gifford, Jerry. "Sermon: A Heritage Builder–Ruth 4." Life Way. First Baptist Church of Franklin, KY, Web. 18 Feb. 2017. http://www. lifeway. com/Article/sermon-ruth-heritage-builder.

"Glean." Merriam Webster, Web. 27 Jan. 2017. <https://www.merriam-webster. com/dictionary/glean>.

Hagensick, Carl. "Faith Hanging On A Thread." The Herald of Christ's Kingdom, 03 Jan. 2003. Web. 14 Feb. 2017. http://www.heraldmag. org/literature/bio_7.htm.

Halley, Henry H. "Ruth Great Grandmother of David: Beginning of Messianic Family." Pocket Bible handbook: an abbreviated Bible commentary. 23rd ed. Grand Rapids, MI: Regency Reference Library, 1965. 175-176.

Henderson, Daniel. Sermon: "Ruth '1God's Kindness on Display." Grace Presbyterian Church (PCA), Blairsville, GA, 12 July 2015.

Henderson, Daniel. Sermon: "Ruth 2From Famine to Plenty." Grace Presbyterian Church (PCA), Blairsville, GA, 19 July 2015.

Henry, Matthew. Ruth–Matthew Henry's Concise Commentary on the Bible. Retrieved January 13, 2017, from https://www.biblegateway.com/resources/commentaries/Matthew-Henry/Ruth/

Hill, Andrew E., and John H. Walton. "Ruth." A survey of the Old Testament. Grand Rapids, MI: Zondervan Pub. House, 2009. 249-253

Hinckley, Karen, ed. A NavPress Bible Study on the Books of Ruth & Esther. Colorado Springs, CO: NavPress, 1987. ISBN 0891090746, 9-60.

Jacobs, Jon. Sermon: "Psalm 11." Grace Presbyterian Church (PCA), Blairsville, GA. 16 January, 2019.

Jastrow, Morris, Jr., Frederic McCurdy, Marcus Jastrow, and Louis Ginzberg. "BAAL-PEOR." JewishEncyclopedia.com, 1906. Web. 28 Feb. 2017. http://jewishencyclopedia.com/articles/2246-baal-peor.

"Joni Eareckson Tada Story." Life Story Foundation. True inspirational stories of faith and life, 2017. Web. 13 Mar. 2017. http://www.joniearecksontadastory. com/.

"Judges of Ancient Israel." Jewish Virtual Library. The Shengold Jewish Encyclopedia, 1998. Web. 31 Jan. 2017. http://www. jewishvirtuallibrary.org/judges-of-ancient-israel.

"7388 Kinsman Redeemer." Bible Gateway, Web. 22 Jan. 2017. https://www. Biblegateway.com

"The Kinsman Redeemer." Grace to You. Web. 7 Feb. 2017. https://www. gty. org/library/sermons-library/80-238.

Knoppers, Gary N., and Jonathan S. Greer. "Deuteronomistic History." Biblical Studies. Oxford Bibliographies, 2017. Web. 9 Mar. 2017. http:// www. oxfordbibliographies.com/view/document/obo9780195393361/ obo-9780195393361-0028. xml.

"Levant." The Free Dictionary by Farlex. Collins English Dictionary – Complete and Unabridged, 12th Edition 2014 © HarperCollins Publishers, 2014. Web. 17 Jan. 2017. http://www. thefreedictionary. com/ Levant.

Lewis, C. S. ""God's Megaphone" by C. S. Lewis." Tolle Lege. 28 July 2010. Web. 14 Feb. 2017. <https://tollelege.wordpress. com/2010/07/28/ gods-megaphone-by-c-s-lewis/>. C. S. Lewis, The Problem of Pain (New York: HarperCollins, 1940/1996), 91.

Lim, Andrew. "Ruth 3:1-18 – Faithful Recklessness vs Prudent Planning." Twotimothytwofifteen. July 21, 2017. Accessed January 03, 2019. https://twotimothytwofifteen.wordpress.com/2015/12/31/ the-book-of-ruth-part-5/.

"Lovingkindness-Definition of Hesed." Precept Austin. April 5, 2018. Accessed January 22, 2019. https://www. preceptaustin. org/ lovingkindness-definition_of_hesed.

Lucado, Max. Books of Ruth and Esther. World Publishing, 1996. 9-41.

MacArthur, John. "Ruth." The MacArthur Study Bible (NASB). Nashville, TN: Thomas Nelson, 2013. 360-367.

MacGregor, G. "Ruth Text, Exegesis and Exposition." The Interpreter's Bible Vol. II. New York: Abingdon Press, 1954. 829-852.

Manor, D. W., PhD. "Ruth." Zondervan illustrated Bible backgrounds commentary (Vol. 2) (J. H. Walton PhD, Ed.). Grand Rapids, MI: Zondervan, 2009. 242-261.

Mays, James, ed. "Ruth." The Harper Collins Bible Commentary. San Francisco, CA: Harper, 2000. 240-244.

"Naomi." All the Women of the Bible – Naomi. Bible Gateway, 1988. Web. 31 Jan. 2017. https://www. biblegateway. com/resources/ all-women-bible/Naomi.

Neuhaus, David M., SJ. "Jesus: Who Do You Think You Are?" Thinking Faith. Web. 13 Feb. 2017. http://www.thinkingfaith.org/articles/ jesus-who-do-you-think-you-are-2-rahab-ruth-and-boaz.

Orr-Stav, Jonathan. "What Is the Real Meaning of the Hebrew Word Hesed in the Bible?" Quora. com. August 21, 2018. Accessed July 22, 2019. https://www. quora. com/ What-is-the-real-meaning-of-the-Hebrew-word-hesed-in-the-Bible.

Pelaia, Ariela. "Ruth Convert to Judaism and Great-Grandmother of King David." About. com. About, Inc., 2017. Web. 31 Jan. 2017. Judaism. about. com/od/jewishpersonalities/a/Ruth-Women-In-theBible. htm.

Piper, John. "Ruth 1: Sweet and Bitter Providence (sermon)." Desiring God. July 1, 1984. Accessed April 24, 2018. https://www. desiringgod. org/messages/ruth-sweet-and-bitter-providence.

Piper, John. "Ruth 2: Under the Wings of God (sermon)." Desiring God. N. p. July 8, 1984. Accessed April 24, 2018. https://www. desiringgod. org/ messages/ruth-under-the-wings-of-god.

Piper, John. "Ruth 3Strategic Righteousness (sermon)." Desiring God. 15 July 1984. Web. 15 Feb. 2017. http://www.desiringgod.org/ messages/ ruth-strategic-righteousness.

Piper, John. "Ruth 4: The Best Is Yet To Come (sermon)." Desiring God. N. 22 July 1984. Web. 14 Feb. 2017. http://www.desiringgod.org/ messages/ruth-the-best-is-yet-to-come>.

"Quorum." Merriam-Webster, Incorporated, 2017. Web. 23 Feb. 2017. <https://www.merriam-webster.com/dictionary/quorum.

"Rahab, The Woman God Took From The Dunghill." Bible Gateway, All the Women in the Bible. Zondervan, 1988. Web. 13 February 2017. https://www. biblegateway. com/resources/all-women-bible/Rahab.

Rea, H., & Gladwell, C. (2014, July). Ruth Obeys God and Finds Love. Retrieved January 11, 2017. http://www. easyenglish. info/bible-commentary/ruth-lbw. htm

"Ruth." Bible Gateway. January 11, 2017. https://www. biblegateway. com/passage/?search=ruth+1-4&version=ASV

Ryrie, C. C., Th. D., Ph. D. (1984). "Ruth." The Ryrie Study Bible (NIV). Chicago, IL: Moody Press.419-426

Sasson, Jack M. The Encyclopedia of Religion. Ed. Mircea Eliade. "Ruth and Naomi" The Encyclopedia of Religion. Vol. 12. New York: Macmillan Publishing Company, 1987. 491-492.

Schechter, Solomon, and Joseph Jacobs. "Levirate Marriage." JewishEncyclopedia.com. Web. 8 Feb. 2017. http://jewishencyclopedia. com/articles/9859-levirate-marriage.

Spurgeon, C. H. "Deciding For God (Ruth 1:16)." Sermon. February 21, 2015. Accessed April 24, 2018. http://www. preceptaustin. org/deciding_for_god_ruth_116#cleaving with a whole heart. Ruth 2:2.

Stamps, Donald C. "Ruth." The Full Life Study Bible (NIV). Grand Rapids: Zondervan House, 1992. 370-376.

Stilley, Lloyd. "Ruth A Loyal Love Story." Sermon, First Baptist Church, Gulf Shores, Alabama. January 1, 2014. Accessed April 24, 2018. https://www. lifeway. com/en/articles/sermon-ruth-loyalty-love-trust-faith.

Strain, David. "The Dead End (Ruth 1:1-5)." Sermon, August 30, 2015, First Presbyterian Church, Jackson, Mississippi, April 30, 2018. https://www. fpcjackson. org/resource-library/sermons/the-dead-end

Strain, David. "The Journey Home (Ruth 1:1-22)." Sermon, September 6, 2015, First Presbyterian Church, Jackson, Mississippi, April 30, 2018. https://www. fpcjackson. org/resource-library/sermons/ the-journey-home/print

Strain, David. "The Way Ahead (Ruth 2:1-23)." Sermon, First Presbyterian Church, Jackson, Mississippi. September 13, 2015. Accessed May 02, 2018. https://www. fpcjackson. org/resource-library/sermons/ the-way-ahead.

Strain, David. "The Wrong Turn? (Ruth 3)." The Wrong Turn? | First Presbyterian Church, Jackson, Mississippi. September 27, 2015. Accessed May 02, 2018. https://www.fpcjackson.org/resource-library/ sermons/the-wrong-turn/print.

Strain, David. "The Gateway to Rest (Ruth 4:1-12)." First Presbyterian Church, Jackson, Mississippi. October 4, 2015. Accessed May 02, 2018. https://www. fpcjackson. org/resource-library/sermons/ the-gateway-to-rest/print.

Strain, David. "The Road to Royalty (Ruth 4:13-22)." First Presbyterian Church, Jackson, Mississippi. October 11, 2015. Accessed May 02, 2018. https://www. fpcjackson. org/resource-library/sermons/ the-road-to-royalty/print.

Thomas, Derek W. H. "Ruth 1: Some Graces Grow Best in Winter." Sermon, June 20, 1999, First Presbyterian Church, Jackson, Mississippi, April 17, 2018. https://www. fpcjackson. org/resource-library/sermons/ some-graces-grow-best-in-winter

Thomas, Derek W. H. "Ruth 1:1-2:23: When Life Tastes Bitter." Sermon, April 21, 1998, First Presbyterian Church, Jackson, Mississippi, April 17, 2018. https://www. fpcjackson. org/resource-library/sermons/ when-life-tastes-bitter

Thomas, Derek W. H. "Models of Love (Ruth 2:1-23)." First Presbyterian Church, Jackson, Mississippi. April 21, 1998. Accessed May 02, 2018. https://www. fpcjackson. org/resource-library/sermons/ models-of-love/ print.

Thomas, Derek W. H. "Single Moabite Woman (Widow) Seeks Attractive Young Man: Marriage Desired (Ruth 3:1-18)." First Presbyterian Church, Jackson, Mississippi. May 6, 2001. Accessed May 02, 2018. https://www. fpcjackson. org/resource-library/sermons/singlemoabite-woman-widow-seeks-attractive-young-man-marriage-desired/print.

Thomas, Derek W. H. "The Perfect Marriage? (Ruth 4)." First Presbyterian Church, Jackson, Mississippi. June 23, 2002. Accessed May 02, 2018. https://www.fpcjackson.org/resource-library/sermons/ the-perfect-marriage—2/print.

Thomas, Geoff. "1:1-15 Blind Unbelief Is Sure to Err." Alfred Place Baptist Church. January 02, 2013. Accessed May 02, 2018. http://www. alfredplacechurch.org.uk/index.php/sermons/ruth-series/11-15-blind-unbelief-is-sure-to-err/.

Thomas, Geoff. "1:16-18 The Great Commitment of Ruth." Alfred Place Baptist Church. January 02, 2013. Accessed May 02, 2018. http:// www. alfredplacechurch.org.uk/index.php/sermons/ ruth-series/116-18-the-great-committment-of-ruth/.

Thomas, Geoff. "1:19-2:3 New Problems Bring New Grace." Alfred Place Baptist Church. January 02, 2013. Accessed May 02, 2018. http://www. alfredplacechurch.org.uk/index.php/sermons/ruth-series/119-23-new-problems-bring-new-grace/.

Thomas, Geoff. "2:14-20 The Nature of a Christian Businessman." Alfred Place Baptist Church. January 02, 2013. Accessed May 02, 2018. http://www. alfredplacechurch. org. uk/index. php/sermons/ ruth-series/214-20-the-nature-of-a-christian-businessman/.

Thomas, Geoff. "3:7 Boaz: A Portrait of a Christian Businessman." Alfred Place Baptist Church. January 02, 2013. Accessed May 02, 2018. http://www. alfredplacechurch. org. uk/index. php/sermons/ ruth-series/37-boaz-a-portrait-of-a-christian-businessman/.

Thomas, Geoff. "3:1-5 May Boaz and Ruth Marry?" Alfred Place Baptist Church. January 02, 2013. Accessed May 02, 2018. http://www. alfredplacechurch. org. uk/index. php/sermons/ ruth-series/31-5-may-boaz-and-ruth-marry/.

Thomas, Geoff. "4:1-13 Boaz and Ruth Are Wed." Alfred Place Baptist Church. January 02, 2013. Accessed May 02, 2018. http://www. alfredplacechurch. org. uk/index. php/sermons/ ruth-series/41-13-boaz-and-ruth-are-wed/.

"Thresh." Merriam Webster, Web. 27 Jan. 2017. <https://www.merriam-webster. com/dictionary/thresh>.

Turrentine, Jan, ed. Cokesbury Adult Bible Study, Summer 2011, 76-82.

"We Are Not Defined By Our Past Ruth 3 (sermon)." University Baptist Church, Web. 14 Feb. 2017. http://universitybaptistchurch. com/?sermons=ruth-3.

"Wet nurse." Merriam Webster, Web. 27 Feb. 2017. https://www. merriam-webster. com/dictionary/wet%20nurse.

"Winnow." Merriam Webster, Web. 27 Jan. 2017. https://www.merriam-webster. com/dictionary/winnow.

Zavada, J. (2015, July 15). Boaz Ancestor of Jesus. Retrieved January 12, 2017, from http://christianity. about. com/od/oldtestamentpeople/ fl/Boaz.htm

Zavada, J. (2015, July 15). Book of Ruth. Retrieved January 12, 2017, from http://christianity. about. com/od/oldtestamentbooks/a/Book-Of-Ruth. htm

Zavada, J. (2015, July 15). Ruth Ancestor of Jesus. Retrieved January 11, 2017, from http://christianity. about. com/od/oldtestamentpeople/fl/Ruth-ndash-Ancestor-of-Jesus.htm

# ESTHER

## THE QUEEN WHO SAVED HER PEOPLE

# DEDICATION

THIS BOOK IS DEDICATED TO THE GLORY OF GOD IN loving memory of my beloved father, The Rev. John Edward Millar Massie. He served the Anglican Church of Canada in Ontario, and the Episcopal Church in Florida and North Carolina. He was truly a kind and gentle man of God.

# BIBLICAL REFERENCES

U nless stated otherwise, scripture quotations are from the HOLY BIBLE, NEW INTERNATIONAL VERSION ® (NIV), copyright © 1973, 1978, 1984, 2011 by International Bible Society.

Other versions of the Bible have been used to show differences in translations. These include the following:

American Standard Version (ASV) Public Domain.

Amplified Bible (AMP) Copyright © 2015 by The Lockman Foundation, La Habra, CA 90631.

BRG Bible (BRG) Blue Red and Gold Letter Edition™ Copyright © 2012 BRG Bible Ministries.

Christian Standard Bible (CSB) The Christian Standard Bible. Copyright © 2017 by Holman Bible Publishers.

Common English Bible (CEB) Copyright © 2011 by Common English Bible.

Complete Jewish Bible (CJB) Copyright © 1998 by David H. Stern.

Darby Translation (DARBY) Public Domain

Douay-Rheims 1899 American Edition (DRA) Public Domain

Easy-to-Read Version (ERV) Copyright © 2006 by Bible League International.

Revised Standard Version (RSV) Revised Standard Version of the Bible, copyright © 1946, 1952, and 1971 the Division of Christian Education of the National Council of the Churches of Christ in the United States of America.

Tree of Life Version (TLV) Tree of Life (TLV) Translation of the Bible. Copyright © 2015 by The Messianic Jewish Family Bible Society.

Wycliffe Bible (WYC) 2001 by Terence P. Noble Young's Literal Translation (YLT) Public Domain.

# ACKNOWLEDGEMENTS

I WOULD LIKE TO THANK THE FOLLOWING MINISTERS, family members, and Christian friends whose advice, prayers, and encouragement made this book possible.

**Nosha Oneal and Khyree Oneal:** Computer experts, proofreaders, advisors, encouragers, and much-loved grandsons

Áine **Massie:** Computer skills, advisor, and formatting

**Renate Craig:** Editor and proofreader

**Bonnie Patterson, Pauline Hebb, Laura Beal, and Veronica Romano:** Proofreaders and advisors

**Judith Leipold:** Jewish advisor

**Nicholas Sommer:** Director of Youth and Family, Grace Presbyterian Church (PCA), Blairsville, Georgia

**The Rev. Bert Daly, Jr.:** Rector, St. Francis of Assisi Anglican-Episcopal Church, Lake Placid, Florida.

**Rev. Valentin Rusu:** Pastor, Seventh Day Adventist Church of Fanin County, Morganton, Georgia

**Rev. Mike Moreau:** Pastor, Central Presbyterian Church (PCA), Kingstree, South Carolina

# INTRODUCTION TO ESTHER

"The grass withers and the flowers fall, but the word of our God endures forever" (Isa. 40:8).

THE AUTHOR OF THE BOOK OF ESTHER IS UNKNOWN, however, biblical scholars agree it was written by an educated Diaspora Jew (Hebrew people dispersed or exiled from their homeland after the Babylonian captivity) who was familiar with the palace of Susa (also called Shushan), King Xerxes, and the language and customs of the Persians. (Although the book was written in Hebrew, some words from the Persian language were also used.[31] Words from languages other than English will be shown in italics.)

This unidentified writer did not comment on worship, faith, prophecy, heaven, or hell. God was not mentioned a single time, but he clearly shows He worked through Queen Esther to save His people from annihilation at the hands of the Persians. The great nineteenth century preacher, Charles Spurgeon, said, "Although the name of God does not occur in the Book of Esther, the Lord Himself is there most conspicuously in every incident which it relates... It has pleased God at

---

31       Posner, Menachem. "What Is the Book of Esther About?–A Summary of the Book of Esther." Judaism, February 27, 2017. https://www.chabad.org/holidays/purim/ article_cdo/aid/3602036/jewish/What-Is-the-Book-of-Esther-About

different times in history to startle the heathen world into a conviction of His presence. "[32] Josephus, the Jewish historian, believed Mordecai (his name means "little man" or "humbled man")[33] penned the book of Esther, while others credit Ezra or Nehemiah with authorship.[34]

The incidents in this narrative took place in the fifth century BC, from 483 to 473 BC, chronologically between Ezra chapters six and seven. There are many references to specific dates (Est. 1:3, 2:12, 2:16, 3:7, 3:12, 8:9).[35] Charles Ryrie, Bible scholar and Christian theologian, theorizes this book was written shortly after the end of Xerxes' reign because his time in power was referred to in the past tense.[36] The contributors to *The Life Application Study Bible* state Esther was written circa 470 BC.[37] The author may have obtained firsthand information from Mordecai, Esther's cousin, who adopted her after her parents died and raised her as his own daughter.[38] God's people were first called Jews in the book of Esther.[39] (The books of Ezra and Nehemiah also use the term Jew. They appear before Esther in the Old Testament; however, most biblical scholars believe Esther was written first.)

32      Spurgeon, Charles Haddon. "Providence–As Seen in the Book of Esther." Spurgeon, November 2, 1874. https://www. spurgeon.org/resource-library/sermons/providence-as-seen-in-the-book-of-esther—2#flipbook/.

33      Stedman, Ray C. "A Pair of Queens." Ray Stedman Ministries, 1963. https://www. raystedman.org/old-testament/esther/a-pair-of-queens.

34      Clarke, Adam, Albert Barnes, Theodore Beza, John Wesley, John Trapp, Thomas Coke, John Gill, et al. "Esther with Book Summary Overview." Verse-by-Verse Bible Commentary.studylight.org. Accessed January 22, 2020. https://www/commentary/esther.html.

35      Dybdahl, Jon L, ed. "Esther." Andrews Study Bible: Light. Depth. Truth. Berrien Springs, MI: Andrews University Press, 2010. p. 613.

36      Ryrie, Charles Caldwell. "The Book of Esther," Ryrie Study Bible: New International Version. Chicago: Moody Publishers, 1986, p. 663.

37      McGrath, Alister E. "Esther," Life Application Study Bible (NIV). Wheaton, IL: Tyndale House Publishers, Inc., 1997.p.821.

38      Stamps, Donald C., and J. Wesley. Adams. "The Book of Esther." The Full Life Study Bible: New International Version (NIV). Grand Rapids, MI: Zondervan Pub. House, 1992. pp.691-693.

39      Tan, Wilson. "The Fall of Vashti." Jubilee Church, January 11, 2010. http://www. jubilee.org.sg/sermons/?sermon_id=86.

This book is named for Esther (her Persian name, which means "star"), also known as Hadassah (her Hebrew name, which means "myrtle"). Only one other book in the Bible is named for a woman, Ruth, the wife of Boaz, mother of Obed, and ancestor of Christ.

Esther was a young Jewish lady, an exile of the tribe of Benjamin, who became the wife and queen of King Xerxes I (his Greek name), also known as Khshayarashan (his Persian name), or Ahasuerus (his Hebrew name, meaning "mighty man"). The title of Xerxes I was "*Shahanshah*," which meant "King of Kings," but it was frequently translated "emperor. "[40] Esther married Xerxes, despite the fact Jews were not to marry outside their race. [41] (This marriage was not Esther's choice.)

Persia was the most powerful nation in the known world. Xerxes came to power in 4486 BC, after the reign of Darius I, and ruled until 465 BC. His kingdom was made up of twenty *satrapies* (areas governed by *satraps*, rulers appointed by the king),[42] which were divided into 127 provinces. It stretched from India to Ethiopia,[43] covering approximately two million square miles.[44] From the description of Xerxes in the book of Esther, he appears to have been weak, capricious, self-centered, vicious, and dominated by his court officials and eunuchs (neutered males). He was quite willing to pass the blame and let others make the difficult decisions.[45]

---

40      Mark, Joshua J. "Xerxes I." Ancient History Encyclopedia. Ancient History Encyclopedia, April 29, 2020. https://www.ancient.eu/Xerxes_I/.

41      Stedman, Ray C. "A Pair of Queens." Ray Stedman Ministries, 1963. https://www. raystedman. org/old-testament/esther/a-pair-of-queens.

42      Buttrick, George Arthur. The Interpreters Bible (Vol 3) the Holy Scriptures in the King James and Revised Standard Versions with General Articles and Introduction, Exegesis, Exposition for Each Book of the Bible. Vol. 3. New York: Abingdon Press, 1954, p. 835.

43      Stamps, Donald C., and J. Wesley. Adams. "The Book of Esther." The Full Life Study Bible: New International Version (NIV). Grand Rapids, MI: Zondervan Pub. House, 1992. pp. 691-693.

44      "Persian Empire Timeline." Math. Accessed April 30, 2020.

45      Buttrick, George Arthur. The Interpreters Bible (Vol 3) the Holy Scriptures in the King James and Revised Standard Versions with General Articles and Introduction, Exegesis, Exposition for Each Book of the Bible. Vol. 3. New York: Abingdon Press, 1954, p. 850.

The real hero in this book is not Mordecai or Esther; it is God. He preserved the Jews, despite seemingly insurmountable adversities. He was and is always faithful, and He will not allow the destruction of His people. His divine purpose will not be thwarted. The Jews were saved by God's will, not through chance, good luck, or human resolve.[46]

The Medes and Persians entered Mesopotamia about 1,000 BC. At first, the Medes ruled over the Persians.[47] Many Jews had been taken by Nebuchadnezzar to Babylon as captives between 598 and 586 BC. In 539 BC, Cyrus the Great defeated the Babylonians and established the Persian Empire.[48] Control of the Jews transferred to Persia. In 538 BC, fifty-five years before the story of Esther took place, Cyrus released the Jews, and allowed them to return to their homeland. Zerubbabel, a Jewish leader and descendant of King David, desired to go back to Jerusalem and rebuild the temple.[49] The king granted his request.[50] Some Jews, led by Zerubbabel, went back (circa 538 to 520 BC).

Because they had some freedom and feared a dangerous trip home (Ezr. 1,2), several hundred thousand, the majority, chose to stay in the land of their captors and establish Jewish communities.[51] They built homes, started businesses, and blended into the life of the Persian kingdom. Some married Persian pagans, while others stayed true to their Jewish

46      Brickner, David. "No Coincidence • Jews for Jesus." Jews for Jesus, March 1, 1998. https://jewsforjesus. org/publications/newsletter/newsletter-mar-1998/ no-coincidence/.

47      Archaeological Study Bible: An Illustrated Walk through Biblical History and Culture: New International Version. Grand Rapids, MI: Zondervan, 2005. "Esther," p. 717.

48      "The Global Message of Esther." ESV Bible. Crossway. Accessed March 9, 2020. https://www.esv.org/resources/esv-global-study-bible/global-message-of-esther/.

49      Barker, William Pierson. "Zerubbabel." Everyone in the Bible. Westwood, NJ: Fleming H. Revell Company, 1966.p. 365.

50      Buttrick, George Arthur. The Interpreters Bible (Vol 3) the Holy Scriptures in the King James and Revised Standard Versions with General Articles and Introduction, Exegesis, Exposition for Each Book of the Bible. Vol. 3. New York: Abingdon Press, 1954, p. 840.

51      Hayford, Jack W. "The Book of Esther." New Spirit Filled Life Bible (NKJV). Nashville, TN: Thomas Nelson Bibles, 2002. P. 632.

faith and kept themselves separate from Gentile ways. Their finances and safety were more important than God's plan for His people's return to the Promised Land. The Persians took no census of its Jewish residents, so estimates of those living in exile differ widely.[52]

About fifty thousand[53] Jewish exiles who returned to Jerusalem entered a time called the "postexilic period" (meaning after the exile).[54] The story of these returning Jews is recorded in the books of Ezra and Nehemiah. The story of Esther began in Persia (now modern-day Iran) in 483 BC.

Esther and her family may have been members of either the second or third generation of the Jewish Diaspora. God's people were forced to adjust to life in a pagan land. The Jewish exiles fasted, celebrated, and mourned, but they were not described as a praying people. Nor were Jerusalem, the Torah, Jewish traditions, or the Temple discussed in this book.

Esther was the only book of the Old Testament not found in the Dead Sea Scrolls.[55] There is also no evidence the people of Qumran observed Purim, the Jewish festival established by Esther.[56] Some scholars believe this indicates the people who concealed the scrolls at Qumran may have felt Esther should not be included in their holy scripture. Martin Luther, the German theologian and reformer, "wanted to pitch it into the River Elbe."[57]

52    Yancey, Philip, and Tim Stafford. "Esther." The Student Bible. Grand Rapids, MI: Zondervan, 1996, p. 512.
53    White, Ellen Gould Harmon. Prophets and Kings. Coldwater, MI: Remnant Publications, 2013. "In the Days of Queen Esther," p. 339.
54    "The Global Message of Esther." ESV Bible. Crossway. Accessed March 9, 2020. https://www.esv.org/resources/esv-global-study-bible/global-message-of-esther/.
55    Leith, Mary Joan Winn. "The Oxford Encyclopedia of the Books of the Bible." Edited by Michael D Coogan. Google Books. Google, 2011, pp. 252-261.
56    Wayne, Luke. "Christian Apologetics & Research Ministry." CARM.org, May 27, 2017. https://carm. org/why-doesnt-the-book-of-esther-directly-mention-god.
57    Barrier, Julie. "Diva or Heroine? What You DON'T Know About Queen Vashti." Preach It Teach It, 2020. https://www. preachitteachit. org/articles/detail/diva-or-heroine-what-you-dont-know-about-queen-vashti/.

God was and is interested in the survival of his people, the Jews. The many "coincidences" described in this book were actually the providence of God. Everything was part of His divine plan. The Jewish Feast of Purim (observed on the fourteenth and fifteenth days of Adar, usually in February or March) celebrates the deliverance of the Jewish people from the genocide planned by the bloodthirsty Haman,[58] prime minister and advisor to King Xerxes.[59] (The word Adar means splendor because the sun was bright and the flowers were lovely at that time.)[60]

The theme of this book is God's providence. He loved and cared for the Jews, even when they were living in a foreign land far from Israel. He worked behind the scenes through both monumental and seemingly insignificant events to protect and redeem His people. Historical and chronological details are consistent throughout the book, and they are helpful in explaining future events in the history of the Hebrew people.[61]

The religion of the ancient Persians was polytheistic. They believed in many gods. Ahura Mazda was "all-god, all-powerful, the creator and sustainer of life," and it was believed he gave birth to all the other gods. Their worship included fire and outside altars, and their places of worship were called fire temples. Little else is known.

Zoroastrianism, a monotheistic faith founded by Zoroaster circa 1500 to 500 BC, came from this early belief system. It was an oral tradition with no written scripture. They believed in one god, and Zoroaster, his

58    Barker, William Pierson. "Haman." Everyone in the Bible. Westwood, NJ: Fleming H. Revell Company, 1966. p. 120.
59    "Purim." Hillel. Hillel International, 2019. https://www. hillel. org/jewish/celebrating-shabbat-and-holidays/purim
60    Clarke, Adam, Albert Barnes, Theodore Beza, John Wesley, John Trapp, Thomas Coke, John Gill, et al. "Esther with Book Summary Esther 3:7" Verse-by-Verse Bible Commentary Accessed January 22, 2020. www.studylightorg/commentary/esther/3-7
61    Dybdahl, Jon L, ed. "Esther." Andrews Study Bible: Light. Depth. Truth. Berrien Springs, MI: Andrews University Press, 2010. pp. 613-14.

prophet, wrote down his prophecies and revelations.[62] They also believed in judgment day, heaven, hell, and a single god named Ahura Mazda. In time, the ancient gods of Persia were demoted to spirits. This remained the chief religion of Persia until the Muslim Conquest (AD 633 to 651).[63]

In the Septuagint, the Greek translation of the Bible, six chapters not in the original Hebrew text were added to the Book of Esther. The Septuagint is often abbreviated LXX (70), which referred to the number of Greek scholars who translated parts of the Bible written in Hebrew or Aramaic into the Greek language. Jerome (a Latin priest and Bible scholar) noted this when he compiled the Latin Vulgate (Latin version of the Bible).[64] Only chapters one through ten are considered canon (divinely inspired, authoritative scripture) by both Jews and Protestant Christians.[65]

There are four major reasons many Christians do not accept the six additional chapters of Esther as canon. First, the Jews, arbiters of the Old Testament, did not include the additions to Esther. Second, it is doubtful the additions were written in Hebrew (or Aramaic). Third, the additions are not judged to have the marks of inspired writing. And fourth, Jesus and the New Testament writers never quoted the additions.[66] Only the ten chapters regarded as canon will be discussed in this book. The additional six sections (107 verses) appear in Roman Catholic and Eastern Orthodox Bible translations.[67]

Susa (Greek Name Sousa, Elamite name Susan or Susun, Hebrew name Shushan) may date to as far back as the Neolithic Age (also called

---

62      Mark, Joshua J. "Ancient Persian Religion." Ancient History Encyclopedia, April 21, 2020. https://www.ancient.eu/Ancient_Persian_Religion/.

63      "Zoroastrianism." History.com. A&E Television Networks, February 13, 2018. https://www. history. com/topics/religion/zoroastrianism.

64      Chaignot, Mary Jane. "Additions to Esther." BibleWise. Accessed April 2, 2020. http://www.biblewise.com/bible_study/apocrypha/additions-esther.php.

65      Brettler, Marc Zvi., Carol A. Newsom, and Pheme Perkins. The New Oxford Annotated Bible: with the Apocryphal/Deuterocanonical Books: New Revised Standard Version. Edited by Michael David. Coogan. NIVed. New York: Oxford University Press, 2001, p. 708.

66      "Rest of Esther (Bible)." Conservapedia. April 9, 2019. Accessed April 22, 2020. https://www.conservapedia.com/Rest_of_Esther_(Bible).

67      BibleGateway. "Additions to Esther"–Encyclopedia of The Bible–Bible Gateway. Accessed April 2, 2020. https://www. biblegateway. com/resources/ encyclopedia-of-the-bible/Additions-Esther.

New Stone Age). In its earliest days, Susa was a religious center with temples to pagan deities. Over time, it was occupied by several different civilizations, and became a commercial and textile producing center. During the Persian Empire, Susa consisted of two parts: the unfortified lower city on the east and the fortified upper city (the citadel of Susa) on the west.[68]

This city is mentioned in the Old Testament books of Esther, Ezra, Daniel, and Nehemiah. Evidence indicates it was occupied continually from about 4,000 BC until it was abandoned in the AD 1400s. A large palace in the upper city and an artisans' village east of Susa have been found and excavated. Disturbances in the area surrounding Susa have delayed digs and made exploration difficult. There were several other capitals in the Persian empire, but Susa is the best known and is mentioned more than any of the others.[69]

Why should we study a book that does not directly mention God? Every word in the Bible is inspired by the Holy Spirit and is therefore important. **"All Scripture is God-breathed and is useful for teaching, rebuking, correcting and training in righteousness, so that the servant of God may be thoroughly equipped for every good work"** (2 Ti. 3:16-17).

Each book of the Bible has its own message. The Book of Esther clearly shows that God was in command of every event in this narrative. God loved His chosen people and protected them. This was far more than being at the right place at the right time. What may seem like coincidences or accidents were really God's divine plan.[70]

Keep in mind, The Book of Esther was written approximately 2,500 years ago. Therefore, the laws, customs and traditions of ancient

68     Archaeological Study Bible: An Illustrated Walk through Biblical History and Culture: New International Version. Grand Rapids, MI: Zondervan, 2005. "Esther," p. 729.
69     Mark, Joshua J. "Susa." Ancient History Encyclopedia. Ancient History Encyclopedia, April 22, 2020. https://www. ancient. eu/susa/.
70     Yancey, Philip, and Tim Stafford. "Esther." The Student Bible. Grand Rapids, MI: Zondervan, 1996, p. 505.

Persia will be discussed. Inserting our modern viewpoint into the lives and rituals of people from the distant past is counterproductive. It is important to be aware of why people did what they did. We cannot fully understand the New Testament without studying the Old Testament.

Many resources have been used in writing this book. When differences of opinion are found, they will be discussed. It is my intention to present information and theories in an unbiased fashion. There is one exception. A few commentators take the position The Book of Esther is historical fiction, or an allegory used to teach a lesson. The characters in this type of writing may or may not be real people.[71] I believe *The Holy Bible* is the inspired (influenced by the Holy Spirit), inerrant (without error in its original language), authoritative (trustworthy) word of God. I further believe every event described in this holy book, from Noah's Ark to Jesus' Resurrection, is true. Therefore, hypotheses to the contrary will not be considered.

Yahweh was the sacred covenant name of the God of Israel. The Hebrew written language did not use vowels. Using our alphabet, this word would be written YHWH. The Hebrews considered His name to be so holy they would not say it aloud. In time, the pronunciation was forgotten. English language Bibles usually use the word LORD (all capital letters) when translating YHWH. The word LORD is not included in the book of Esther. Quotations from other books of the Bible have been used in writing this book.

Luke Wayne declared, "God hid Himself from His people in their time of exile, but God did not forsake them. God is still faithful to His covenant, and in His secret providence, He was protecting them and prospering them even while He was punishing them and correcting them for their sins against Him. "[72]

We are His creation. There is a purpose for every human being; no person is worthless to God. He is always faithful and keeps His promises. Esther surrendered her life to God's divine will, and He used her in a mighty way to save the lives of His people.

---

71      Tan, Wilson. "The Fall of Vashti." Jubilee Church, January 11, 2010. http://www. jubilee.org.sg/sermons/?sermon_id=86.

72      Wayne, Luke. "Christian Apologetics & Research Ministry." CARM.org, May 27, 2017. https://carm. org/why-doesnt-the-book-of-esther-directly-mention-god.

# ESTHER CHAPTER 1

## ESTHER 1:1-8

**1** **This is what happened during the time of Xerxes** [Hebrew Ahasuerus], **the Xerxes who ruled over 127 provinces stretching from India** [the area drained by the Indus River in present-day Pakistan] **to Cush** [or Ethiopia, Upper Nile region, northern Sudan][73]**: 2 At that time King Xerxes reigned from his royal throne in the citadel of Susa, 3 and in the third year of his reign he gave a banquet for all his nobles and officials. The military leaders of Persia and Media** [northwest Iran]**, the princes, and the nobles of the provinces were present.**

**4 For a full 180 days he displayed the vast wealth of his kingdom and the splendor and glory of his majesty. 5 When these days were over, the king gave a banquet, lasting seven days, in the enclosed garden of the king's palace, for all the people from the least to the greatest who were in the citadel of Susa. 6 The garden had hangings of white and blue linen, fastened with cords of white linen and purple material to silver rings on marble pillars. There were couches of gold and silver on a mosaic pavement of porphyry** (igneous rock similar to granite)**, marble, mother-of-pearl, and other costly stones. 7 Wine was served in goblets of gold, each one different from the other, and the royal wine was abundant, in keeping with the king's liberality.**

---

73      Ryrie, Charles Caldwell. "The Book of Esther," Ryrie Study Bible: New International Version. Chicago: Moody Publishers, 1986, p. 664

**8 By the king's command each guest was allowed to drink with no restrictions, for the king instructed all the wine stewards to serve each man what he wished.**

XERXES I (SON OF KING DARIUS I AND QUEEN ATOSSA)[74] was the absolute monarch (ruler with total dictatorial power) of a huge empire that stretched from India on the east, to the Mediterranean Sea on the west, and from the Caspian Sea and Black Sea in the north to Cush (Ethiopia) in the south.[75] Ethiopia was a country that touched southern Egypt and was irrigated by branches of the Upper Nile. According to Herodotus, the ancient Greek historian, both India and Ethiopia were ruled by Xerxes.[76] He was one of the richest men in the known world.[77] Xerxes ruled from 486 BC to 465 BC.[78]

Susa was a beautiful city located about 225 miles east of Babylon at the edge of the Mesopotamian Plain in the foothills of the Zagros Mountains. Darius I chose Susa (one of six main capital cities, 150 miles north of the Persian Gulf)[79] as his primary capital city and his winter residence because of its strategic location.[80] It was surrounded

---

74    Tomasino, Anthony. "Esther." Zondervan Illustrated Bible Backgrounds Commentary. Edited by John H. Walton. Vol. 3. Grand Rapids (Mich.): Zondervan, 2009, p. 470.

75    Clarke, Adam, Albert Barnes, Theodore Beza, John Wesley, John Trapp, Thomas Coke, John Gill, et al. "Esther with Book Summary Esther 1:15" Verse-by-Verse Bible Commentary Accessed January 22, 2020. https://www.studylight.org/commentary/esther/1-15.html.

76    Clarke, Adam, Albert Barnes, Theodore Beza, John Wesley, John Trapp, Thomas Coke, John Gill, et al. "Esther with Book Summary Esther 1:1" Verse-by-Verse Bible Commentary Accessed January 22, 2020. https://www.studylight.org/commentary/esther/1-1. html.

77    McGrath, Alister E. "Esther," Life Application Study Bible (NIV). Wheaton, IL: Tyndale House Publishers, Inc., 1997. p. 823.

78    Stamps, Donald C., and J. Wesley. Adams. "The Book of Esther." The Full Life Study Bible: New International Version (NIV). Grand Rapids, MI: Zondervan Pub. House, 1992. p. 694.

79    Buttrick, George Arthur. The Interpreters Bible (Vol 3) the Holy Scriptures in the King James and Revised Standard Versions with General Articles and Introduction, Exegesis, Exposition for Each Book of the Bible. Vol. 3. New York: Abingdon Press, 1954, p. 835.

80    Tomasino, Anthony. "Esther." Zondervan Illustrated Bible Backgrounds Commentary. Edited by John H. Walton. Vol. 3. Grand Rapids (Mich.): Zondervan, 2009, p. 473.

by rich agricultural land. Aristotle, an ancient Greek philosopher and scientist, revealed the city contained "a wonderful royal palace, shining with gold, amber, and ivory."[81] Throughout the summer, Susa became terribly hot, so during those oppressive months, the capital moved north to Ecbatana.[82] However, even though the Book of Esther reported on events covering several years, the author did not indicate Xerxes held court in any other city.[83]

In the third year of his reign (483 BC), Xerxes gathered important government officials (perhaps his elite bodyguards known as the Ten Thousand Immortals)[84] and princes from throughout Persia and Media for a huge banquet at Susa.[85] This festivity was held to celebrate Xerxes' victory in a war with Egypt as well as to plan for an upcoming war against the Greeks. Wars were not always fought to defend the land from invaders. Sometimes battles were waged to gain more land, power, and wealth.[86]

It was common for Persians to use feasts to debate important matters.[87] These were lavish, lengthy celebrations where the king could

81    Clarke, Adam, Albert Barnes, Theodore Beza, John Wesley, John Trapp, Thomas Coke, John Gill, et al. "Esther with Book Summary Esther 1:2" Verse-by-Verse Bible Commentary  Accessed January 22, 2020.
https://www.studylight.org/commentary/esther/1. 2. html.
82    Tomasino, Anthony. "Esther." Zondervan Illustrated Bible Backgrounds Commentary. Edited by John H. Walton. Vol. 3. Grand Rapids (Mich.): Zondervan, 2009, p.474.
83    Buttrick, George Arthur. The Interpreters Bible (Vol 3) the Holy Scriptures in the King James and Revised Standard Versions with General Articles and Introduction, Exegesis, Exposition for Each Book of the Bible. Vol. 3. New York: Abingdon Press, 1954, p. 835.
84    Buttrick, George Arthur. The Interpreters Bible (Vol 3) the Holy Scriptures in the King James and Revised Standard Versions with General Articles and Introduction, Exegesis, Exposition for Each Book of the Bible. Vol. 3. New York: Abingdon Press, 1954, p. 836.
85    Hayford, Jack W. "The Book of Esther." New Spirit Filled Life Bible (NKJV). Nashville, TN: Thomas Nelson Bibles, 2002. P. 634.
86    McGrath, Alister E. "Esther," Life Application Study Bible (NIV). Wheaton, IL: Tyndale House Publishers, Inc., 1997. p. 823.
87    Clarke, Adam, Albert Barnes, Theodore Beza, John Wesley, John Trapp, Thomas Coke, John Gill, et al. "Esther with Book Summary Esther 1:3" Verse-by-Verse Bible Commentary  Accessed January 22, 2020.
https://www.studylight.org/commentary/esther/1-3. html.

flaunt his wealth and the splendor of his court. Such banquets were also given after victories or on other state occasions. The guests may have attended in turns, then returned to their duties at home.[88] There were ten feasts, or banquets, depicted in the Book of Esther (Est. 1:3-4, 1:5, 1:9, 2:18, 3:15, 5:5, 7:1, 8:17, 9:17, 9:18). Scholars do not agree if the event described in Est. 3:15 was a banquet or just a time of drinking and relaxation.[89]

The first feast, held for the nobles and high officials, lasted six months. The seven-day banquet was for everyone not included in the first feast, regardless of age, class, or occupation. All residents of the capital city were invited.[90] The king was not concerned with the pleasure or condition of his subjects. This was a way for him to enjoy himself and display his wealth and generosity to the common people. The palace was not large enough to accommodate a multitude estimated to be nearly fifteen thousand people, so festivities moved outside to the garden. (The gardens of Persians palaces usually contained trees, fountains, plants, and animals from many parts of the known world.) This was a time of great merriment. All groups participated.[91] Food and alcohol were unlimited at both banquets. Everyone could eat and drink as much as he pleased.

The palace and gardens were festively decorated. Awnings in the royal colors, white and blue or violet, and brightly colored linen curtains hung from linen cords fastened to marble columns with silver rings.

---

88      Clarke, Adam, Albert Barnes, Theodore Beza, John Wesley, John Trapp, Thomas Coke, John Gill, et al. "Esther with Book Summary Esther 1:4" Verse-by-Verse Bible Commentary  Accessed January 22, 2020. https://www.studylight.org/commentary/esther/1-4. html.
89      "Intro to Esther." Biblica, October 8, 2016. https://www. biblica. com/ resources/ scholar-notes/niv-study-bible/intro-to-esther/.
90      Florence, Anna Carter. "Listen Download mp3 Print The Woman Who Just Said No." Day 1 @ 75. Columbia Theological Seminary, Decatur, GA, November 11, 2007.  https://day1.org/weekly-broadcast/5d9b820ef71918cdf2002672/the_woman_who_just_said_no.
91      Clarke, Adam, Albert Barnes, Theodore Beza, John Wesley, John Trapp, Thomas Coke, John Gill, et al. "Esther with Book Summary Esther 1:5" Verse-by-Verse Bible Commentary  Accessed January 22, 2020. https://www.studylight.org/commentary/esther/1-5. html.

Not only were these curtains and awnings beautiful and decorative, they also protected the guests from wind, heat, and dust. The colorful marble pavement was probably brought in from the Zagros Mountains. This decoration was typical of Persian palaces and temples of that period.[92]

Some experts believe the couches were made of solid gold and silver,[93] covered with gold or silver colored cloth made of soft lambs' wool. Others suggest furniture had wooden frames that were inlaid with precious metal. Ancient people often did not sit upright to eat as we do today. The guests reclined on these beautiful couches (some translations say beds or sofas) to eat or visit with their friends.[94]

Herodotus, the Greek historian wrote, "Persians are very fond of wine, and drink it in large quantities… It is also their general practice to deliberate upon affairs of weight when they are drunk… Sometimes, however, they are sober at the first deliberation, but in this case, they always reconsider the matter under the influence of wine."[95]

Food and royal wine (possibly Chalybonian wine from Syria or wine of Helbon) were served in a variety of golden vessels, further proof of the king's vast treasure. (These vessels were of different sizes and shapes, indicating they were made by various artisans and not mass produced.)[96] Some have hypothesized these were the golden vessels Nebuchadnezzar looted from the temple in Jerusalem in 586 BC. [97] After 70 years in exile

92      Clarke, Adam, Albert Barnes, Theodore Beza, John Wesley, John Trapp, Thomas Coke, John Gill, et al. "Esther with Book Summary Esther 1:6" Verse-by-Verse Bible Commentary  Accessed January 22, 2020.
https://www.studylight.org/commentary/esther/1-6. html.
93      Tomasino, Anthony. "Esther." Zondervan Illustrated Bible Backgrounds Commentary. Edited by John H. Walton. Vol. 3. Grand Rapids (Mich.): Zondervan, 2009, p.476.
94      Clarke, Adam, Albert Barnes, Theodore Beza, John Wesley, John Trapp, Thomas Coke, John Gill, et al. "Esther with Book Summary Esther 1:6".
95      Yancey, Philip, and Tim Stafford. "Esther." The Student Bible. Grand Rapids, MI: Zondervan, 1996, p. 507.
96      Tomasino, Anthony. "Esther." Zondervan Illustrated Bible Backgrounds Commentary. Edited by John H. Walton. Vol. 3. Grand Rapids (Mich.): Zondervan, 2009, p. 477.
97      Clarke, Adam, Albert Barnes, Theodore Beza, John Wesley, John Trapp, Thomas Coke, John Gill, et al. "Esther with Book Summary Esther 1:7" Verse-by-Verse Bible Commentary  Accessed January 22, 2020.
https://www.studylight.org/commentary/esther/1-7. html.

(516 BC), the Jews were allowed to return to Jerusalem, taking much of the plundered treasure with them.[98] Since those vessels were returned to Zerubbabel by Cyrus (Ezra 1:7) prior to Xerxes' banquet (circa 483 BC), this theory is false.

**Moreover, King Cyrus brought out the articles belonging to the temple of the LORD, which Nebuchadnezzar had carried away from Jerusalem and had placed in the temple of his god** [or gods] (Ezra 1:7). The guests could eat and drink as much or as little as they chose. They were not required to take more wine than they wanted or thought sensible. [99] Xerxes respected the habits and choices of his guests and issued a special order that stated people could not be compelled to drink. [100]

## ESTHER 1:9-12

**9 Queen Vashti also gave a banquet for the women in the royal palace of King Xerxes. 10 On the seventh day, when King Xerxes was in high spirits from wine, he commanded the seven eunuchs who served him—Mehuman, Biztha, Harbona, Bigtha, Abagtha, Zethar, and Karkas— 11 to bring before him Queen Vashti, wearing her royal crown, in order to display her beauty to the people and nobles, for she was lovely to look at. 12 But when the attendants delivered the king's command, Queen Vashti refused to come. Then the king became furious and burned with anger.**

Vashti was King Xerxes' wife. Her name, probably meaning "beautiful," "the best," or "the beloved," was uncommon in the ancient world. It is possible it might have been her title, rather than her actual name. [101] Nothing is known of her family. She may have been the daughter

98      Dolphin, Lambert. "The Treasures of the Temple," June 5, 2019. http:// ldolphin. org/ TMTRS.html.
99      Engelbrecht Edward A. "Esther." The Lutheran Study Bible: English Standard Version. Saint Louis: Concordia Publishing House, 2004. P. 762.
100     Clarke, Adam, Albert Barnes, Theodore Beza, John Wesley, John Trapp, Thomas Coke, John Gill, et al. "Esther with Book Summary Esther 1:8" Verse-by-Verse Bible Commentary Accessed January 22, 2020.
https://www.studylight.org/commentary/esther/1-8. html.
101     Tomasino, Anthony. "Esther." Zondervan Illustrated Bible Backgrounds Commentary. Edited by John H. Walton. Vol. 3. Grand Rapids (Mich.): Zondervan,

of Cyrus, or possibly the granddaughter of Nebuchadnezzar. It has also been suggested she may have been Xerxes' sister or even his daughter, since such marriages were common in Persia at that time. Daniel Whedon proposes she may not have been the queen-consort (king's wife who has no power to rule) or even one of his inferior wives. Instead, she could have been the king's favorite concubine (king's mistress, of lower social class than a wife). This theory is doubtful. At a drunken party, it would be more common to summon a concubine than a wife. Concubines could expect a summons to display their beauty, but surely not the queen.[102] If Vashti had been merely a concubine, it is unlikely the king would have sent a formal command delivered by seven eunuchs. Nor would a concubine have dared to defy the king's command.

Persia was a patriarchal society dominated by men. Most biblical scholars assert women were virtual slaves, considered to be the property of their husbands and completely under their control,[103] although some experts believe there is evidence women did have certain rights. The treatment of women described in this book indicates the first statement is more likely to be correct. A marriage of equals was unusual. The Greek historian, Herodotus, observed, "Persians considered it the greatest insult to say a man was worse than a woman."[104]

Xerxes owned Vashti and he wanted to show her off.[105] Wives' value was in their beauty and their ability to produce children. With no offspring to inherit a king's throne, the empire would fall apart.[106]

---

2009, p.477.

102    Tomasino, Anthony. "Esther." Zondervan Illustrated Bible Backgrounds Commentary. Edited by John H. Walton. Vol. 3. Grand Rapids (Mich.): Zondervan, 2009, p.479.

103    Clarke, Adam, Albert Barnes, Theodore Beza, John Wesley, John Trapp, Thomas Coke, John Gill, et al. "Esther with Book Summary Esther 1:9" Verse-by-Verse Bible Commentary. Accessed January 22, 2020. https://www.studylight.org/commentary/esther/1-9. html.

104    Tomasino, Anthony. "Esther." Zondervan Illustrated Bible Backgrounds Commentary. Edited by John H. Walton. Vol. 3. Grand Rapids (Mich.): Zondervan, 2009, p.480.

105    Wilcox, Ashley M. "LESSONS FROM VASHTI (ESTHER 1:10-22)," July 3, 2017. https://www. ashleymwilcox. com/blog/2017/7/3/lessons-from-vashti.

106    Stedman, Ray C. "A Pair of Queens." Ray Stedman Ministries, 1963. https:// www. raystedman. org/old-testament/esther/a-pair-of-queens.

A few historians say wives accompanied their husbands to banquets,[107] but the vast majority believe it was not the custom for ladies in Persia to mix with men in public. The men had their festivity in the courtyard, and the women feasted inside the royal house. Women were not allowed to attend men's festivals.

Since no mention of wine was made, it is not known if Vashti served alcohol to her guests. However, her husband, King Xerxes, served his guests a great deal of wine. While no-one was forced to drink, most had. The king was "merry with wine." In other words, he was intoxicated. Common sense is one of the first casualties of drunkenness. [108] Intemperance can lead to poor choices and disaster.

Often Eastern kings had limited close relationships with their spouses, not seeing each other for long periods of time. They usually had harems and showed little if any regard for their wives. True respect comes from shared love and thoughtfulness, not from threats and forced submission.[109]

Xerxes sent seven eunuchs to summon Vashti to the men's banquet. (Eunuchs oversaw the royal harem and looked after the women. Some translations use the word "chamberlains," who were officers who managed the king's household.) Vashti bravely refused to go. This was not the spiteful rebuff of a woman who did not want to leave her own party. Only prostitutes took part in such banquets. She was protecting

107    Tomasino, Anthony. "Esther." Zondervan Illustrated Bible Backgrounds Commentary. Edited by John H. Walton. Vol. 3. Grand Rapids (Mich.): Zondervan, 2009, p.478.
108    Clarke, Adam, Albert Barnes, Theodore Beza, John Wesley, John Trapp, Thomas Coke, John Gill, et al. "Esther with Book Summary Esther 1:10" Verse-by-Verse Bible Commentary Accessed January 22, 2020.
https://www.studylight.org/commentary/esther/1-10. html.
109    McGrath, Alister E. "Esther," Life Application Study Bible (NIV). Wheaton, IL: Tyndale House Publishers, Inc., 1997. p. 824.

her own honor and reputation as well as her husband's.[110] It has also been suggested she may have been expecting a child and did not wish to appear publicly in that condition. Anaxerxes, the son of Vashti and Xerxes, was born in 483 BC. [111]

Persian kings were often thought of as gods. When they spoke, immediate compliance was expected.[112] Xerxes ordered Vashti to bring her royal crown in order to display her beauty to those present. (No description was given of the crown. It may have been a tall, stiff cloth or felt cap decorated with gems and blue and white ribbons.[113] It could also have been a jeweled turban.)[114] Some believe his instructions implied she was to wear only her crown.[115] To do such a thing would have been degrading and immoral. Philip Harrelson does not believe she was ordered to appear nude. He thinks Xerxes expected her to be clad in her beautiful royal clothing, wearing her crown without a veil, which was considered indiscreet and socially inappropriate.[116] Either way, a modest Persian woman displaying herself before a group of drunken men was totally unacceptable.

---

110    Clarke, Adam, Albert Barnes, Theodore Beza, John Wesley, John Trapp, Thomas Coke, John Gill, et al. "Esther with Book Summary Esther 1:10" Verse-by-Verse Bible Commentary  Accessed January 22, 2020.
https://www.studylight.org/commentary/esther/1-10. html.
111    McGrath, Alister E. "Esther," Life Application Study Bible (NIV). Wheaton, IL: Tyndale House Publishers, Inc., 1997. p. 823.
112    McGrath, Alister E. "Esther," Life Application Study Bible (NIV). Wheaton, IL: Tyndale House Publishers, Inc., 1997. p. 824.
113    Clarke, Adam, Albert Barnes, Theodore Beza, John Wesley, John Trapp, Thomas Coke, John Gill, et al. "Esther with Book Summary Esther 1:11" Verse-by-Verse Bible Commentary  Accessed January 22, 2020.
https://www.studylight.org/commentary/esther/1. html.
114    Clarke, Adam, Albert Barnes, Theodore Beza, John Wesley, John Trapp, Thomas Coke, John Gill, et al. "Esther with Book Summary Esther 1:8" Verse-by-Verse Bible Commentary  Accessed January 22, 2020.
https://www.studylight.org/commentary/esther/1-8. html.
115    Tomasino, Anthony. "Esther." Zondervan Illustrated Bible Backgrounds Commentary. Edited by John H. Walton. Vol. 3. Grand Rapids (Mich.): Zondervan, 2009, p.478.
116    Harrelson, Philip. "The Veil Of Vashti." Sermon Central, January 31, 2009. https://www. sermoncentral. com/sermons/ the-veil-of-vashti-philip-harrelson-sermon-on-holiness-131608.

When the king ordered her to come, she was required to obey. Disobedience could cost her everything: her crown, her prosperity and luxuries, and most terrifying, her life.[117] It is possible the queen knew her husband was drunk and not in full command of his senses. The customs and laws of Persia kept married women from such impropriety. She might have assumed when he became sober, he would condemn her for coming to the feast and behaving in an immodest fashion.[118]

## ESTHER 1:13-18

**13 Since it was customary for the king to consult experts in matters of law and justice, he spoke with the wise men who understood the times 14 and were closest to the king—Karshena, Shethar, Admatha, Tarshish, Meres, Marsena and Memukan, the seven nobles of Persia and Media who had special access to the king and were highest in the kingdom.**

**15 "According to law, what must be done to Queen Vashti?" he asked. "She has not obeyed the command of King Xerxes that the eunuchs have taken to her."**

**16 Then Memukan replied in the presence of the king and the nobles, "Queen Vashti has done wrong, not only against the king but also against all the nobles and the peoples of all the provinces of King Xerxes. 17 For the queen's conduct will become known to all the women, and so they will despise their husbands and say, 'King Xerxes commanded Queen Vashti to be brought before him, but she would not come.' 18 This very day the Persian and Median women of the nobility who have heard about the queen's conduct will respond to all the king's nobles in the same way. There will be no end of disrespect and discord."**

117     Barrier, Julie. "Diva or Heroine? What You DON'T Know About Queen Vashti." Preach It Teach It, 2020. https://www. preachitteachit. org/articles/detail/diva-or-heroine-what-you-dont-know-about-queen-vashti/.
118     Clarke, Adam, Albert Barnes, Theodore Beza, John Wesley, John Trapp, Thomas Coke, John Gill, et al. "Esther with Book Summary Esther 1:12" Verse-by-Verse Bible Commentary  Accessed January 22, 2020. https://www.studylight.org/commentary/esther/1-12. html.

The king was furious and humiliated. His queen had dared to disobey his direct order and insulted his rather large ego. He could not allow her to get away with such defiance. Something had to be done, so he discussed the matter with his trusted advisors. Several translations use the term "wise men" rather than "experts," leading some to incorrectly assume these men were astrologers. The seven nobles Xerxes consulted were well educated in history, customs, and the laws of Persia. These men may have been left over from a group of counselors formed by Darius.[119] They were the highest princes in Persia, possibly his privy counselors (the ruler's advisors), who were called on when needed (also referred to by Herodotus and Ezra in Ezr. 7:14). They were very influential, and Xerxes held them in high regard. Wise advisors could make or break the monarchy. Second in power just below the king, they were able to give him well-informed advice. Persians often drank wine while conducting their consultations, which may well have affected the outcome.[120]

Persian subjects rarely saw their king, but the seven most important families had regular access to him. The ruler's wife was required to come from one of these families,[121] but there are examples, in addition to Esther, where this rule was not followed.

It is much better to have a code of law than to be at the mercy of a cruel or unstable despot. The drunken, enraged Xerxes could have reacted harshly and had Vashti murdered immediately, but he acted according to the law. He called in his counselors and asked for their advice. He tried to shift the blame from his own drunken behavior to his wife's righteous refusal. What could he legally do? What was a proper punishment?[122]

---

119    Tomasino, Anthony. "Esther." Zondervan Illustrated Bible Backgrounds Commentary. Edited by John H. Walton. Vol. 3. Grand Rapids (Mich.): Zondervan, 2009, p.479.

120    Clarke, Adam, Albert Barnes, Theodore Beza, John Wesley, John Trapp, Thomas Coke, John Gill, et al. "Esther with Book Summary Esther 1:13" Verse-by-Verse Bible Commentary  Accessed January 22, 2020.
https://www.studylight.org/commentary/esther/1-13. html.

121    Clarke, Adam, Albert Barnes, Theodore Beza, John Wesley, John Trapp, Thomas Coke, John Gill, et al. "Esther with Book Summary Esther 1:14" Verse-by-Verse Bible Commentary  Accessed January 22, 2020.
https://www.studylight.org/commentary/esther/1-14. html.

122    Clarke, Adam, Albert Barnes, Theodore Beza, John Wesley, John Trapp, Thomas

It is quite possible the king and his seven advisors were too intoxicated to know right from wrong, or they may have been committed to keeping women in their place of servitude.

Vashti had done nothing wrong; her hostile, inebriated husband certainly had. There was a problem far more serious than punishing Vashti, which may be difficult for twenty-first century individuals from developed countries to understand. The princes saw her disobedience as a threat not only to the king, but also to all the men in the kingdom.[123] If the ladies of the kingdom learned that Vashti had gotten away with disobeying Xerxes, they might stand up to their husbands and defy them.[124] Such behavior would cause strife in the families. The men couldn't allow that to happen.[125] They had to make an example of the queen and punish her in a way that would discourage other women from doing the same thing. Wives were considered property and had a much lower status than their husbands. Property could not be allowed to disobey its owners.

## ESTHER 1:19-22

**19 "Therefore, if it pleases the king, let him issue a royal decree and let it be written in the laws of Persia and Media, which cannot be repealed, that Vashti is never again to enter the presence of King**

---

Coke, John Gill, et al. "Esther with Book Summary Esther 1:15" Verse-by-Verse Bible Commentary Accessed January 22, 2020.

https://www.studylight.org/commentary/esther/1-15. html.

123     Clarke, Adam, Albert Barnes, Theodore Beza, John Wesley, John Trapp, Thomas Coke, John Gill, et al. "Esther with Book Summary Esther 1:16" Verse-by-Verse Bible Commentary Accessed January 22, 2020.

https://www.studylight.org/commentary/esther/1-16. html.

124     Clarke, Adam, Albert Barnes, Theodore Beza, John Wesley, John Trapp, Thomas Coke, John Gill, et al. "Esther with Book Summary Esther 1:17" Verse-by-Verse Bible Commentary Accessed January 22, 2020.

https://www.studylight.org/commentary/esther/1-17. html.

125     Clarke, Adam, Albert Barnes, Theodore Beza, John Wesley, John Trapp, Thomas Coke, John Gill, et al. "Esther with Book Summary Esther 1:18" Verse-by-Verse Bible Commentary Accessed January 22, 2020.

https://www.studylight.org/commentary/esther/1-18. html.

**Xerxes. Also let the king give her royal position to someone else who is better than she. 20 Then when the king's edict is proclaimed throughout all his vast realm, all the women will respect their husbands, from the least to the greatest."**

**21 The king and his nobles were pleased with this advice, so the king did as Memukan proposed. 22 He sent dispatches to all parts of the kingdom, to each province in its own script and to each people in their own language, proclaiming that every man should be ruler over his own household, using his native tongue.**

Many pagan people believed Persian kings were gods. Their word was law.[126] Permanent laws in the Persian Empire became part of the constitution and were not to be amended or repealed[127] (Daniel 6:8, 6:15). If the king had not signed his decree into law, he could have ignored the proclamation and reinstated Vashti as queen.

Memukan was a cunning and underhanded politician. He suggested a harsh sentence to send a stern message to all the women of the Persian Empire. Vashti was to be banned from the king's presence, and her position was to be given to a more worthy woman. The king and queen would be divorced.[128] (Leniency was often seen as weakness. The king could not admit he had made a mistake demanding Vashti appear before his drunken friends.) The women of the empire were also included in this edict. **"All the women will respect their husbands, from the least to the greatest"** (verse 20). They were to honor and obey their husbands, whether they were peasants or princes. The implied threat was, if they did not abide by the decree, they too would be divorced and left destitute. [129] At a time when few women had jobs outside the home, this was a serious

126     McGrath, Alister E. "Esther," Life Application Study Bible (NIV). Wheaton, IL: Tyndale House Publishers, Inc., 1997. p. 824.

127     Hayford, Jack W. "The Book of Esther." New Spirit Filled Life Bible (NKJV). Nashville, TN: Thomas Nelson Bibles, 2002. P. 634.

128     Clarke, Adam, Albert Barnes, Theodore Beza, John Wesley, John Trapp, Thomas Coke, John Gill, et al. "Esther with Book Summary Esther 1:19" Verse-by-Verse Bible Commentary Accessed January 22, 2020.
https://www.studylight.org/commentary/esther/1-19. html.

129     Clarke, Adam, Albert Barnes, Theodore Beza, John Wesley, John Trapp, Thomas Coke, John Gill, et al. "Esther with Book Summary Esther 1:20" Verse-by-Verse Bible Commentary Accessed January 22, 2020.
https://www.studylight.org/commentary/esther/1-20. html.

threat. The king and his advisors unanimously approved Memucan's proposal. He signed, sealed, and registered the law so that it could not be overturned. This pleased the advisors, because their authority was safeguarded.[130] The king further decreed the husbands were to rule over their households. In instances of mixed marriages, the wives and children were required to speak the husband's native language.[131] It is unknown how such a law could be enforced.

Xerxes' empire had excellent roads and a postal system comparable to the American Pony Express. Riders on horseback sped information and decrees from the king to his subjects in all parts of the kingdom. In describing this method of communication, Herodotus proclaimed, "Neither snow nor rain, nor heat, nor gloom of night, stays these valiant couriers from the swift completion of their appointed rounds,"[132] a quote familiar today when referring to the United States Postal Service.

This harsh sentence was a part of God's perfect plan. Vashti had to be banished to make a place for Esther, the woman He had chosen to rescue His people. It is important to note, despite conflicting reports, Vashti was not killed. Historical documents attest she later became an important advisor to her son, Anaxerxes.[133]

Copies of the king's decree were sent to every province in the empire. They were written in a variety of languages to ensure everyone understood Xerxes' intent. (Aramaic was used for royal decrees, while Elamite, Akkadian, and Persian were used for inscriptions.)[134] Some

---

130    Clarke, Adam, Albert Barnes, Theodore Beza, John Wesley, John Trapp, Thomas Coke, John Gill, et al. "Esther with Book Summary Esther 1:21" Verse-by-Verse Bible Commentary  Accessed January 22, 2020. https://www.studylight.org/commentary/esther/1-21. html.

131    Ryrie, Charles Caldwell. "The Book of Esther," Ryrie Study Bible: New International Version. Chicago: Moody Publishers, 1986, p. 664.

132    Tomasino, Anthony. "Esther." Zondervan Illustrated Bible Backgrounds Commentary. Edited by John H. Walton. Vol. 3. Grand Rapids (Mich.): Zondervan, 2009, p.480.

133    Engelbrecht Edward A. "Esther." The Lutheran Study Bible: English Standard Version. Saint Louis: Concordia Publishing House, 2004. p. 762.

134    Buttrick, George Arthur. The Interpreters Bible (Vol 3) the Holy Scriptures in the King James and Revised Standard Versions with General Articles and Introduction, Exegesis, Exposition for Each Book of the Bible. Vol. 3. New York: Abingdon Press, 1954, p. 839.

languages could be printed on parchment with a quill, while others were pressed into clay tablets with a stick or stylus.[135] Edward Englebrecht suggests these documents may have also been translated into Egyptian hieroglyphics, Greek, Lycian, and Hebrew.[136] Scribes not only recorded the king's orders or other important information, sometimes they had the duty to make sure his orders were obeyed.[137]

135    Tomasino, Anthony. "Esther." Zondervan Illustrated Bible Backgrounds Commentary. Edited by John H. Walton. Vol. 3. Grand Rapids (Mich.): Zondervan, 2009, p. 497.

136    Engelbrecht Edward A. "Esther." The Lutheran Study Bible: English Standard Version. Saint Louis: Concordia Publishing House, 2004. p. 762.

137    Tomasino, Anthony. "Esther." Zondervan Illustrated Bible Backgrounds Commentary. Edited by John H. Walton. Vol. 3. Grand Rapids (Mich.): Zondervan, 2009, p. 498

# ESTHER CHAPTER 2

Texts found in Mesopotamia dating to 465-405 BC verify there were many Jewish inhabitants in Persia during the time covered in the book of Esther. The historian Herodotus referred to a list of the king's benefactors recorded in Persian archives (Est. 2:22).[138]

## ESTHER 2: 1-4

**1 Later when King Xerxes' fury had subsided, he remembered Vashti and what she had done and what he had decreed about her. 2 Then the king's personal attendants proposed, "Let a search be made for beautiful young virgins for the king. 3 Let the king appoint commissioners in every province of his realm to bring all these beautiful young women into the harem at the citadel of Susa. Let them be placed under the care of Hegai, the king's eunuch, who is in charge of the women; and let beauty treatments be given to them. 4 Then let the young woman who pleases the king be queen instead of Vashti." This advice appealed to the king, and he followed it.**

It is not known how long after Xerxes divorced Vashti these events took place. It could have been a few months or more than a year later.[139]

---

138    Archaeological Study Bible: An Illustrated Walk through Biblical History and Culture: New International Version. Grand Rapids, MI: Zondervan, 2005. "Esther," p. 720.
139    Clarke, Adam, Albert Barnes, Theodore Beza, John Wesley, John Trapp, Thomas Coke, John Gill, et al. "Esther with Book Summary Esther 2:1" Verse-by-Verse Bible Commentary  Accessed January 22, 2020.
https://www.studylight.org/commentary/esther/2:1. html.

Charles Ryrie suggests this incident probably occurred in 479 BC,[140] after Xerxes was defeated near the city of Plataea at the end of the second Persian attack on Greece.[141] The king was probably lonely and missed his former wife and the enjoyable times they had spent together. After his temper cooled and he was no longer drunk, he may have regretted his cruelty and impulsive behavior. Anger and alcohol are a dangerous combination. A person who acts in rage or drunkenness will often live to regret his foolish acts. Not only had he hurt Vashti, he had also made himself miserable.[142] However, because she had defied him and humiliated him in front of his friends, he had divorced her and expelled her from the kingdom.[143] His decree could not be revoked, so the king's attendants proposed a solution to his loneliness.

Wives were usually chosen from one of the ruling families, although sometimes this tradition was ignored. Political connections were far more important than simple beauty. The method suggested by the king's attendants, a beauty pageant, was unheard of. (The term "virgin" simply meant a young female eligible for marriage, not the meaning we have today.) These beautiful young ladies were to come from every province, class, and ethnic group. Even non-Persians were included. The process of gathering potential brides and preparing them for the king probably took two or three years.[144]

140    Ryrie, Charles Caldwell. "The Book of Esther," Ryrie Study Bible: New International Version. Chicago: Moody Publishers, 1986, p. 665.

141    "Battle of Plataea." Wikipedia. Wikimedia Foundation, March 26, 2020. https:// en.wikipedia.org/wiki/Battle_of_Plataea.

142    Clarke, Adam, Albert Barnes, Theodore Beza, John Wesley, John Trapp, Thomas Coke, John Gill, et al. "Esther with Book Summary Esther 2:1" Verse-by-Verse Bible Commentary Accessed January 22, 2020
. https://www.studylight.org/commentary/esther/2:1. html.

143    McGrath, Alister E. "Esther," Life Application Study Bible (NIV). Wheaton, IL: Tyndale House Publishers, Inc., 1997. p. 825.

144    Clarke, Adam, Albert Barnes, Theodore Beza, John Wesley, John Trapp, Thomas Coke, John Gill, et al. "Esther with Book Summary Esther 2:3" Verse-by-Verse Bible Commentary Accessed January 22, 2020. https://www.studylight.org/commentary/esther/2-3. html.

"Harem" meant "house of women." There was one dwelling for the young women before they were introduced to Xerxes.[145] He provided separate residences for his wives and concubines.[146]

The young ladies were under the strict control of Hegai, the chamberlain. (All chamberlains were eunuchs.) The contenders were purified (cleansed from impurities) and treated with oils and perfumes to prepare them for the royal beauty contest. John Gill suggests they may have been as young as twelve or fourteen.[147]

This is a story of self-indulgence, not a sweet fairy tale about a lucky Jewish girl who falls in love with a handsome king, marries him, and lives happily ever after. Women in ancient Persia were frequently abused and treated as property rather than valued as human beings. Few young ladies willingly volunteered to enter Xerxes' beauty pageant; most were abducted against their will.

Through the misery and hardship of the beauty pageant and life in the Persian court, Esther rose to become the queen of Persia and the savior of her people. What people intended for evil; God used for good. What may appear strange or impulsive to us became a part of God's perfect plan for His people.

## ESTHER 2:5-7

**5 Now there was in the citadel of Susa a Jew of the tribe of Benjamin, named Mordecai son of Jair, the son of Shimei, the son of Kish, 6 who had been carried into exile from Jerusalem by Nebuchadnezzar king of Babylon, among those taken captive with**

---

145    Clarke, Adam, Albert Barnes, Theodore Beza, John Wesley, John Trapp, Thomas Coke, John Gill, et al. "Esther with Book Summary Esther 2:3" Verse-by-Verse Bible Commentary  Accessed January 22, 2020.
https://www.studylight.org/commentary/esther/2:3. html.
146    Tomasino, Anthony. "Esther." Zondervan Illustrated Bible Backgrounds Commentary. Edited by John H. Walton. Vol. 3. Grand Rapids (Mich.): Zondervan, 2009, pp. 480-481.
147    Clarke, Adam, Albert Barnes, Theodore Beza, John Wesley, John Trapp, Thomas Coke, John Gill, et al. "Esther with Book Summary Esther 2:4" Verse-by-Verse Bible Commentary  Accessed January 22, 2020.
https://www.studylight.org/commentary/esther/2-4. html.

**Jehoiachin** [Hebrew Jeconiah, a variant of Jehoiachin] **king of Judah. 7 Mordecai had a cousin named Hadassah, whom he had brought up because she had neither father nor mother. This young woman, who was also known as Esther, had a lovely figure and was beautiful. Mordecai had taken her as his own daughter when her father and mother died.**

The name Mordecai was commonplace at that time. It meant "servant of Marduk," the chief Babylonian god. Even though he came from a Jewish family, Mordecai's parents may have chosen a name that was common in the land in which they lived. It was customary for people to have both a Gentile and a Hebrew name, although no additional name was revealed. [148]

In verse 6, the author states, **"Mordecai had been carried into exile from Jerusalem by Nebuchadnezzar, king of Babylon."** The deportation was in 598 BC, which would mean he was over one hundred years old, perhaps as old as one hundred forty, at the time Xerxes ruled.[149] The Hebrew text could also mean his family, rather than Mordecai himself, was taken into exile. Even though he could have been an old man, it is far more likely he was the great grandson of Kish, one of the men who was captured along with King Jehoiachin.[150] Albert Barnes estimates Mordecai was about thirty or forty, and Esther was about twenty.[151]

148    Tomasino, Anthony. "Esther." Zondervan Illustrated Bible Backgrounds Commentary. Edited by John H. Walton. Vol. 3. Grand Rapids (Mich.): Zondervan, 2009, p.481.
149    Clarke, Adam, Albert Barnes, Theodore Beza, John Wesley, John Trapp, Thomas Coke, John Gill, et al. "Esther with Book Summary Esther 2:5" Verse-by-Verse Bible Commentary  Accessed January 22, 2020.
https://www.studylight.org/commentary/esther/2-5. html.
150    McGrath, Alister E. "Esther," Life Application Study Bible (NIV). Wheaton, IL: Tyndale House Publishers, Inc., 1997. p. 825.
151    Clarke, Adam, Albert Barnes, Theodore Beza, John Wesley, John Trapp, Thomas Coke, John Gill, et al. "Esther with Book Summary Esther 2:5" Verse-by-Verse Bible Commentary  Accessed January 22, 2020.
https://www.studylight.org/commentary/esther/2-5. html.

The tribe of Benjamin came from a land located between the tribes of Judah in the north, and Israel in the south. The two kingdoms frequently fought over land. When many Israelites were deported,[152] Benjamin was under the control of Judah, and therefore allowed to stay in their land. Kish and Jehoiachin, not the Benjamites, were carried into exile. [153]

Mordecai's cousin, Hadassah (Hebrew name), was also known as Esther (Persian name derived from "Ishtar," the pagan goddess of love, war,[154] and the planet Venus).[155] Because both her parents were deceased, Mordecai raised her as his own daughter.[156] According to the Targum (an ancient Aramaic paraphrase of the Hebrew Bible, circa first century AD), Esther's father died before her birth, and her mother died shortly after her delivery. Esther was the daughter of Mordecai's uncle,[157] therefore, they were first cousins. She was an attractive young lady, respected, proficient in social skills, and well-prepared spiritually to do God's will.[158]

## ESTHER 2:8-9

**8 When the king's order and edict had been proclaimed, many young women were brought to the citadel of Susa and put under the care of Hegai. Esther also was taken to the king's palace and entrusted**

152  Hayford, Jack W. "The Book of Esther." New Spirit Filled Life Bible (NKJV). Nashville, TN: Thomas Nelson Bibles, 2002. P. 635.

153  Tomasino, Anthony. "Esther." Zondervan Illustrated Bible Backgrounds Commentary. Edited by John H. Walton. Vol. 3. Grand Rapids (Mich.): Zondervan, 2009, pp. 481-482.

154  Pryke, Louise. "Ishtar." Ancient History Encyclopedia, April 7, 2020. https://www. ancient. eu/ishtar/.

155  "Esther." Wikipedia. Wikimedia Foundation, March 8, 2020. https://en.wikipedia. org/wiki/Esther

156  Tomasino, Anthony. "Esther." Zondervan Illustrated Bible Backgrounds Commentary. Edited by John H. Walton. Vol. 3. Grand Rapids (Mich.): Zondervan, 2009, p.482.

157  Clarke, Adam, Albert Barnes, Theodore Beza, John Wesley, John Trapp, Thomas Coke, John Gill, et al. "Esther with Book Summary Esther 2;7" Verse-by-Verse Bible Commentary Accessed January 22, 2020. https://www.studylight.org/commentary/esther/2-7. html.

158  Hayford, Jack W. "The Book of Esther." New Spirit Filled Life Bible (NKJV). Nashville, TN: Thomas Nelson Bibles, 2002. p. 635.

**to Hegai, who had charge of the harem. 9 She pleased him and won his favor. Immediately he provided her with her beauty treatments and special food. He assigned to her seven female attendants selected from the king's palace and moved her and her attendants into the best place in the harem.**

Esther and all the other young women were taken by force to the citadel. Persian kings were powerful tyrants who could do as they wished with their subjects, particularly women.[159] This was far more than a contest where the winners remained in the harem, and the others went home to their families to live normal lives as before. They all became wives or concubines and remained with the other women, even after a winner was chosen.[160] Tragically, these young ladies often never saw their families again.[161]

Esther greatly pleased and impressed Hegai. The special food Xerxes provided (verse 9) was the same as provided for other wives and concubines, however, the chief eunuch served her personally. She ate what the other ladies ate, not a kosher diet (food prepared according to the requirements of Jewish dietary law). Had she requested specially cooked meals, her religion would have been disclosed.[162] Seven maidens, one for each day of the week, were given to her to fulfill all her needs.

159    Clarke, Adam, Albert Barnes, Theodore Beza, John Wesley, John Trapp, Thomas Coke, John Gill, et al. "Esther with Book Summary Esther 2:8" Verse-by-Verse Bible Commentary  Accessed January 22, 2020.
https://www.studylight.org/commentary/esther/2-8. html.
160    Tomasino, Anthony. "Esther." Zondervan Illustrated Bible Backgrounds Commentary. Edited by John H. Walton. Vol. 3. Grand Rapids (Mich.): Zondervan, 2009, p.482.
161    Clarke, Adam, Albert Barnes, Theodore Beza, John Wesley, John Trapp, Thomas Coke, John Gill, et al. "Esther with Book Summary Esther 2:1" Verse-by-Verse Bible Commentary  Accessed January 22, 2020.
https://www.studylight.org/commentary/esther/2:1. html.
162    Tomasino, Anthony. "Esther." Zondervan Illustrated Bible Backgrounds Commentary. Edited by John H. Walton. Vol. 3. Grand Rapids (Mich.): Zondervan, 2009, p.482.

## ESTHER 2:10-11

**10 Esther had not revealed her nationality and family background, because Mordecai had forbidden her to do so. 11 Every day he walked back and forth near the courtyard of the harem to find out how Esther was and what was happening to her.**

Fearing for her safety, Mordecai instructed Esther to hide her Jewish heritage to protect her from anti-Semitism.[163] (Anti-Semitism is a relatively new word, coined about 1875. However, the distrust and dislike of minority groups has existed from the beginning of time.)[164] Persians did not dislike Jews more than any other foreigners. All captured ethnicities were held in low esteem. Had her religion been known, she might never have been presented to the king.[165] Xerxes did not discover her true background until after their marriage (Est. 7:4)

Every day Mordecai walked back and forth in front of the women's house to check on the welfare of his cousin. The harem was off limits to all men except the king and the eunuchs. (John Trapp suggests Mordecai might have been a eunuch, although there is no biblical evidence of this.) Mordecai may have been a royal porter in charge of one of the gates, so his presence in the court would not have seemed strange. Since men were not allowed to visit the king's harem, Mordecai might have gotten special consent from the chief eunuch. It is also conceivable the eunuch may have been giving him regular reports on Esther's welfare.[166]

---

163    Hayford, Jack W. "The Book of Esther." New Spirit Filled Life Bible (NKJV). Nashville, TN: Thomas Nelson Bibles, 2002. P. 635.

164    Buttrick, George Arthur. The Interpreters Bible (Vol 3) the Holy Scriptures in the King James and Revised Standard Versions with General Articles and Introduction, Exegesis, Exposition for Each Book of the Bible. Vol. 3. New York: Abingdon Press, 1954, p. 848.

165    Clarke, Adam, Albert Barnes, Theodore Beza, John Wesley, John Trapp, Thomas Coke, John Gill, et al. "Esther with Book Summary Esther 2:10" Verse-by-Verse Bible Commentary Accessed January 22, 2020. https://www.studylight.org/commentary/esther/2-10. html.

166    Tomasino, Anthony. "Esther." Zondervan Illustrated Bible Backgrounds Commentary. Edited by John H. Walton. Vol. 3. Grand Rapids (Mich.): Zondervan, 2009, p.482.

## ESTHER 2:12-14

**12 Before a young woman's turn came to go in to King Xerxes, she had to complete twelve months of beauty treatments prescribed for the women, six months with oil of myrrh and six with perfumes and cosmetics. 13 And this is how she would go to the king: Anything she wanted was given her to take with her from the harem to the king's palace. 14 In the evening she would go there and in the morning return to another part of the harem to the care of Shaashgaz, the king's eunuch who was in charge of the concubines. She would not return to the king unless he was pleased with her and summoned her by name.**

Only physically attractive women were selected for the king. Esther underwent twelve months of intensive beauty treatments to prepare her for God's sovereign plan for her life.[167] Myrrh, a precious spice, was used in medicines and cosmetics. [Oil of myrrh was also used to anoint the tabernacle and the priests (Ex. 30:23).] The expensive, fragrant oil was massaged into the skin of the candidates to moisturize their skin in the hot, dry climate of Persia.[168] During this time they were also trained in Persian customs and etiquette.[169] Twelve months seems an excessively long time for beauty treatments. Matthew Poole, Joseph Benson, and others suggest there may have been another reason for this lengthy delay. In the days before paternity tests, the king wanted to be sure all babies born to his wives or concubines were his.[170]

167    Hayford, Jack W. "The Book of Esther." New Spirit Filled Life Bible (NKJV). Nashville, TN: Thomas Nelson Bibles, 2002. P. 635.

168    Tomasino, Anthony. "Esther." Zondervan Illustrated Bible Backgrounds Commentary. Edited by John H. Walton. Vol. 3. Grand Rapids (Mich.): Zondervan, 2009, p.484.

169    Engelbrecht Edward A. "Esther." The Lutheran Study Bible: English Standard Version. Saint Louis: Concordia Publishing House, 2004. p. 764.

170    Clarke, Adam, Albert Barnes, Theodore Beza, John Wesley, John Trapp, Thomas Coke, John Gill, et al. "Esther with Book Summary Esther 2:12" Verse-by-Verse Bible Commentary  Accessed January 22, 2020. https://www.studylight.org/commentary/esther/2-12. html.

## ESTHER 2:15-18

**15 When the turn came for Esther (the young woman Mordecai had adopted, the daughter of his uncle Abihail) to go to the king, she asked for nothing other than what Hegai, the king's eunuch who was in charge of the harem, suggested. And Esther won the favor of everyone who saw her. 16 She was taken to King Xerxes in the royal residence in the tenth month, the month of Tebeth, in the seventh year of his reign.**

**17 Now the king was attracted to Esther more than to any of the other women, and she won his favor and approval more than any of the other virgins. So he set a royal crown on her head and made her queen instead of Vashti. 18 And the king gave a great banquet, Esther's banquet, for all his nobles and officials. He proclaimed a holiday throughout the provinces and distributed gifts with royal liberality.**

Esther was taken before the king in either December 479 BC or January 478 BC.[171] The beauty contestants could take anything they wanted, such as clothes, jewels, or whatever else they thought would make them more attractive to the king. Esther knew Hegai was familiar with Xerxes and understood what would make him happy, so she wisely took only what the eunuch suggested.[172] God's work can be seen in Esther's appearance. King Xerxes chose her to be his queen because he found her to be the most beautiful young lady in his kingdom. [173]

Esther became the wife and queen of a pagan monarch approximately four years after his divorce from Vashti. [174] Jewish marriages to Gentiles

171    Clarke, Adam, Albert Barnes, Theodore Beza, John Wesley, John Trapp, Thomas Coke, John Gill, et al. "Esther with Book Summary Esther 2:16" Verse-by-Verse Bible Commentary Accessed January 22, 2020.
https://www.studylight.org/commentary/esther/2-16. html.
172    Clarke, Adam, Albert Barnes, Theodore Beza, John Wesley, John Trapp, Thomas Coke, John Gill, et al. "Esther with Book Summary Esther 2:13" Verse-by-Verse Bible Commentary Accessed January 22, 20
20. https://www.studylight.org/commentary/esther/2-13. html.
173    Hirsch, Emil G, John Dyneley Prince, and Solomon Schechter. "Esther." ESTHER JewishEncyclopedia. com, 1906. http://www. jewishencyclopedia. com/articles/5872-esther.
174    Ryrie, Charles Caldwell. "The Book of Esther," Ryrie Study Bible: New

were strongly discouraged, but not actually prohibited. Jews were forbidden to marry Hittites, Girgashites, Amorites, Canaanites, Perizzites, Hivites. and Jebusites, but they were not banned from marrying Persians (Dt. 7:1-4).

It was God's plan to put Esther in the important position of queen so she would be available when His people were in danger.[175] Esther's true importance was not her great beauty. Cruel or unjust people can be physically attractive. Her value to both God and her people was her bravery in the face of brutality and death. Provoking King Xerxes could have resulted in her death, but ignoring a terrible situation could have led to the annihilation of her Jewish countrymen.[176] Even when we do not understand, God's sovereign plan is always right.

Xerxes **"proclaimed a holiday"** (verse 18). The commentators of *The Interpreter's Bible* speculate this could have been a reduction of taxes, reduction or forgiveness of tribute (money or valuables paid to the ruler), a release of prisoners, a furlough (leave of absence) from military service, or a release from work. To show off his immense wealth, he gave away many extravagant gifts.[177]

Notice, as Mordecai had commanded, Esther continued to hide her Hebrew identity. She became Xerxes' most important wife, so all the lesser wives and concubines had to show her tremendous respect. Placing the royal crown on her head, perhaps only a purple and white headband, indicated she was the king's favorite and should be honored as such. [178]

---

International Version. Chicago: Moody Publishers, 1986, p. 666.
175    McGrath, Alister E. "Esther," Life Application Study Bible (NIV). Wheaton, IL: Tyndale House Publishers, Inc., 1997. p. 825
176    Fulkerson, Jason. "Sermon: The Courage of Esther." Reformed Church in America, August 5, 2019. https://www. rca. org/resources/sermon-courage-esther.
177    Buttrick, George Arthur. The Interpreters Bible (Vol 3) the Holy Scriptures in the King James and Revised Standard Versions with General Articles and Introduction, Exegesis, Exposition for Each Book of the Bible. Vol. 3. New York: Abingdon Press, 1954, p. 845.
178    Clarke, Adam, Albert Barnes, Theodore Beza, John Wesley, John Trapp, Thomas Coke, John Gill, et al. "Esther with Book Summary Esther 2:10" Verse-by-Verse Bible Commentary Accessed January 22, 2020. https://www.studylight.org/commentary/esther/2-10. html.

She moved to a special chamber, while the other women returned to the quarters reserved for the rest of his harem.

Persian men were permitted to have numerous wives and concubines. Concubines did not have the same rights and responsibilities as wives. Sometimes they were prisoners of war or slaves, but some were noble women. If the queen was infertile, a baby born to a concubine was the father's lawful heir. Life in the harem was closely regulated by the eunuchs in charge.[179] The chief duty of the harem was to serve the king and be ready to come to him at a moment's notice.[180]

According to the Greeks, Esther's banquet lasted seven days, but the historian Josephus stated they celebrated an entire month. This celebration was held to demonstrate Xerxes' great love and respect for his new queen.[181]

## ESTHER 2:19-23

**19 When the virgins were assembled a second time, Mordecai was sitting at the king's gate. 20 But Esther had kept secret her family background and nationality just as Mordecai had told her to do, for she continued to follow Mordecai's instructions as she had done when he was bringing her up.**

**21 During the time Mordecai was sitting at the king's gate, Bigthana** [Hebrew Bigthan, a variant of Bigthana] **and Teresh, two of the king's officers who guarded the doorway, became angry and conspired to assassinate King Xerxes. 22 But Mordecai found out about the plot and told Queen Esther, who in turn reported it to**

---

179    Tomasino, Anthony. "Esther." Zondervan Illustrated Bible Backgrounds Commentary. Edited by John H. Walton. Vol. 3. Grand Rapids (Mich.): Zondervan, 2009, p.484-485.

180    McGrath, Alister E. "Esther," Life Application Study Bible (NIV). Wheaton, IL: Tyndale House Publishers, Inc., 1997. p. 825.

181    Clarke, Adam, Albert Barnes, Theodore Beza, John Wesley, John Trapp, Thomas Coke, John Gill, et al. "Esther with Book Summary Esther 2:18" Verse-by-Verse Bible Commentary Accessed January 22, 2020.
https://www.studylight.org/commentary/esther/2-18. html.

**the king, giving credit to Mordecai. 23 And when the report was investigated and found to be true, the two officials were impaled on poles. All this was recorded in the book of the annals in the presence of the king.**

Even though Xerxes was delighted with Esther, he called a second group of young ladies to be added to his harem. It was during this time Mordecai saved the king's life.[182]

The king's gate, located in the eastern wall, was the main entrance to the upper part of the city. Rooms built into the wall on either side of the gate could be used for meetings or to house troops. Many of the king's administrators also lived in the king's gate. [183]

The gate was a place to conduct business, legal proceedings, and hear interesting gossip. Mordecai was not just idly resting by the gate. It is believed he held some position of authority in the king's service, although none was described. Once when he was sitting at the gate, Mordecai overheard two of the officers planning to assassinate the king. (No explanation was given for their murderous scheme. Thomas Coke suggests they might have been loyal to Vashti and resented Xerxes divorcing her and replacing her with Esther.)[184] He immediately reported the conspiracy to Queen Esther, and she told Xerxes. (This is the first time she was referred to by her title, Queen Esther.)[185] She made sure Xerxes knew the information came from Mordecai but did not disclose he was her cousin.[186]

182    Clarke, Adam, Albert Barnes, Theodore Beza, John Wesley, John Trapp, Thomas Coke, John Gill, et al. "Esther with Book Summary Esther 2:19" Verse-by-Verse Bible Commentary  Accessed January 22, 2020. https://www.studylight.org/commentary/esther/2-19. html.

183    Tomasino, Anthony. "Esther." Zondervan Illustrated Bible Backgrounds Commentary. Edited by John H. Walton. Vol. 3. Grand Rapids (Mich.): Zondervan, 2009, p.485.

184    Clarke, Adam, Albert Barnes, Theodore Beza, John Wesley, John Trapp, Thomas Coke, John Gill, et al. "Esther with Book Summary Esther 2:21" Verse-by-Verse Bible Commentary  Accessed January 22, 2020. https://www.studylight.org/commentary/esther/2-21. html.

185    Engelbrecht Edward A. "Esther." The Lutheran Study Bible: English Standard Version. Saint Louis: Concordia Publishing House, 2004. p. 765.

186    Buttrick, George Arthur. The Interpreters Bible (Vol 3) Exposition for Each Book of the Bible. Vol. 3. New York: Abingdon Press, 1954, p. 845.

When the king investigated the report and found it was true, he had the officials executed. Some biblical translations say the men were hanged on gallows (CSB, ESV, etc.), while others indicate they were hanged on a tree (KJ21, BRG, ASV, etc.). The Hebrew word translated "gallows" literally means "wooden object" or "tree". This did not mean they were hanged by the neck until they died, because that was not a Persian form of capital punishment. Their chosen method of execution was impaling the victim on a stake or pike until he died. Sometimes they crucified the condemned, allowing them to die of exposure.[187]

Even though she was a grown woman and married to the king, Esther continued to obey Mordecai, just as she had as a child. He had instructed her not to divulge her Jewish heritage, and her obedience may have saved her life.[188]

Scribes were always available to the king to record every important event that took place during his reign.[189] Some of the information provided by secular as well as biblical historians has come from these chronicles (diaries). They have been used to verify the accuracy of various incidents recorded in scripture.

Each detail in this book is important. The scribes carefully recorded Mordecai's warning to the king, and it became part of the permanent history of the empire. These were the same records read to Xerxes during the night he had insomnia (Est. 6:1-3).

---

187    Tomasino, Anthony. "Esther." Zondervan Illustrated Bible Backgrounds Commentary. Edited by John H. Walton. Vol. 3. Grand Rapids (Mich.): Zondervan, 2009, p.485.

188    Tomasino, Anthony. "Esther." Zondervan Illustrated Bible Backgrounds Commentary. Edited by John H. Walton. Vol. 3. Grand Rapids (Mich.): Zondervan, 2009, pp. 485-486.

189    Clarke, Adam, Albert Barnes, Theodore Beza, John Wesley, John Trapp, Thomas Coke, John Gill, et al. "Esther with Book Summary Esther 2:23" Verse-by-Verse Bible Commentary  Accessed January 22, 2020. https://www.studylight.org/commentary/esther/2-23. html.

# ESTHER CHAPTER 3

MANY HISTORIANS HAVE QUESTIONED THE LIKELIHOOD of a Jewish man, Mordecai, becoming an influential member of the Persian Empire. No secular records have yet been found that verify his existence. A cuneiform tablet, dating to the end of Darius I's rule or the beginning of Xerxes I's rule, mentions a scribe or government official named Marduka. According to the book of Esther, Mordecai was a royal official who sat at the king's gate (Est. 2:19, 5:13, 6:10). Later he was advanced to a higher position (Est. 8:2). It is possible Marduka and Mordecai are the same person.[190]

Archaeologists discovered another ancient tablet with an inscription stating Mardukaya was an official during Xerxes' reign.[191] Remember, many people had more than one name. Esther was also called Hadassah. Xerxes was known as Khshayarashan and Ahasuerus. Some biblical scholars believe Mardukaya was Mordecai.[192]

190     Archaeological Study Bible: An Illustrated Walk through Biblical History and Culture: New International Version. Grand Rapids, MI: Zondervan, 2005. "Esther," p. 721.
191     McGrath, Alister E. "Esther," Life Application Study Bible (NIV). Wheaton, IL: Tyndale House Publishers, Inc., 1997. p. 836.
192     Buttrick, George Arthur. The Interpreters Bible (Vol 3) the Holy Scriptures in the King James and Revised Standard Versions with General Articles and Introduction, Exegesis, Exposition for Each Book of the Bible. Vol. 3. New York: Abingdon Press, 1954, p. 835.

## ESTHER 3:1-2

**1 After these events, King Xerxes honored Haman son of Hammedatha, the Agagite, elevating him and giving him a seat of honor higher than that of all the other nobles. 2 All the royal officials at the king's gate knelt down and paid honor to Haman, for the king had commanded this concerning him. But Mordecai would not kneel down or pay him honor.**

The period of time that had elapsed is unknown. It could have been as much as five years.[193] Haman was an Amalekite, nomadic people descended from Esau (Gen. 36:12, 36:15). [The descendants of Esau had long been enemies of the Jewish descendants of Isaac (Ex. 17:16; Dt. 25:17-19)].[194] The genocidal Haman was filled with prejudice and bigotry against Jews in general and Mordecai in particular. Satan, the father of lies, certainly influenced the self-important Haman. Even though he had free will, he opted to persecute God's people.

Haman definitely was not a member of the seven noble families of Persia that served as the king's advisors. He was advanced to a higher position, but the precise description of his title in the king's court is not known. He has been referred to as Xerxes' *vizier* (high official) or prime minister, but that has not been verified. It has also been suggested he could have been the head of the king's bodyguards, or perhaps an inspector in charge of the *satraps* (provincial governors). [195]

Unwisely, Xerxes appointed the malevolent Haman as his second in command. Only the king was more powerful. He even raised Haman's chair to a higher level than the princes, an important distinction in the

---

193      Hayford, Jack W. "The Book of Esther." New Spirit Filled Life Bible (NKJV). Nashville, TN: Thomas Nelson Bibles, 2002. P. 636.
194      Ryrie, Charles Caldwell. "The Book of Esther," Ryrie Study Bible: New International Version. Chicago: Moody Publishers, 1986, p. 666.
195      Tomasino, Anthony. "Esther." Zondervan Illustrated Bible Backgrounds Commentary. Edited by John H. Walton. Vol. 3. Grand Rapids (Mich.): Zondervan, 2009, p.487.

Persian court.[196] Everyone except Mordecai bowed before him.[197] No explanation was given for Mordecai's refusal to kneel down and pay honor to Haman. (In Persian society, kneeling, bowing, and prostration were common ways people of lower rank showed respect to their superiors.)[198] One story, told by rabbis, asserted that Haman carried an idol with him, so Mordecai declined to honor the idol. There is no proof of this story. It is more probable the Jewish Mordecai, being loyal to God, refused to pay homage to a pagan Amalekite, particularly if he claimed divinity as Xerxes did.[199]

Some scholars believe Haman was a person of low birth who rose to importance in Xerxes' court. Upper class Persians probably would not have shown him honor. Haman was ready to fight anyone he thought was not exhibiting proper respect.[200] Jews bowed before God, not men or idols.[201] What seems like foolishness and disregard for his own safety was really a demonstration of his faith in God, the final authority in all things. He worshipped God, and God alone. Mordecai was God's servant and did what was right, even though his action endangered his life. He obeyed God rather than Haman. [202]

---

196     Clarke, Adam, Albert Barnes, Theodore Beza, John Wesley, John Trapp, Thomas Coke, John Gill, et al. "Esther with Book Summary Esther 3:1" Verse-by-Verse Bible Commentary  Accessed January 22, 2020. https://www.studylight.org/commentary/esther/3-1. html.

197     Yancey, Philip, and Tim Stafford. "Esther." The Student Bible. Grand Rapids, MI: Zondervan, 1996, p. 509.

198     Buttrick, George Arthur. The Interpreters Bible (Vol 3) the Holy Scriptures in the King James and Revised Standard Versions with General Articles and Introduction, Exegesis, Exposition for Each Book of the Bible. Vol. 3. New York: Abingdon Press, 1954, p. 848.

199     Ryrie, Charles Caldwell. "The Book of Esther," Ryrie Study Bible: New International Version. Chicago: Moody Publishers, 1986, p. 666.

200     Buttrick, George Arthur. The Interpreters Bible (Vol 3) the Holy Scriptures in the King James and Revised Standard Versions with General Articles and Introduction, Exegesis, Exposition for Each Book of the Bible. Vol. 3. New York: Abingdon Press, 1954, p. 849.

201     McGrath, Alister E. "Esther," Life Application Study Bible (NIV). Wheaton, IL: Tyndale House Publishers, Inc., 1997. p. 825.

202     McGrath, Alister E. "Esther," Life Application Study Bible (NIV). Wheaton, IL: Tyndale House Publishers, Inc., 1997. p. 826.

## ESTHER 3:3-6

**3 Then the royal officials at the king's gate asked Mordecai, "Why do you disobey the king's command?" 4 Day after day they spoke to him but he refused to comply. Therefore they told Haman about it to see whether Mordecai's behavior would be tolerated, for he had told them he was a Jew.**

**5 When Haman saw that Mordecai would not kneel down or pay him honor, he was enraged. 6 Yet having learned who Mordecai's people were, he scorned the idea of killing only Mordecai. Instead Haman looked for a way to destroy all Mordecai's people, the Jews, throughout the whole kingdom of Xerxes.**

The servants were concerned for Mordecai's safety. They tried to reason with him and convince him to bow before Haman, but he refused. He revealed he was a Jew, which was unknown prior to this time. Jews were forbidden to give divine honor to a human being.[203] This was not deemed to be a good excuse to dishonor Haman. Apparently, he had not noticed Mordecai's refusal until he was told. Haman was an Amalekite, sworn enemies of the Jews.[204] Haman transferred his hatred of Mordecai to all Jewish people. Humiliating or killing Mordecai was not enough revenge for Haman. He wanted to slaughter all the Jews.[205] This was a bitter, long standing blood feud between the Jews and Amalekites that began during the exodus from Egypt and continued for many centuries (Ex. 17:8-16; Dt. 25:17-19; Nu. 24:1-7; 1 Sa. 15; 1 Ch. 4:43). [206]

---

203     Clarke, Adam, Albert Barnes, Theodore Beza, John Wesley, John Trapp, Thomas Coke, John Gill, et al. "Esther with Book Summary Esther 3:3" Verse-by-Verse Bible Commentary  Accessed January 22, 2020.
https://www.studylight.org/commentary/esther/3-3. html.
204     Engelbrecht Edward A. "Esther." The Lutheran Study Bible: English Standard Version. Saint Louis: Concordia Publishing House, 2004. p. 765.
205     Clines, David J. A. "Esther." The HarperCollins Bible Commentary. Edited by James Luther Mays. San Francisco, CA: Harper San Francisco, 2000, p. 355.
206     Buttrick, George Arthur. The Interpreters Bible (Vol 3) the Holy Scriptures in the King James and Revised Standard Versions with General Articles and Introduction, Exegesis, Exposition for Each Book of the Bible. Vol. 3. New York: Abingdon Press, 1954, p. 847.

Both the Law Code of Hammurabi and scripture taught the concept of proportional retribution. This meant the punishment had to be equal to the crime (Lev. 24:17-22). Haman's plan to murder all the Israelites because one Jew had offended him was disproportionate. [207]

There is precedent. In the eleventh century BC, God told Saul, the first king of Israel, to kill all the Amalekites (1 Sa. 15). King Saul disobeyed God and allowed the king, Agag, and some animals to live. Haman was a descendant of King Agag. King Saul, Esther, and Mordecai were all members of the tribe of Benjamin, sworn enemies of the Amalekites. Haman was the first person recorded in the Bible to plan the genocide of all the Jews in the kingdom.[208]

## ESTHER 3:7-11

**7 In the twelfth year of King Xerxes, in the first month, the month of Nisan, the pur (that is, the lot) was cast in the presence of Haman to select a day and month. And the lot fell on** [Septuagint; Hebrew does not have 'And the lot fell on'] **the twelfth month, the month of Adar.**

**8 Then Haman said to King Xerxes, "There is a certain people dispersed among the peoples in all the provinces of your kingdom who keep themselves separate. Their customs are different from those of all other people, and they do not obey the king's laws; it is not in the king's best interest to tolerate them. 9 If it pleases the king, let a decree be issued to destroy them, and I will give ten thousand talents** [about 375 tons or about 340 metric tons] **of silver to the king's administrators for the royal treasury."**

**10 So the king took his signet ring from his finger and gave it to Haman son of Hammedatha, the Agagite, the enemy of the Jews. 11 "Keep the money," the king said to Haman, "and do with the people as you please."**

---

207     Tomasino, Anthony. "Esther." Zondervan Illustrated Bible Backgrounds Commentary. Edited by John H. Walton. Vol. 3. Grand Rapids (Mich.): Zondervan, 2009, p.488.

208     Stamps, Donald C., and J. Wesley. Adams. "The Book of Esther." The Full Life Study Bible: New International Version (NIV). Grand Rapids, MI: Zondervan Pub. House, 1992. p. 696.

The twelfth year of King Xerxes' reign was approximately 510 BC. Esther had been the queen for more than four years. Nisan, the first month of the Jewish calendar, falls in March or April in our calendar (the Gregorian calendar). This was also the beginning of the year in the Babylonian calendar and the official time to cast lots.[209] It was the time they believed their pagan gods would decide people's futures. Haman was very superstitious[210] and may have thought this was the ideal moment to set the time for his evil plans.[211] His diviners (soothsayers, prophets of the occult) cast lots to determine the appropriate date to murder the Jews. Babylonians believed the gods exhibited their superhuman guidance through the casting of lots. The method used is unknown.[212] This result was a part God's plan. The planned date of attack was eleven months away, giving time for Mordecai to contact Esther, who in turn was able to make her plea to the king for the lives of her condemned fellow Jews.[213] God's design frequently involves human activities and responsibilities. [214] There are no coincidences in God's sovereign plan.

Haman began his conversation with the king by telling the truth. The Jews in Persia did not blend in with their pagan captors. They deliberately maintained their separateness and refused to allow their faith and culture to be diluted by foreign gods and idols. The Jews followed the Mosaic law, which protected them from cultural and religious assimilation. Devout Jews avoided anything that was non-Jewish. They did not allow the pagan culture around them to defile their way of life.

209      Clarke, Adam, Albert Barnes, Theodore Beza, John Wesley, John Trapp, Thomas Coke, John Gill, et al. "Esther with Book Summary Esther 3:7" Verse-by-Verse Bible Commentary Accessed January 22, 2020. https://www.studylight.org/commentary/esther/3-7. html.

210      Ryrie, Charles Caldwell. "The Book of Esther," Ryrie Study Bible: New International Version. Chicago: Moody Publishers, 1986, p. 667.

211      Hayford, Jack W. "The Book of Esther." New Spirit Filled Life Bible (NKJV). Nashville, TN: Thomas Nelson Bibles, 2002. P. 635.

212      Tomasino, Anthony. "Esther." Zondervan Illustrated Bible Backgrounds Commentary. Edited by John H. Walton. Vol. 3. Grand Rapids (Mich.): Zondervan, 2009, p.488.

213      McGrath, Alister E. "Esther," Life Application Study Bible (NIV). Wheaton, IL: Tyndale House Publishers, Inc., 1997. p. 825.

214      Stamps, Donald C., and J. Wesley. Adams. "The Book of Esther." The Full Life Study Bible: New International Version (NIV). Grand Rapids, MI: Zondervan Pub. House, 1992. p. 698

Racial and religious prejudice of their neighbors helped the Jews survive, no matter where they were. Even though they were dispersed throughout the kingdom, they continued to eat kosher foods and keep the Sabbath. [215]

Haman was shrewd and spiteful. His prejudice can be seen in the way he aimed suspicion at the Jews, people whose customs and religion differed from the Persians.[216] His goal was to convince Xerxes the Jewish people were disloyal. The Persians frequently allowed conquered people to keep their own customs and laws if they did not disturb the peace.

That was not a problem to King Xerxes. In order to provoke the king's wrath, Haman falsely claimed the Jews had refused to obey his laws. [217] The selfish Xerxes felt everything and everyone existed for his benefit and pleasure. Haman convinced him the Jews were defiant, which presented a major problem. The king was more than happy to do whatever was necessary to force compliance.[218] Notice, Haman never mentioned his wounded pride or the long-standing hostility between his ancestors, the Amalekites, and the Jews. He only mentioned those things he felt would make Xerxes angry. The foolish, self-important king frequently made hasty decisions with little debate or thought.

After that, Haman offered the King a huge bribe or *bakshish* (provide a gift for a favor) equal to about two thirds of the annual budget of Persia. Xerxes handed Haman his signet ring and told him to keep the money. Allowing Haman to use the king's signet ring was an act of trust and friendship. (The signet ring, probably made of metal, wood, or

---

215      Buttrick, George Arthur. The Interpreters Bible (Vol 3) the Holy Scriptures in the King James and Revised Standard Versions with General Articles and Introduction, Exegesis, Exposition for Each Book of the Bible. Vol. 3. New York: Abingdon Press, 1954, p. 849-852.

216      Dybdahl, Jon L, ed. "Esther." Andrews Study Bible: Light. Depth. Truth. Berrien Springs, MI: Andrews University Press, 2010. P. 617.

217      Brettler, Marc Zvi., Carol A. Newsom, and Pheme Perkins. The New Oxford Annotated Bible: with the Apocryphal/Deuterocanonical Books: New Revised Standard Version. Edited by Michael David. Coogan. NIVed. New York: Oxford University Press, 2001, p. 713.

218      Tomasino, Anthony. "Esther." Zondervan Illustrated Bible Backgrounds Commentary. Edited by John H. Walton. Vol. 3. Grand Rapids (Mich.): Zondervan, 2009, p.488.

bone, was the same as the king's signature. [219] A cylindrical signet was sometimes worn around a person's neck on a cord. The impression of the seal was pressed into wax or clay to authenticate documents or to seal something closed. )[220] This ring gave Haman limitless power and vast authority. It was basically a transfer of power from the king to Haman. Xerxes would pay for the elimination of the Jews himself, and Haman could do as he wished.[221] Persian law prohibited executions based on the testimony of only one man. The king acted on Haman's testimony alone, which was forbidden.

Albert Barnes explains there are two interpretations for Xerxes' comment to **"keep the money"** (Est. 3:10). Most scholars believe Xerxes refused to take the money and returned it to Haman, while a few think the king may have taken the bribe and awarded Haman the property of the Jews he planned to murder.[222] Typically, the winner of any conflict got the plunder.[223]

## ESTHER 3:12-15

**12 Then on the thirteenth day of the first month the royal secretaries were summoned. They wrote out in the script of each province and in the language of each people all Haman's orders to the king's satraps, the governors of the various provinces and the nobles of the various peoples. These were written in the name of**

219     McGrath, Alister E. "Esther," Life Application Study Bible (NIV). Wheaton, IL: Tyndale House Publishers, Inc., 1997. p. 828.

220     Archaeological Study Bible: An Illustrated Walk through Biblical History and Culture: New International Version. Grand Rapids, MI: Zondervan, 2005. "Esther," p. 728.

221     Tomasino, Anthony. "Esther." Zondervan Illustrated Bible Backgrounds Commentary. Edited by John H. Walton. Vol. 3. Grand Rapids (Mich.): Zondervan, 2009, p.489.

222     Clarke, Adam, Albert Barnes, Theodore Beza, John Wesley, John Trapp, Thomas Coke, John Gill, et al. "Esther with Book Summary Esther 3:11" Verse-by-Verse Bible Commentary  Accessed January 22, 2020.
 https://www.studylight.org/commentary/esther/3-11. html.

223     Buttrick, George Arthur. The Interpreters Bible (Vol 3) the Holy Scriptures in the King James and Revised Standard Versions with General Articles and Introduction, Exegesis, Exposition for Each Book of the Bible. Vol. 3. New York: Abingdon Press, 1954, p. 850.

King Xerxes himself and sealed with his own ring. 13 Dispatches were sent by couriers to all the king's provinces with the order to destroy, kill and annihilate all the Jews—young and old, women and children—on a single day, the thirteenth day of the twelfth month, the month of Adar, and to plunder their goods. 14 A copy of the text of the edict was to be issued as law in every province and made known to the people of every nationality so they would be ready for that day.

15 The couriers went out, spurred on by the king's command, and the edict was issued in the citadel of Susa. The king and Haman sat down to drink, but the city of Susa was bewildered.

On the day before Passover, Xerxes issued an empire-wide command to kill all the Jewish men, women, and children in any way they found acceptable. Afterward, the victors could steal the property of the dead Jews as a reward for their part in the slaughter.[224] Then, as if nothing important had happened, the king and Haman sat down for a drink.

John Gill suggests Haman may have prepared a banquet for Xerxes to demonstrate his gratitude for the King's bloodthirsty edict. [225] The people of Susa, both pagan and Jew, were astounded by this proclamation. Not all Persians were anti-Semitic. Many had Jewish friends, family members, and business associates. They were horrified at the genocide planned for the thirteenth of Adar. Most people were loyal to the Jews and opposed to Haman.[226]

224    Clarke, Adam, Albert Barnes, Theodore Beza, John Wesley, John Trapp, Thomas Coke, John Gill, et al. "Esther with Book Summary Esther 3:13" Verse-by-Verse Bible Commentary  Accessed January 22, 2020.
https://www.studylight.org/commentary/esther/3-13. html.
225    Clarke, Adam, Albert Barnes, Theodore Beza, John Wesley, John Trapp, Thomas Coke, John Gill, et al. "Esther with Book Summary Esther 3:15" Verse-by-Verse Bible Commentary  Accessed January 22, 2020.
https://www.studylight.org/commentary/esther/3-15. html.
226    Clarke, Adam, Albert Barnes, Theodore Beza, John Wesley, John Trapp, Thomas Coke, John Gill, et al. "Esther with Book Summary Esther 3:15" Verse-by-Verse Bible Commentary  Accessed January 22, 2020.
https://www.studylight.org/commentary/esther/3-15. html.

Many have questioned why the Jews did not leave Persia when they heard of Haman's plan. Daniel Whedon explains the Jews were in bondage under the control of the Persians. They could not leave without permission from the king. Escape was virtually impossible.[227]

Haman's edict was sent to all parts of the kingdom. Not only were letters given to all the governors, but copies were also displayed in public places so that everyone knew what was expected. Haman, their tormentor, probably enjoyed the terror he was inflicting on the Jewish people.[228]

The persecutors could do as they wished to the persecuted. They were indifferent to the plight of those they considered inferior. Even though the Jews were the only targets of this edict, Persians who had intermarried and had children with the Jews were also in danger.[229]

227    Clarke, Adam, Albert Barnes, Theodore Beza, John Wesley, John Trapp, Thomas Coke, John Gill, et al. "Esther with Book Summary Esther 3:13" Verse-by-Verse Bible Commentary Accessed January 22, 2020.
https://www.studylight.org/commentary/esther/3-13. html.
228    Clarke, Adam, Albert Barnes, Theodore Beza, John Wesley, John Trapp, Thomas Coke, John Gill, et al. "Esther with Book Summary Esther 3:14" Verse-by-Verse Bible Commentary Accessed January 22, 2020.
https://www.studylight.org/commentary/esther/3-14. html.
229    Clarke, Adam, Albert Barnes, Theodore Beza, John Wesley, John Trapp, Thomas Coke, John Gill, et al. "Esther with Book Summary Esther 3:15" Verse-by-Verse Bible Commentary Accessed January 22, 2020.
https://www.studylight.org/commentary/esther/3-15. html.

# ESTHER CHAPTER 4

I N THE 1970s, A FRENCH ARCHAEOLOGICAL EXPEDITION
found the gatehouse of the king's gate (Est. 2:19-21, 3:2-3, 4:2, 4:6,
5:9, 5:13, 6:10, 6:12). An inscription from Xerxes, in three languages,
commemorated its construction by Darius. The Greek historian,
Herodotus, wrote of petitioners waiting outside the gate.[230]

## ESTHER 4:1-3

**1 When Mordecai learned of all that had been done, he tore
his clothes, put on sackcloth and ashes, and went out into the city,
wailing loudly and bitterly. 2 But he went only as far as the king's
gate, because no one clothed in sackcloth was allowed to enter it.
3 In every province to which the edict and order of the king came,
there was great mourning among the Jews, with fasting, weeping and
wailing. Many lay in sackcloth and ashes.**

The act of tearing one's clothes was a dramatic way to express strong
feelings, such as grief, anger, or indignation (see Ge. 37:29-30, 37:34;
Jos. 7:6; 1 Ki. 21:27; Ezr. 9:3). Sackcloth, a dark-colored, course material
that was woven from goat or camel hair, was often used to make sacks.
Clothing made from this material was customarily worn to show grief
or mourning after a person had torn his clothes. Rolling in ashes or

---

230    Archaeological Study Bible: An Illustrated Walk through Biblical History and
Culture: New International Version. Grand Rapids, MI: Zondervan, 2005. "Esther," p.
722.

rubbing them on a person's body was another visible sign of suffering[231] (see also Jnh. 3:6; 2 Sa. 3:31, 12:16; 2 Ki. 6:30, 19:1, and many more). These demonstrations of grief were also used by the Persians. According to Daniel Whedon and George Haydock, when news of Xerxes' defeat by the Greeks reached Susa, the people tore their clothes and wailed in despair.[232]

Mordecai was a patriot who deeply loved his people. As a man of faith, he believed his God would come to the aid of the Jews, however, the author gave no indication he prayed for mercy.[233] Though he was extremely distraught, his grief did not cloud his judgment. A public display of tearing his clothes, putting on sackcloth, and wailing were not the acts of a man fearing for his own life. He feared for his countrymen, the people of God. Many believe his cry was addressed to God, not Xerxes.[234] Mordecai's public mourning was copied by many other Jews throughout the kingdom.[235]

No-one wearing sackcloth could enter the king's gate. Such clothing was forbidden by Xerxes' dress code.[236] Public displays of grief were against the law. Mordecai's sorrow could not be hidden. The king was not to be exposed to such suffering because it could cause him despair as well. Persians saw this as an evil omen (sign, premonition). John Trapp

231     Tomasino, Anthony. "Esther." Zondervan Illustrated Bible Backgrounds Commentary. Edited by John H. Walton. Vol. 3. Grand Rapids (Mich.): Zondervan, 2009, p.490.

232     Clarke, Adam, Albert Barnes, Theodore Beza, John Wesley, John Trapp, Thomas Coke, John Gill, et al. "Esther with Book Summary Esther 4:1" Verse-by-Verse Bible Commentary Accessed January 22, 2020. https://www/commentary/esther/4-1.html.

233     Clarke, Adam, Albert Barnes, Theodore Beza, John Wesley, John Trapp, Thomas Coke, John Gill, et al. "Esther with Book Summary Esther 4:2" Verse-by-Verse Bible Commentary Accessed January 22, 2020. https://www.studylight.org/commentary/esther/4-2. html.

234     Buttrick, George Arthur. The Interpreters Bible (Vol 3) the Holy Scriptures in the King James and Revised Standard Versions with General Articles and Introduction, Exegesis, Exposition for Each Book of the Bible. Vol. 3. New York: Abingdon Press, 1954, p. 841.

235     Dybdahl, Jon L, ed. "Esther." Andrews Study Bible: Light. Depth. Truth. Berrien Springs, MI: Andrews University Press, 2010. p. 618.

236     Engelbrecht Edward A. "Esther." The Lutheran Study Bible: English Standard Version. Saint Louis: Concordia Publishing House, 2004. p. 766.

explained, "The kings and couriers of Persia must see no sad sight lest their mirth should be marred, and themselves surprised with heaviness and horror. "[237] The only way for Mordecai to enter the gate would be to change his clothes. This he refused to do. Removing the outward signs of grief would not remove its cause.

## ESTHER 4:4-8

**4 When Esther's eunuchs and female attendants came and told her about Mordecai, she was in great distress. She sent clothes for him to put on instead of his sackcloth, but he would not accept them. 5 Then Esther summoned Hathak, one of the king's eunuchs assigned to attend her, and ordered him to find out what was troubling Mordecai and why.**

**6 So Hathak went out to Mordecai in the open square of the city in front of the king's gate. 7 Mordecai told him everything that had happened to him, including the exact amount of money Haman had promised to pay into the royal treasury for the destruction of the Jews. 8 He also gave him a copy of the text of the edict for their annihilation, which had been published in Susa, to show to Esther and explain it to her, and he told him to instruct her to go into the king's presence to beg for mercy and plead with him for her people.**

When Esther heard of Mordecai's display of grief, she immediately sent him fresh clothes. (It is possible her servants knew of both her relationship to Mordecai and her religion, but her husband definitely did not.) Esther was now the queen. She had many responsibilities, but she sincerely loved Mordecai and could not ignore his suffering.

Little information reached Esther, so it was necessary to send Hathak (also spelled Hathach) the eunuch to determine the reason for Mordecai's distress.[238] Xerxes had appointed Hathak to both serve his wife and observe her conduct. The king was a jealous and suspicious

237    Clarke, Adam, Albert Barnes, Theodore Beza, John Wesley, John Trapp, Thomas Coke, John Gill, et al. "Esther with Book Summary Esther 4:4" Verse-by-Verse Bible Commentary  Accessed January 22, 2020.
https://www.studylight.org/commentary/esther/4-4. html.
238    Engelbrecht Edward A. "Esther." The Lutheran Study Bible: English Standard Version. Saint Louis: Concordia Publishing House, 2004. p. 765.

man. It is possible the eunuch was an old man who had been rewarded with this position for his faithful service.[239] Xerxes' wives and concubines were under constant scrutiny, so there was no way for Esther to sneak away to meet with Mordecai.[240] Obviously Esther trusted the eunuch's discretion since she sent him to speak to her cousin.

Mordecai knew the exact amount of Haman's bribe, but the source of his information is unknown. It is possible he had an upper level official feeding him information, but there is no proof of this theory. He gave Hathak a transcribed copy of the decree calling for the destruction of the Jewish people. Mordecai instructed the eunuch to explain it to the queen. No mention is made of Esther reading the king's decree for herself. It has been suggested the edict was written in a language she did not know, so it would be necessary to translate the words into Aramaic for Esther to understand. Less than five percent of ancient Jewish men could read, and the percentage for women was unquestionably lower. Royal women were taught many skills, such as horsemanship and martial arts, but no mention was made of literacy. Quite likely Esther was illiterate; therefore, an educated person was required to read the document to her.[241]

## ESTHER 4:9-17

**9 Hathak went back and reported to Esther what Mordecai had said.**

**10 Then she instructed him to say to Mordecai, 11 "All the king's officials and the people of the royal provinces know that for any man**

---

239    Clarke, Adam, Albert Barnes, Theodore Beza, John Wesley, John Trapp, Thomas Coke, John Gill, et al. "Esther with Book Summary Esther 4:5" Verse-by-Verse Bible Commentary Accessed January 22, 2020.
https://www.studylight.org/commentary/esther/4-5. html.
240    Clarke, Adam, Albert Barnes, Theodore Beza, John Wesley, John Trapp, Thomas Coke, John Gill, et al. "Esther with Book Summary Esther 4:10" Verse-by-Verse Bible Commentary Accessed January 22, 2020.
https://www.studylight.org/commentary/esther/4-10. html.
241    Tomasino, Anthony. "Esther." Zondervan Illustrated Bible Backgrounds Commentary. Edited by John H. Walton. Vol. 3. Grand Rapids (Mich.): Zondervan, 2009, pp. 490-491.

or woman who approaches the king in the inner court without being summoned the king has but one law: that they be put to death unless the king extends the gold scepter to them and spares their lives. But thirty days have passed since I was called to go to the king."

12 When Esther's words were reported to Mordecai, 13 he sent back this answer: "Do not think that because you are in the king's house you alone of all the Jews will escape. 14 For if you remain silent at this time, relief and deliverance for the Jews will arise from another place, but you and your father's family will perish. And who knows but that you have come to your royal position for such a time as this?"

15 Then Esther sent this reply to Mordecai: 16 "Go, gather together all the Jews who are in Susa, and fast for me. Do not eat or drink for three days, night or day. I and my attendants will fast as you do. When this is done, I will go to the king, even though it is against the law. And if I perish, I perish."

17 So Mordecai went away and carried out all of Esther's instructions.

Hathak, Esther's faithful messenger, returned from his meeting with Mordecai with a request. He instructed Esther to appear before Xerxes and ask for mercy for her people. Esther was the queen, but Mordecai still had great influence in her life. However, instead of telling her what to do, as he had when she was small, he pleaded with her to make an appeal to her husband.

Persian law was harsh. The king could summon people to his court, but any person daring to appear before him without an invitation could be killed, unless the king chose to spare his or her life. It would seem reasonable for Esther to request a meeting with her husband, but communication between the couple was limited. They lived in separate homes and did not eat together. Xerxes had hundreds of other concubines and lesser wives to keep him company. The king had not summoned Esther for thirty days, which did not indicate a close husband-wife relationship. Queens or members of the harem may go days, months, or even years without seeing the king.[242] She may have feared she had angered him in some way, so was hesitant to request a meeting with him. Esther feared for her life.

There was another possible reason for Esther's hesitation. Haman may have been Xerxes' *chiliarch* (commander of 1,000 men). If that were the case, Esther would have had to ask Haman to be admitted to the throne room. He would have demanded to know the reason for her uninvited visit, putting her in tremendous danger.[243]

Adam Clarke hypothesizes, "It is very likely that this wicked man (Haman) had endeavored to draw the king's attention from the queen, that his affection might be lessened, as he must have known something of the relationship between her and Mordecai, and consequently viewed her as a person who, in all probability, might stand much in the way of the accomplishments of his designs. I cannot but think that he had been the cause why Esther had not seen the king for thirty days."[244]

She told her cousin his request could cause her death if she invaded the king's privacy uninvited. Persian kings were usually kept away from their subjects. This policy was designed to protect the king's safety as well as emphasize his imperial standing. All business was conducted through his ministers, so he would not have to be troubled with the everyday business of the empire or bothersome subjects asking for favors. This restriction applied to his wife as well. (This was not a new law created by Xerxes or Haman. It had existed for many years, and all the king's subjects were familiar with it.)[245] It is possible she also thought of Vashti who had been divorced and banished for disobedience.

242    Engelbrecht Edward A. "Esther." The Lutheran Study Bible: English Standard Version. Saint Louis: Concordia Publishing House, 2004. p. 767.
243    Tomasino, Anthony. "Esther." Zondervan Illustrated Bible Backgrounds Commentary. Edited by John H. Walton. Vol. 3. Grand Rapids (Mich.): Zondervan, 2009, p. 491.
244    Clarke, Adam, Albert Barnes, Theodore Beza, John Wesley, John Trapp, Thomas Coke, John Gill, et al. "Esther with Book Summary Esther 4:11" Verse-by-Verse Bible Commentary. Accessed January 22, 2020.
https://www.studylight.org/commentary/esther/4-11. html.
245    Clarke, Adam, Albert Barnes, Theodore Beza, John Wesley, John Trapp, Thomas Coke, John Gill, et al. "Esther with Book Summary Esther 4:11" Verse-by-Verse Bible Commentary. Accessed January 22, 2020.

Mordecai pressured Esther and spoke persuasively.[246] He told the queen she and her family would die if she did nothing. He believed if Esther refused, God would send another person to deliver the Jews, and she would miss the opportunity to serve God and His people.[247] Mordecai trusted God. He believed, based on His previous deliverances and saving grace, God would rescue His people, whether through Esther or another person. His promises never fail. God was involved in the day-to-day life of the empire in order to save His people. He often used human activities to accomplish His sovereign purposes.[248]

Esther had a difficult choice to make. There was no neutral or safe action. The fact she was a queen would not protect her from the fate faced by all the other Jews in the empire. Esther agreed to do as Mordecai asked. Her reply to his request demonstrated her great loyalty to her cousin and to her people. Knowing she needed God's help, the queen responded with courage and faith. She was willing to risk everything: her security, her possessions, and even her life for the welfare of her people. This was more than a single person could do in her own strength.

Every person had a part to play. First, they must seek God's will and pray Esther would find favor in the king's sight. The Jewish people, the queen, and her attendants would fast. [Robert Jamieson suggests Esther might have chosen Jewish ladies or proselytes (converts to Judaism) to be her assistants.][249]

---

https://www.studylight.org/commentary/esther/4-11. html.

246    Ryrie, Charles Caldwell. "The Book of Esther," Ryrie Study Bible: New International Version. Chicago: Moody Publishers, 1986, p. 668

247    Hayford, Jack W. "The Book of Esther." New Spirit Filled Life Bible (NKJV). Nashville, TN: Thomas Nelson Bibles, 2002. p. 635.

248    Stamps, Donald C., and J. Wesley. Adams. "The Book of Esther." The Full Life Study Bible: New International Version (NIV). Grand Rapids, MI: Zondervan Pub. House, 1992. p. 698.

249    Clarke, Adam, Albert Barnes, Theodore Beza, John Wesley, John Trapp, Thomas Coke, John Gill, et al. "Esther with Book Summary Esther 4:16" Verse-by-Verse Bible Commentary. Accessed January 22, 2020. https://www./commentary/esther/4-16. html.

They would neither eat nor drink for three days. (In ancient times, part of a day counted as a whole day when reckoning time.[250] Therefore, the fast was for one full day, two nights, and two partial days.)[251] Then the queen would go before the king, even though such an act could result in her murder.[252]

The author did not mention prayer, but it is implied in the request, since fasting and prayer were usually linked (2 Sa. 12:16; Da. 9:3; Jnh. 3:5-9; Ezr. 8:21-23).[253]

God was in control. Mordecai obviously expected Him to come to the aid of His people, and Esther greatly needed His protection. In verse 16 she told her cousin, **"I will go to the king, even though it is against the law. And if I perish, I perish."** No matter the cost to her personally, Esther was ready to do God's will, and trust Him to take care of everything else. The brave queen willingly risked her life to save her people. God used both Mordecai and Esther in His divine plan. He honors those who obey Him.[254]

Up until this time, Esther always obeyed Mordecai's orders. Their roles had now changed. Esther had taken charge, and Mordecai carried out all her instructions (verse 17).[255]

250      Ryrie, Charles Caldwell. "The Book of Esther," Ryrie Study Bible: New International Version. Chicago: Moody Publishers, 1986, p. 669.

251      Clarke, Adam, Albert Barnes, Theodore Beza, John Wesley, John Trapp, Thomas Coke, John Gill, et al. "Esther with Book Summary Esther 4:16" Verse-by-Verse Bible Commentary. Accessed January 22, 2020. https://www./commentary/esther/4-16. html.

252      Hayford, Jack W. "The Book of Esther." New Spirit Filled Life Bible (NKJV). Nashville, TN: Thomas Nelson Bibles, 2002. p. 635.

253      Buttrick, George Arthur. The Interpreters Bible (Vol 3) the Holy Scriptures in the King James and Revised Standard Versions with General Articles and Introduction, Exegesis, Exposition for Each Book of the Bible. Vol. 3. New York: Abingdon Press, 1954, p. 855.

254      Stamps, Donald C., and J. Wesley. Adams. "The Book of Esther." The Full Life Study Bible: New International Version (NIV). Grand Rapids, MI: Zondervan Pub. House, 1992. p. 698.

255      Clines, David J. A. "Esther." The HarperCollins Bible Commentary. Edited by James Luther Mays. San Francisco, CA: Harper San Francisco, 2000, p. 356.

# ESTHER CHAPTER 5

EVEN THOUGH ESTHER'S EXISTENCE CANNOT BE corroborated with secular sources, some historians believe it is possible Amestris, referred to by Herodotus, was actually Esther, since their names are linguistically related. Others believe Amestris was Vashti. Neither theory can be confirmed.

There are also many similarities between archaeological evidence found in Susa and details recorded in the book of Esther. The author definitely knew a great deal about Persian customs, life, and vocabulary.[256]

## ESTHER 5:1-4

**1 On the third day Esther put on her royal robes and stood in the inner court of the palace, in front of the king's hall. The king was sitting on his royal throne in the hall, facing the entrance. 2 When he saw Queen Esther standing in the court, he was pleased with her and held out to her the gold scepter that was in his hand. So Esther approached and touched the tip of the scepter.**

**3 Then the king asked, "What is it, Queen Esther? What is your request? Even up to half the kingdom, it will be given you."**

256    Archaeological Study Bible: An Illustrated Walk through Biblical History and Culture: New International Version. Grand Rapids, MI: Zondervan, 2005. "Esther," p. 724.

**4 "If it pleases the king," replied Esther, "let the king, together with Haman, come today to a banquet I have prepared for him."**

On the fifteenth day of Nisan, Esther bravely went to see the king. She surely had good reason to be apprehensive. Xerxes had not called for her in a month. Had he already grown tired of her? Appearing before the autocratic, unpredictable king uninvited could result in her death. Esther dressed in her royal robes and stood where her husband would notice her. The king sat in his throne room on a raised chair with a footstool. The chair was either solid gold or made of wood that was inlaid with gold and covered with a beautiful tapestry. If any person other than the king sat in the chair, he or she would be executed. [257]

The door to his throne room was kept open, so he could see into the inner court where Esther waited. Fortunately, he was pleased to see her and extended his golden scepter, a sign of mercy, so she could enter and speak to him. Esther touched the tip of his scepter, which showed her respect and admiration for the king.

In all existing paintings or reliefs portraying Persian kings, whether standing or sitting, the monarch was always shown holding an elongated, tapered staff in his right hand with the base resting on the ground. Sometimes the staff had a small ball attached to the top. This scepter was an important symbol of his royal status and absolute authority, and the king kept it with him at all times.[258]

In the ruins of the palace at Persepolis, ancient carvings have been found that depict a soldier, holding a huge axe, standing behind Xerxes' throne.[259] Such a frightening sight was a grim reminder the queen was risking her life to speak to her husband. There is definite irony shown

---

257     Clarke, Adam, Albert Barnes, Theodore Beza, John Wesley, John Trapp, Thomas Coke, John Gill, et al. "Esther with Book Summary Esther 5:1" Verse-by-Verse Bible Commentary. Accessed January 22, 2020.
https://www.studylight.org/commentary/esther/5-1. html.
258     Clarke, Adam, Albert Barnes, Theodore Beza, John Wesley, John Trapp, Thomas Coke, John Gill, et al. "Esther with Book Summary Esther 5:2" Verse-by-Verse Bible Commentary. Accessed January 22, 2020.
https://www.studylight.org/commentary/esther/5-2. html.
259     Strain, David. "Gallows Humor." First Presbyterian Church, Jackson, Mississippi, June 23, 2013. https://www.fpcjackson.org/resource-library/sermons/gallows-humor.

here. In chapter one, Queen Vashti was expelled and divorced because she refused to come when her husband called for her. Esther risked everything to approach Xerxes uninvited, but the king extended his scepter to show she was welcome.

God heard the countless prayers offered for Esther and touched the heart of the king. Xerxes was glad to see his wife, addressed her as "Queen Esther," and requested to know her petition. In fact, he offered her anything she wanted, up to half his kingdom.[260] Amazingly, she did not beg for the lives of her people. Instead, she invited the king and Haman to a banquet.

There are three theories for Haman's invitation. Perhaps she invited her enemy so he would not suspect she had any hidden agenda. She also knew Xerxes was very fond of Haman, so inviting him would make the king happy and he would be more apt to grant her request. The third theory is the most likely. She invited him so she could accuse him face-to-face, in front of Xerxes, at the appropriate time. In the king's presence, it would be difficult to make up an excuse, harm Esther, or flee to safety.

She may have known accepting her husband's offer literally would be unwise. Subtlety was more sensible.[261] She was careful to follow Persian etiquette. First she asked for a small favor (come to the banquet), then when the time was right, she would present the real issue to the king.[262] Her goal was to gain the king's favor so he would be more receptive to her request. (This banquet occurred three days after Mordecai notified Esther of Haman's proclamation.)[263]

Banquets involved the consumption of a great deal of alcohol. The feast would start with drinking wine and eating fruit and sugary treats.

260     Engelbrecht Edward A. "Esther." The Lutheran Study Bible: English Standard Version. Saint Louis: Concordia Publishing House, 2004. p. 768.

261     Clines, David J. A. "Esther." The HarperCollins Bible Commentary. Edited by James Luther Mays. San Francisco, CA: Harper San Francisco, 2000, p. 356.

262     Tomasino, Anthony. "Esther." Zondervan Illustrated Bible Backgrounds Commentary. Edited by John H. Walton. Vol. 3. Grand Rapids (Mich.): Zondervan, 2009, p. 494.

263     Tomasino, Anthony. "Esther." Zondervan Illustrated Bible Backgrounds Commentary. Edited by John H. Walton. Vol. 3. Grand Rapids (Mich.): Zondervan, 2009, p. 498.

After an hour or so, the main course was served with water to drink (called the banquet of meats). After the food was consumed and the table cleared, fruit and more wine were served (called the banquet of wine). Drinking excessively was expected.[264]

Esther's banquet was unusual. The king always ate alone, and his guests dined in a nearby room. At the queen's feast, they drank and ate together, which Haman considered a great honor.[265]

Xerxes again offered to give Esther up to half of his kingdom. This was a common saying that meant he would give her anything that was reasonable. Sometimes Persian kings gave their wives entire cities.

## ESTHER 5:5-8

**5 "Bring Haman at once," the king said, "so that we may do what Esther asks." So the king and Haman went to the banquet Esther had prepared.**

**6 As they were drinking wine, the king again asked Esther, "Now what is your petition? It will be given you. And what is your request? Even up to half the kingdom, it will be granted."**

**7 Esther replied, "My petition and my request is this: 8 If the king regards me with favor and if it pleases the king to grant my petition and fulfill my request, let the king and Haman come tomorrow to the banquet I will prepare for them. Then I will answer the king's question."**

Rather than disclose her true petition, Esther invited Xerxes and Haman to another banquet. Only then would she reveal what she wanted. Notice, she said if he was willing to grant her petition, he and Haman would attend a banquet the next night. In other words, if they

264    Clarke, Adam, Albert Barnes, Theodore Beza, John Wesley, John Trapp, Thomas Coke, John Gill, et al. "Esther with Book Summary Esther 5:6" Verse-by-Verse Bible Commentary. studylight. org. Accessed January 22, 2020. https://www. studylight. org/commentary/esther/5-6. html.
265    Clarke, Adam, Albert Barnes, Theodore Beza, John Wesley, John Trapp, Thomas Coke, John Gill, et al. "Esther with Book Summary Esther 5:8" Verse-by-Verse Bible Commentary. Accessed January 22, 2020. https://www. studylight. org/commentary/esther/5-8. html.

came to the second banquet, Xerxes agreed to grant her request.[266] Esther was very wise. She would wait for God's perfect timing before she made her request. Haman had no idea she had any secret motive, so he was thrilled by her outwardly wonderful invitation. His pride would be his downfall. **"Pride goes before destruction, a haughty spirit before a fall"** (Pr. 16:18). **"In his pride the wicked man does not seek Him; in all his thoughts there is no room for God"** (Ps.10:4). **"When pride comes, then comes disgrace, but with humility comes wisdom"** (Pr. 11:2). The higher Haman's standing rose, the farther he had to fall. God humbles the self-important.[267]

### ESTHER 5:9-12

**9 Haman went out that day happy and in high spirits. But when he saw Mordecai at the king's gate and observed that he neither rose nor showed fear in his presence, he was filled with rage against Mordecai. 10 Nevertheless, Haman restrained himself and went home.**

**Calling together his friends and Zeresh, his wife, 11 Haman boasted to them about his vast wealth, his many sons, and all the ways the king had honored him and how he had elevated him above the other nobles and officials. 12 "And that's not all," Haman added. "I'm the only person Queen Esther invited to accompany the king to the banquet she gave. And she has invited me along with the king tomorrow."**

Haman was delighted with himself. He called together his friends and his wife to brag about his many sons, his immense wealth, the great honor bestowed upon him by the king, and most impressive, his invitation to a second banquet with the king and queen. He had such a high opinion of himself, he clearly viewed his invitation from Esther as a special honor, not a setup for his demise.

Persians considered fathering many sons was a sign of impressive manhood. In fact, each year the king gave a gift to the man with the most

---

266     Clines, David J. A. "Esther." The HarperCollins Bible Commentary. Edited by James Luther Mays. San Francisco, CA: Harper San Francisco, 2000, p. 356.
267     Engelbrecht Edward A. "Esther." The Lutheran Study Bible: English Standard

sons.[268] Legend speculates Haman may have had as many as 208 children with a variety of women, but there is no corroboration for this story. According to the Greek historian Herodotus, next to military heroism, the greatest accomplishment any Persian man could have was being the father of many sons.[269] Daughters and the health of the mother(s) were not considered important.

Despite Haman's great fortune, he had a major dilemma. Earlier, when he went to the king's gate, he saw the hated Mordecai and was filled with rage. Once again, Mordecai had refused to show Haman the honor he believed he was due. This was a major violation of Persian protocol. Mordecai obviously knew of Haman's evil decree to murder the Jews, so he refused to show him even the smallest amount of civil respect.[270]

Haman's most obvious sins were greed and pride. Though he held the second highest position in the kingdom, he was completely miserable. Mordecai's admiration should not have been needed for his happiness. He was so consumed with anger and hatred, he could not enjoy even the great honor of dining with the king and queen. The intolerable snub of one Jewish man was all he could think about.[271] Haman restrained himself and hurried home. Mordecai served the king, possibly as his doorkeeper, so he was therefore under his royal protection. Haman could not take violent revenge on his Jewish enemy, because such an act would reflect badly on Xerxes and result in his own death.[272]

268    Tomasino, Anthony. "Esther." Zondervan Illustrated Bible Backgrounds Commentary. Edited by John H. Walton. Vol. 3. Grand Rapids (Mich.): Zondervan, 2009, p. 494.

269    Clarke, Adam, Albert Barnes, Theodore Beza, John Wesley, John Trapp, Thomas Coke, John Gill, et al. "Esther with Book Summary Esther 5:11" Verse-by-Verse Bible Commentary. studylight. org. Accessed January 22, 2020.

270    Clarke, Adam, Albert Barnes, Theodore Beza, John Wesley, John Trapp, Thomas Coke, John Gill, et al. "Esther with Book Summary Esther 5:9" Verse-by-Verse Bible Commentary. studylight. org. Accessed January 22, 2020. https://www. studylight. org/commentary/esther/5-9. html.

271    McGrath, Alister E. "Esther," Life Application Study Bible (NIV). Wheaton, IL: Tyndale House Publishers, Inc., 1997. p. 830.

272    Clarke, Adam, Albert Barnes, Theodore Beza, John Wesley, John Trapp, Thomas Coke, John Gill, et al. "Esther with Book Summary Esther 5:10" Verse-by-Verse Bible Commentary. studylight. org. Accessed January 22, 2020. https://www. studylight. org/commentary/esther/5-10. html.

## ESTHER 5:13-15

**13 "But all this gives me no satisfaction as long as I see that Jew Mordecai sitting at the king's gate."**

**14 His wife Zeresh and all his friends said to him, "Have a pole set up, reaching to a height of fifty cubits,** [about 75 feet or 23 meters] **and ask the king in the morning to have Mordecai impaled on it. Then go with the king to the banquet and enjoy yourself." This suggestion delighted Haman, and he had the pole set up.**

Haman had wealth, prestige, and power, but he was not satisfied. Mordecai had humiliated him publicly, so he felt degrading and punishing Mordecai in a public spectacle was necessary. An execution witnessed by large numbers of people would disgrace Mordecai and fill Haman's enemies with fear so they would not dare oppose him. [273]

His wife and friends were sympathetic. They understood his rage. He could not enjoy his good fortune as long as Mordecai refused to show him the respect he desired. Zeresh (meaning "gold") and his friends suggested Haman should set up a tall pole in his courtyard that could be seen from all over Susa. It would be used to impale Mordecai. This pole was to be three times the usual length used for executing prisoners. (The pole would be enormous to match the bloodthirsty Haman's massive ego.)[274] This murder must not appear to be personal revenge; therefore, authorization by Xerxes was necessary.[275] He could ask the king to execute Mordecai in the morning, leaving the rest of the day to enjoy himself and attend the royal banquet.

Guilt or remorse were not feelings Haman understood. He had no respect for human life. His thirst for power and respect led to bloodlust.

---

273    Clarke, Adam, Albert Barnes, Theodore Beza, John Wesley, John Trapp, Thomas Coke, John Gill, et al. "Esther with Book Summary Esther 5:14" Verse-by-Verse Bible Commentary. studylight. org. Accessed January 22, 2020. https://www. studylight. org/commentary/esther/5-14. html.

274    Ritchie, Paul. "Esther 5-7 'Seeming Coincidences, Perfect Timing and an Irresistible Force'." Esther 5-7 'Seeming coincidences, perfect timing and an irresistible force', January 7, 2009. http://paulritchieblog. blogspot. com/2009/01/esther-5-7-seeming-coincidences-perfect. html.

275    Clines, David J. A. "Esther." The HarperCollins Bible Commentary. Edited by James Luther Mays. San Francisco, CA: Harper San Francisco, 2000, p. 356.

He could not tolerate any more interruptions to his evil plot. Haman unlawfully prepared for the execution of a man who had not been convicted of a crime.[276]

276    Clarke, Adam, Albert Barnes, Theodore Beza, John Wesley, John Trapp, Thomas Coke, John Gill, et al. "Esther with Book Summary Esther 7:9" Verse-by-Verse Bible Commentary. studylight. org. Accessed January 22, 2020. https://www. studylight. org/commentary/esther/7-9. html.

# Esther Chapter 6

G OD'S HAND COULD BE SEEN IN THE DEVELOPMENT of this unlikely story. After the first feast, Mordecai once again snubbed Haman at the king's gate. This insult intensified his fury so much he had a pole erected to impale the impertinent Jew. That was the perfect setup for the next day's banquet.

## ESTHER 6:1-9

1 That night the king could not sleep; so he ordered the book of the chronicles, the record of his reign, to be brought in and read to him. 2 It was found recorded there that Mordecai had exposed Bigthana and Teresh, two of the king's officers who guarded the doorway, who had conspired to assassinate King Xerxes.

3 "What honor and recognition has Mordecai received for this?" the king asked.

"Nothing has been done for him," his attendants answered.

4 The king said, "Who is in the court?" Now Haman had just entered the outer court of the palace to speak to the king about impaling Mordecai on the pole he had set up for him.

5 His attendants answered, "Haman is standing in the court."

"Bring him in," the king ordered.

**6 When Haman entered, the king asked him, "What should be done for the man the king delights to honor?"**

**Now Haman thought to himself, "Who is there that the king would rather honor than me?" 7 So he answered the king, "For the man the king delights to honor, 8 have them bring a royal robe the king has worn and a horse the king has ridden, one with a royal crest placed on its head. 9 Then let the robe and horse be entrusted to one of the king's most noble princes. Let them robe the man the king delights to honor, and lead him on the horse through the city streets, proclaiming before him, 'This is what is done for the man the king delights to honor!'"**

Many translations refer to the officers in verse two as "chamberlains" (KJ21, ASV, BRG, DARBY, and others) or "doorkeepers" (AMP, NASB, NLV, and others). Doorkeepers guarded the entrance to cities, public buildings, and the homes of the rich, while chamberlains managed the noble's household. [277] Either could have been present at that time.

God supervised and controlled every part of this story. No detail was too large or too small. The king was apparently not ill or in pain. By God's design, he had insomnia. He could have called for a musician or one of his wives or concubines to keep him company, but instead, he ordered his servant to read to him from the Book of Chronicles, the official Persian recorded history. (Canon Rawlinson speculated the king may have been unable to read. However, Xerxes was part of a noble family. He would have been trained for his royal duties from an early age. It is unlikely his education would have neglected literacy.)[278]

The Book of Chronicles was not a dry historical narrative. Information was recorded in verse, and these epic poems were the work of the finest poets in Persia. The scribes recorded the names of "royal benefactors" (sponsors, patrons, supporters) who had served the king well or who had performed great deeds for him, and therefore deserved to be recognized

277    Hayford, Jack W. "The Book of Esther." New Spirit Filled Life Bible (NKJV). Nashville, TN: Thomas Nelson Bibles, 2002. p. 638.
278    Clarke, Adam, Albert Barnes, Theodore Beza, John Wesley, John Trapp, Thomas Coke, John Gill, et al. "Esther with Book Summary Esther 6:1" Verse-by-Verse Bible Commentary. studylight. org. Accessed January 22, 2020. https://www. studylight. org/commentary/esther/6-1. html.

and honored. Their names were placed on a special roll so the king could make sure they were properly rewarded. This sometimes took months or years. Nothing appearing in this chronicle was ever forgotten. By reviewing the information recorded in this important journal, monarchs could learn from events in their own lives or in the lives of their ancestors or enemies.[279]

Was it merely happenstance the king listened to the story of how Mordecai had overheard the plot to murder the king and saved his life? Was it coincidence that the king had neglected to honor Mordecai? Certainly not! This "oversight" was a divinely ordained God-incidence that was all part of His sovereign plan. Persian kings had a reputation for quickly rewarding those who had performed some outstanding service.[280]

When Xerxes realized he had not rewarded Mordecai for saving his life, he decided to honor him without delay.[281] God caused Xerxes' apparent memory lapse so Mordecai would be rewarded at the right time. He continually orchestrated incidents to further His plan to redeem His people.

Like the king, Haman may also have had insomnia. Was his sleep interrupted by his hatred of Mordecai or anticipation of his enemy's impending demise? He arrived at the court very early, anxious to request Mordecai's execution. His convenient arrival was part of God's preordained timetable.

Haman stood in the outer court waiting to be summoned to Xerxes' bedroom. Even the second in command could not enter without being

---

279    Clarke, Adam, Albert Barnes, Theodore Beza, John Wesley, John Trapp, Thomas Coke, John Gill, et al. "Esther with Book Summary Esther 6:2" Verse-by-Verse Bible Commentary. studylight. org. Accessed January 22, 2020. https://www. studylight. org/commentary/esther/6-2. html.

280    Tomasino, Anthony. "Esther." Zondervan Illustrated Bible Backgrounds Commentary. Edited by John H. Walton. Vol. 3. Grand Rapids (Mich.): Zondervan, 2009, p. 495.

281    Clines, David J. A. "Esther." The HarperCollins Bible Commentary. Edited by James Luther Mays. San Francisco, CA: Harper San Francisco, 2000, p. 356.

called. Since he was the first person available in the palace, the king sent for him to ask his advice.[282] Xerxes immediately began to discuss rewarding the honored man. This gave Haman no chance to propose his malicious plan.

Xerxes had no idea Haman was plotting a murder. He asked his arrogant official how to pay homage to an unnamed man he wished to honor. Xerxes was careful not to reveal the honoree's name, possibly hoping to receive unbiased suggestions. Of course, the self-centered Haman assumed the king wanted to honor him. Without a moment's hesitation, he went into great detail describing various ways Xerxes could pay tribute to this great unidentified man.[283] The extraordinary tributes suggested by Haman were probably far more extravagant than anything the king or his servants could have imagined.

Dr. David Strain proposed Haman was really suggesting Xerxes should declare him to be the king's equal, his surrogate, or perhaps even his heir. The narcissistic prime minister had made himself into his own idol. His list of outrageous rewards was ridiculous.[284] The recognition he requested for himself was now bestowed upon Mordecai. His world was falling apart.

The king's clothes were very important. Anyone fortunate enough to publicly wear his garments would receive great honor and respect. Even the horse wore a turban that looked like a crown.[285] Ancient reliefs (artistic work in which part of the scene protruded from the background) have been discovered that show horses wearing crown-like decorations on their heads.[286]

---

282    Clarke, Adam, Albert Barnes, Theodore Beza, John Wesley, John Trapp, Thomas Coke, John Gill, et al. "Esther with Book Summary Esther 6:5" Verse-by-Verse Bible Commentary. studylight. org. Accessed January 22, 2020. https://www. studylight. org/commentary/esther/6-5. html.

283    Engelbrecht Edward A. "Esther." The Lutheran Study Bible: English Standard Version. Saint Louis: Concordia Publishing House, 2004. p. 769.

284    Strain, David. "The Man Who the King Delights to Honor." First Presbyterian Church, Jackson, Mississippi, June 30, 2013. https://www.fpcjackson.org/resource-library/ sermons/the-man-who-the-king-delights-to-honor.

285    Engelbrecht Edward A. "Esther." The Lutheran Study Bible: English Standard Version. Saint Louis: Concordia Publishing House, 2004. p. 769.

286    Buttrick, George Arthur. The Interpreters Bible (Vol 3) the Holy Scriptures in the King James and Revised Standard Versions with General Articles and Introduction,

## ESTHER 6:10-11

**10 "Go at once," the king commanded Haman. "Get the robe and the horse and do just as you have suggested for Mordecai the Jew, who sits at the king's gate. Do not neglect anything you have recommended."**

**11 So Haman got the robe and the horse. He robed Mordecai, and led him on horseback through the city streets, proclaiming before him, "This is what is done for the man the king delights to honor!"**

The arrogant Haman must have smiled as he waited to hear Xerxes say he was the man to be honored. He had planned all the wonderful accolades for himself, but that was not to be. The great man was Mordecai the Jew who sat at the king's gate! Xerxes was very careful to specify exactly who he wanted to honor, so there was no room for mistakes. Haman knew who Mordecai was and longed for his death more than anything in the world. Haman had gone to the king to plan his murder, and now he was in charge of paying high honors to his enemy. God planned it, Xerxes ordered it, and Haman was forced to carry it out.

The king said to hurry. He wanted Mordecai's honors performed before Esther's feast. A delay would have been seen as refusing to carry out Xerxes' decree.[287] Haman could not afford to antagonize the all-powerful king.

The fact Xerxes was anxious to honor a Jew implied he may not have known the full extent of the decree Haman issued in his name.[288] Mordecai was a humble man. He wanted no glory, only the safety of his people. Nevertheless, he was given all the rewards and tributes Haman longed for.

Exegesis, Exposition for Each Book of the Bible. Vol. 3. New York: Abingdon Press, 1954, p. 859.

287     Clarke, Adam, Albert Barnes, Theodore Beza, John Wesley, John Trapp, Thomas Coke, John Gill, et al. "Esther with Book Summary Esther 6:10" Verse-by-Verse Bible Commentary. studylight. org. Accessed January 22, 2020. https://www. studylight. org/commentary/esther/6-10. html.

288     Engelbrecht Edward A. "Esther." The Lutheran Study Bible: English Standard Version. Saint Louis: Concordia Publishing House, 2004. p. 769.

The faithful Mordecai would not have been awarded an entire suit of clothes. Rather, he was given a coat or cloak that had been previously worn by the king. This was an obvious sign of his royal approval. Xerxes' robes were purple and embellished with gold. They were unique and easily recognized by the residents of the palace and city.[289]

Xerxes' mount was a beautiful charger brought from Armenia. The fact Mordecai was allowed to ride the king's decorated horse demonstrated the monarch's immense gratitude.[290] Wearing the king's clothes or riding his horse without special authorization from the king would have been considered treason. The offender would pay for this transgression with his life. Not only was Mordecai honored with the king's robe and horse, the second most important man in the kingdom acted as his herald. This surely would have raised Mordecai's standing in the eyes of his friends and acquaintances.[291] Obviously, Haman could not request the execution of the man Xerxes planned to honor.

Persian kings and nobles always rode, either on a horse or in a chariot. True gentlemen never walked to their destinations. Peasants never rode. They walked.[292] This practice must have infuriated Haman as he walked before the king's horse. Even though this task was to be done by a high ranking official, Haman must have felt like a slave. He paraded Mordecai through the streets of the most important parts of the city proclaiming,

**"This is what is done for the man the king delights to honor!"** (verse 11). This was a complete reversal of fortune. By God's design, Haman served in the role of Mordecai's servant. Instead of witnessing

---

289    Clarke, Adam, Albert Barnes, Theodore Beza, John Wesley, John Trapp, Thomas Coke, John Gill, et al. "Esther with Book Summary Esther 6:8" Verse-by-Verse Bible Commentary. studylight. org. Accessed January 22, 2020. https://www. studylight. org/commentary/esther/6-8. html.

290    Tomasino, Anthony. "Esther." Zondervan Illustrated Bible Backgrounds Commentary. Edited by John H. Walton. Vol. 3. Grand Rapids (Mich.): Zondervan, 2009, p. 495.

291    Dybdahl, Jon L, ed. "Esther." Andrews Study Bible: Light. Depth. Truth. Berrien Springs, MI: Andrews University Press, 2010. p. 620.

292    Clarke, Adam, Albert Barnes, Theodore Beza, John Wesley, John Trapp, Thomas Coke, John Gill, et al. "Esther with Book Summary Esther 6:8" Verse-by-Verse Bible Commentary. studylight. org. Accessed January 22, 2020. https://www. studylight. org/commentary/esther/6-8. html.

Mordecai's execution, Haman extravagantly honored him in front of the entire town. Obviously this was a great honor for Mordecai, but it may have also been intended to encourage other people to serve the king and be rewarded in a similar way.[293]

## ESTHER 6:12-14

**12 Afterward Mordecai returned to the king's gate. But Haman rushed home, with his head covered in grief, 13 and told Zeresh his wife and all his friends everything that had happened to him.**

**His advisers and his wife Zeresh said to him, "Since Mordecai, before whom your downfall has started, is of Jewish origin, you cannot stand against him—you will surely come to ruin!" 14 While they were still talking with him, the king's eunuchs arrived and hurried Haman away to the banquet Esther had prepared.**

Despite his royal tribute as Xerxes' rescuer earlier in the day, Mordecai returned to his position at the king's gate. He understood it was important to go back to his job and stay near Esther.[294] John Gill suggests he may have also "returned to his sackcloth and fasting."[295]

Covering one's head was an ancient sign of mourning for the dead (2 Sa. 15:30),[296] but in Haman's case, it clearly showed disgrace, self-consciousness, and embarrassment.[297] With great outrage, Haman returned to his house as quickly as possible and recounted the traumatic events of his day to his wife and friends.

---

293    Tomasino, Anthony. "Esther." Zondervan Illustrated Bible Backgrounds Commentary. Edited by John H. Walton. Vol. 3. Grand Rapids (Mich.): Zondervan, 2009, p. 495.

294    Hayford, Jack W. "The Book of Esther." New Spirit Filled Life Bible (NKJV). Nashville, TN: Thomas Nelson Bibles, 2002. p. 639.

295    Clarke, Adam, Albert Barnes, Theodore Beza, John Wesley, John Trapp, Thomas Coke, John Gill, et al. "Esther with Book Summary Esther 6:12" Verse-by-Verse Bible Commentary. studylight. org. Accessed January 22, 2020. https://www. studylight. org/commentary/esther/6-12. html.

296    Tomasino, Anthony. "Esther." Zondervan Illustrated Bible Backgrounds Commentary. Edited by John H. Walton. Vol. 3. Grand Rapids (Mich.): Zondervan, 2009, p. 495.

297    Tomasino, Anthony. "Esther." Zondervan Illustrated Bible Backgrounds Commentary. Edited by John H. Walton. Vol. 3. Grand Rapids (Mich.): Zondervan,

Instead of comforting the distraught man, they predicted his doom and defeat. In Esther 6:13 in the Septuagint, Zeresh's quote reads, **"Since Mordecai, before whom your downfall has started, is of Jewish origin, you cannot stand against him—you will surely come to ruin, for the living God is with him!"** Most Bible scholars believe this was added later, because a pagan would not have made such a statement. She might have said "his god," but surely not "the living God. "[298]

When Haman's wife and friends realized Mordecai was a Jew, they knew he was doomed.[299] Some translations of the Bible (KJ21, ASV, AMPC, DARBY, ESV, and others) call these friends "wise men." John Gill suggests these men may have been soothsayers or magicians Haman employed to advise him on important matters.[300] Since they had previously advised the tyrant to harm Mordecai the Jew, they were not very wise. Many of Haman's problems were caused because he took their advice. Even though the king still trusted Haman and he had not lost his high position in the king's court, his downfall was imminent. An Amalekite could not possibly triumph over God and His people.[301]

After the day he had been through, Haman was in no mood for a party. Perhaps he feared more horror awaited him, however, snubbing the king and queen by staying home was not an option. The eunuchs came to escort him to Esther's feast, because it was common for honored guests to be ushered to banquets or other important gatherings.[302]

2009, p. 495.

298    Clarke, Adam, Albert Barnes, Theodore Beza, John Wesley, John Trapp, Thomas Coke, John Gill, et al. "Esther with Book Summary Esther 6:13" Verse-by-Verse Bible Commentary. studylight. org. Accessed January 22, 2020. https://www. studylight. org/commentary/esther/6-13. html.

299    Ryrie, Charles Caldwell. "The Book of Esther," Ryrie Study Bible: New International Version. Chicago: Moody Publishers, 1986, p. 670.

300    Clarke, Adam, Albert Barnes, Theodore Beza, John Wesley, John Trapp, Thomas Coke, John Gill, et al. "Esther with Book Summary Esther 6:13" Verse-by-Verse Bible Commentary. studylight. org. Accessed January 22, 2020. https://www. studylight. org/commentary/esther/6-13. html.

301    Buttrick, George Arthur. The Interpreters Bible (Vol 3) the Holy Scriptures in the King James and Revised Standard Versions with General Articles and Introduction, Exegesis, Exposition for Each Book of the Bible. Vol. 3. New York: Abingdon Press, 1954, p. 860.

302    Dybdahl, Jon L, ed. "Esther." Andrews Study Bible: Light. Depth. Truth. Berrien Springs, MI: Andrews University Press, 2010. pp. 620.

# ESTHER CHAPTER 7

THE BIBLE IS NOT THE ONLY RESOURCE CONTAINING evidence of Xerxes. Archaeologists have excavated the Susa palace and found governmental documents from Xerxes' reign. Herodotus, the historian, also provided a great deal of information about the king and life at the Persian court.[303]

## ESTHER 7:1-6

**1 So the king and Haman went to Queen Esther's banquet, 2 and as they were drinking wine on the second day, the king again asked, "Queen Esther, what is your petition? It will be given you. What is your request? Even up to half the kingdom, it will be granted."**

**3 Then Queen Esther answered, "If I have found favor with you, Your Majesty, and if it pleases you, grant me my life—this is my petition. And spare my people—this is my request. 4 For I and my people have been sold to be destroyed, killed and annihilated. If we had merely been sold as male and female slaves, I would have kept quiet, because no such distress would justify disturbing the king** [or I would have kept quiet, but the compensation our adversary offers cannot be compared with the loss the king would suffer]. **"**

---

303    Archaeological Study Bible: An Illustrated Walk-through Biblical History and Culture: New International Version. Grand Rapids, MI: Zondervan, 2005. "Esther," p. 726.

**5 King Xerxes asked Queen Esther, "Who is he? Where is he— the man who has dared to do such a thing?"**

**6 Esther said, "An adversary and enemy! This vile Haman!" Then Haman was terrified before the king and queen.**

Verse two refers to a time called the "banquet of wine" (KJ21, ASV, BRG, GNV, and others). This was the time after the feast when the guests relaxed, talked, and drank wine.[304] Haman was a witness, but not a participant of this conversation. It was between the king and queen only. Esther showed great deference to her husband, and he responded with sincere interest.[305] Once again, Xerxes offered Esther half his kingdom. (This was the third time the king made this proposal.)[306] Xerxes was intelligent enough to realize the queen's invitation to a feast was not the real topic of her petition. God unquestionably kept the matter of Esther's request in the front of his mind.

Queen Esther was in full control of the situation. She was not interested in wealth or land, nor did she ask for half the kingdom. She made a sincere request: to spare her life and the lives of her people. She used the same words Haman had used in his fiendish decree. Wisely, she tied her own safety to that of her Jewish people. Evidently the king had seen no connection between his wife and the previously unnamed people Haman wanted to destroy (Est. 3:8). Now he finally realized who they were and understood their fate could affect his queen.[307] This was probably the time Xerxes realized his beloved wife was Jewish.

Esther pointed out the king would lose a great deal of tax revenue if the Jews were slaughtered. Acknowledging Haman's bribe and how the genocide would affect the king's finances (verse 4) was a wise move.[308]

---

304    Hayford, Jack W. "The Book of Esther." New Spirit Filled Life Bible (NKJV). Nashville, TN: Thomas Nelson Bibles, 2002. p. 639.

305    Engelbrecht Edward A. "Esther." The Lutheran Study Bible: English Standard Version. Saint Louis: Concordia Publishing House, 2004. p. 769.

306    Clarke, Adam, Albert Barnes, Theodore Beza, John Wesley, John Trapp, Thomas Coke, John Gill, et al. "Esther with Book Summary Esther 7:2" Verse-by-Verse Bible Commentary. studylight. org. Accessed January 22, 2020. https://www. studylight. org/commentary/esther/7-2. html.

307    Dybdahl, Jon L, ed. "Esther." Andrews Study Bible: Light. Depth. Truth. Berrien Springs, MI: Andrews University Press, 2010. p. 620.

308    309 Ryrie, Charles Caldwell. "The Book of Esther," Ryrie Study Bible: New

From Esther's comment, **"For I and my people have been sold to be destroyed, killed and annihilated"** (Est. 7:4), we may assume Esther believed Xerxes had accepted Haman's bribe (Est. 3:9). In this context, "sell" does not mean to exchange a product for money. As in Judges 4:9, the word "sell" means to deliver up to one's enemies. The **"loss the king would suffer"** (Est. 3:4) referred to the loss of the ten thousand talents of Haman's bribe.[309] This huge payoff could not replace the tax money Xerxes would lose if many thousands of his innocent subjects were killed. The loss of taxes from the Jews was not a one-time event. The deficit would have been permanent. Every year his revenue would dwindle. The cost would far exceed the enormous bribe. [310]

In a very short time, Esther revealed the nature of her request, her true religion, and the fact that Haman was the foe who had dreamed up such a vile scheme. She too was under the same death sentence as her Jewish brothers and sisters.

Slavery was common in the days of Xerxes. Some historians believe as much as half the population was enslaved. The illiterate worked in farming or household duties, and the well-educated performed clerical tasks. Slaves were property and had few rights. They could be bought or sold, branded, or even forced to become eunuchs or concubines. Impoverished residents sometimes had to sell themselves or their families into slavery to avoid starvation or to pay a debt. Esther's comment in verses three and four pointed out to King Xerxes that if the Jews did not deserve to be sold as slaves, they certainly did not deserve to be murdered as Haman planned.[311]

---

International Version. Chicago: Moody Publishers, 1986, p. 670.

309    Buttrick, George Arthur. The Interpreters Bible (Vol 3) the Holy Scriptures in the King James and Revised Standard Versions with General Articles and Introduction, Exegesis, Exposition for Each Book of the Bible. Vol. 3. New York: Abingdon Press, 1954, p. 861.

310    Clarke, Adam, Albert Barnes, Theodore Beza, John Wesley, John Trapp, Thomas Coke, John Gill, et al. "Esther with Book Summary Esther 7:4" Verse-by-Verse Bible Commentary. studylight. org. Accessed January 22, 2020. https://www.studylight. org/commentary/esther/7-4. html.

311    Tomasino, Anthony. "Esther." Zondervan Illustrated Bible Backgrounds Commentary. Edited by John H. Walton. Vol. 3. Grand Rapids (Mich.): Zondervan, 2009, p. 495.

Xerxes seemed to be oblivious to what was happening in his empire. He did not appear to comprehend the magnitude of Haman's bloody death warrant against the Jews. Esther quoted the edict word-for-word using a variety of alarming words (destroyed, killed, annihilated) to get the king's attention and convince him her plight was urgent. Slowly he understood and became enraged. The king realized Esther's words were true and demanded to know the name of the wicked person who had conceived this ethnic cleansing.[312]

Without hesitation Esther bravely pointed the finger of guilt at the wicked Haman, but at the same time she was also pointing an accusatory finger at her husband. The edict against the Jewish people was still in force. Haman was the mastermind, but he had tricked Xerxes into going along with his proposal. The king apparently chose not to remember the part he had played in this murderous plan. He had heartlessly agreed to mass murder without asking who the intended victims were. Human beings may be deceived, but God never is. He knew exactly what Haman's true motives were. The LORD preordained Haman's downfall at just the right time. The wicked Amalekite risked his life, position, and everything he owned for his malevolent scheme, and he lost spectacularly.

## ESTHER 7:7-10

**7 The king got up in a rage, left his wine and went out into the palace garden. But Haman, realizing that the king had already decided his fate, stayed behind to beg Queen Esther for his life.**

**8 Just as the king returned from the palace garden to the banquet hall, Haman was falling on the couch where Esther was reclining.**

**The king exclaimed, "Will he even molest the queen while she is with me in the house?"**

**As soon as the word left the king's mouth, they covered Haman's face. 9 Then Harbona, one of the eunuchs attending the king, said, "A pole reaching to a height of fifty cubits** [about 75 feet or about 23 meters] **stands by Haman's house. He had it set up for Mordecai, who spoke up to help the king."**

---

312      Clines, David J. A. "Esther." The HarperCollins Bible Commentary. Edited by James Luther Mays. San Francisco, CA: Harper San Francisco, 2000, p. 357.

**The king said, "Impale him on it!" 10 So they impaled Haman on the pole he had set up for Mordecai. Then the king's fury subsided.**

Esther's words greatly distressed the king. The man who plotted to kill his queen was his friend, the prime minister. The king was used to having advisors, and suddenly he had no one to help guide him. The sight of Haman disgusted him. In frustration and rage he went out into the garden to think and regain his self-control. (This was the same garden where Xerxes had held a feast nine years previously when Vashti had disobeyed him.)[313]

Xerxes realized he was partly to blame for this murderous proclamation. When a Persian king left the room after delivering a death sentence, it meant there was no chance for clemency.[314] Even though he had not actually condemned Haman to death, his actions spoke clearly.

Oddly, the king left the malevolent Haman in the room with his wife. This was strictly against Persian protocol. Only the king could be alone with any of the ladies in his harem. When Xerxes went outside to the garden, Haman should have left also.[315]

Haman believed he was going to die, so he stayed behind to plead his case with Esther. She was reclining on a couch, as was the ancient custom. (Some translations, such as KJ21, BRG, DRA, and WYC say bed.) In his terror, the frantic man violated palace etiquette by approaching Esther

---

313    Clarke, Adam, Albert Barnes, Theodore Beza, John Wesley, John Trapp, Thomas Coke, John Gill, et al. "Esther with Book Summary Esther 7:7" Verse-by-Verse Bible Commentary. studylight. org. Accessed January 22, 2020. https://www. studylight. org/commentary/esther/7-7. html.
314    Clarke, Adam, Albert Barnes, Theodore Beza, John Wesley, John Trapp, Thomas Coke, John Gill, et al. "Esther with Book Summary Esther 7:7" Verse-by-Verse Bible Commentary. studylight. org. Accessed January 22, 2020. https://www. studylight. org/commentary/esther/7-7. html.
315    Archaeological Study Bible: An Illustrated Walk-through Biblical History and Culture: New International Version. Grand Rapids, MI: Zondervan, 2005. "Esther," p. 715.

too closely.[316] As he moved toward the queen, he threw himself onto the couch. (It is ironic, the man who wanted to murder the Jews of Persia because Mordecai the Jew refused to bow before him was now bowing before the Jewish Esther, his enemy's cousin, to beg for her mercy.)[317]

At that moment, Xerxes returned. Seeing Haman's position, he incorrectly assumed his prime minister was attempting to defile his wife. Attacking the queen was treason. Dishonoring the queen also dishonored the king.[318] Even though Esther obviously knew Haman had not attacked her, she said nothing in his defense.

The king's charge was inaccurate. The arrogant bully was guilty of plotting to murder Mordecai, Esther, and thousands of innocent Jews, but he was not guilty of defiling the queen. Perhaps Xerxes knew this, but charging him with violating his wife was a convenient way to get rid of the problem once and for all. Ironically, Haman was sentenced to death for a crime he did not commit. Covering the faces of prisoners who were condemned to death was routine in Persia,[319] as well as in Greece and Rome.[320]

316    Hayford, Jack W. "The Book of Esther." New Spirit Filled Life Bible (NKJV). Nashville, TN: Thomas Nelson Bibles, 2002. p. 639.
317    Ritchie, Paul. "Esther 5-7 'Seeming Coincidences, Perfect Timing and an Irresistible Force'." Esther 5-7 'Seeming coincidences, perfect timing and an irresistible force', January 7, 2009. http://paulritchieblog. blogspot. com/2009/01/esther-5-7-seeming-coincidences-perfect. html.
318    Brettler, Marc Zvi., Carol A. Newsom, and Pheme Perkins. The New Oxford Annotated Bible: with the Apocryphal/Deuterocanonical Books: New Revised Standard Version. Edited by Michael David. Coogan. NIVed. New York: Oxford University Press, 2001, p. 717.
319    Tomasino, Anthony. "Esther." Zondervan Illustrated Bible Backgrounds Commentary. Edited by John H. Walton. Vol. 3. Grand Rapids (Mich.): Zondervan, 2009, p. 496.
320    Buttrick, George Arthur. The Interpreters Bible (Vol 3) the Holy Scriptures in the King James and Revised Standard Versions with General Articles and Introduction, Exegesis, Exposition for Each Book of the Bible. Vol. 3. New York: Abingdon Press, 1954, p. 862.

Haman's malicious plan completely backfired. Xerxes sentenced his wicked prime minister to be impaled on the pole he had planned for Mordecai, the man who had saved the king's life.[321] There was no trial. Xerxes' word was law. The man who had shown no mercy was now given no mercy. The chamberlains led him away to be impaled.

**"Do not be deceived: God cannot be mocked. A man reaps what he sows"** (Gal. 6:7)

---

321    Clines, David J. A. "Esther." The HarperCollins Bible Commentary. Edited by James Luther Mays. San Francisco, CA: Harper San Francisco, 2000, p. 357.

# ESTHER CHAPTER 8

E VEN THOUGH HAMAN WAS DEAD, THE EDICT against the Jewish people was still in force. Since it was written in Xerxes' name and sealed with his signet ring (Est. 3:22), it was irrevocable. The king faced a major crisis.[322]

## ESTHER 8:1-2

**1 That same day King Xerxes gave Queen Esther the estate of Haman, the enemy of the Jews. And Mordecai came into the presence of the king, for Esther had told how he was related to her. 2 The king took off his signet ring, which he had reclaimed from Haman, and presented it to Mordecai. And Esther appointed him over Haman's estate.**

When any traitor betrayed the king, all the person's property, including his servants, animals, and money was forfeited. (The historians Josephus and Herodotus verified this information.)[323] Xerxes seized Haman's property and gave it to his queen. Esther revealed Mordecai was her cousin and the foster-father who had raised her after the deaths of her parents. As a reward for his loyalty and service to the king, Mordecai

---

322    Clines, David J. A. "Esther." The HarperCollins Bible Commentary. Edited by James Luther Mays. San Francisco, CA: Harper San Francisco, 2000, p. 357.
323    Archaeological Study Bible: An Illustrated Walk through Biblical History and Culture: New International Version. Grand Rapids, MI: Zondervan, 2005. "Esther," p. 727.

was given Haman's position as second in command below Xerxes.[324] Matthew Poole and Robert Jamieson believe he was also made one of the seven princes (or seven counselors).[325] Ten of Haman's sons were killed on Adar 13. The fate of Haman's wife and any remaining children is unknown.

Xerxes decided the edict was not really his problem. After all, he had been tricked by Haman. The king knew Mordecai was a brave man with great knowledge and understanding, so he solved the problem by handing his signet ring to Mordecai. (This was a sign of the king's friendship as well as Mordecai's authority.) Now the decree was Mordecai's responsibility. [326] The signet ring allowed him to sign royal edicts. This was the same power Haman had misused.[327]

## ESTHER 8:3-6

**3 Esther again pleaded with the king, falling at his feet and weeping. She begged him to put an end to the evil plan of Haman the Agagite, which he had devised against the Jews. 4 Then the king extended the gold scepter** (symbol of royal authority) **to Esther and she arose and stood before him.**

**5 "If it pleases the king," she said, "and if he regards me with favor and thinks it the right thing to do, and if he is pleased with me, let an order be written overruling the dispatches that Haman son of Hammedatha, the Agagite, devised and wrote to destroy the Jews in all the king's provinces. 6 For how can I bear to see disaster fall on my people? How can I bear to see the destruction of my family?"**

---

324    Tomasino, Anthony. "Esther." Zondervan Illustrated Bible Backgrounds Commentary. Edited by John H. Walton. Vol. 3. Grand Rapids (Mich.): Zondervan, 2009, p. 497.

325    Clarke, Adam, Albert Barnes, Theodore Beza, John Wesley, John Trapp, Thomas Coke, John Gill, et al. "Esther with Book Summary Esther 8:1" Verse-by-Verse Bible Commentary. studylight. org. Accessed January 22, 2020. https://www. studylight. org/commentary/esther/8-1. html.

326    Clines, David J. A. "Esther." The HarperCollins Bible Commentary. Edited by James Luther Mays. San Francisco, CA: Harper San Francisco, 2000, p. 357.

327    Engelbrecht Edward A. "Esther." The Lutheran Study Bible: English Standard Version. Saint Louis: Concordia Publishing House, 2004. p. 770.

Xerxes extended his royal scepter to Esther as a sign of royal favor, not to grant permission to approach the king (Est. 5:2).

Even though Haman had been executed, the king's order to slaughter the Jews was still legally binding. Esther fell prostrate at the king's feet, crying. This was the position of a humble supplicant. Wisely, she placed all the blame on Haman. She did not request riches or half the kingdom, as Xerxes had previously offered. She respectfully begged her husband to spare the life of the Jewish people, which of course, included Esther.[328] Haman's order would not just lead to persecution, oppression, and hardship. It would result in the total annihilation of the Persian Jews. The situation seemed hopeless. Xerxes could not override his own decree even if he wanted to.[329]

## ESTHER 8:7-11

**7 King Xerxes replied to Queen Esther and to Mordecai the Jew, "Because Haman attacked the Jews, I have given his estate to Esther, and they have impaled him on the pole he set up. 8 Now write another decree in the king's name in behalf of the Jews as seems best to you, and seal it with the king's signet ring—for no document written in the king's name and sealed with his ring can be revoked."**

**9 At once the royal secretaries were summoned—on the twenty-third day of the third month, the month of Sivan. They wrote out all Mordecai's orders to the Jews, and to the satraps, governors and nobles of the 127 provinces stretching from India to Cush [Upper Nile region]. These orders were written in the script of each province**

---

328     Clarke, Adam, Albert Barnes, Theodore Beza, John Wesley, John Trapp, Thomas Coke, John Gill, et al. "Esther with Book Summary Esther 8:5" Verse-by-Verse Bible Commentary. studylight. org. Accessed January 22, 2020. https://www. studylight. org/commentary/esther/8-5. html.

329     Stamps, Donald C., and J. Wesley. Adams. "The Book of Esther." The Full Life Study Bible: New International Version (NIV). Grand Rapids, MI: Zondervan Pub. House, 1992. p. 700.

and the language of each people and also to the Jews in their own script and language. 10 Mordecai wrote in the name of King Xerxes, sealed the dispatches with the king's signet ring, and sent them by mounted couriers, who rode fast horses especially bred for the king.

11 The king's edict granted the Jews in every city the right to assemble and protect themselves; to destroy, kill and annihilate the armed men of any nationality or province who might attack them and their women and children, [Or province, together with the women and children, who might attack them] and to plunder the property of their enemies.

Seventy days had elapsed since Haman cast lots to determine the date to carry out his slaughter. For over two months the Jews had feared total destruction. (It was now Sivan 23, which was late May or early June in the Gregorian calendar.) Using Xerxes' signet ring, Haman had issued an irrevocable decree to kill all the Jews. Since Haman's order could not be rescinded, it was necessary for Mordecai to issue a second edict that gave the Jews the right to assemble (or build up an army). Such a decree would essentially neutralize Haman's declaration.[330]

Notice, the author made a point to emphasize Mordecai's religion, calling him Mordecai the Jew. Prior to this order, the Jews would surely have fought back, but now they could gather together to form a militia to defend themselves against the enemies who wanted to destroy them. Without this order, building up their defenses would have been classified as rebellion.

Mordecai gathered the royal secretaries (scribes) to dictate a new document. He devised an ingenious solution to the problem created by Haman's edict. Mordecai's decree did not reverse the first decree, but it essentially invalidated it by permitting the Jews to defend themselves against anyone trying to carry out Haman's orders.[331] The new decree

---

330    Clarke, Adam, Albert Barnes, Theodore Beza, John Wesley, John Trapp, Thomas Coke, John Gill, et al. "Esther with Book Summary Esther 8:8" Verse-by-Verse Bible Commentary. studylight. org. Accessed January 22, 2020. https://www. studylight. org/commentary/esther/8-8. html.
331    Tomasino, Anthony. "Esther." Zondervan Illustrated Bible Backgrounds Commentary. Edited by John H. Walton. Vol. 3. Grand Rapids (Mich.): Zondervan,

was translated into the languages spoken by all the people of the kingdom so it could be read and understood. The decree was carried to all parts of the kingdom by men on horseback.[332] Nobody could claim ignorance. The Jews had nearly nine months to prepare.

## ESTHER 8:12-17

**12 The day appointed for the Jews to do this in all the provinces of King Xerxes was the thirteenth day of the twelfth month, the month of Adar. 13 A copy of the text of the edict was to be issued as law in every province and made known to the people of every nationality so that the Jews would be ready on that day to avenge themselves on their enemies.**

**14 The couriers, riding the royal horses, went out, spurred on by the king's command, and the edict was issued in the citadel of Susa.**

**15 When Mordecai left the king's presence, he was wearing royal garments of blue and white, a large crown of gold, and a purple robe of fine linen. And the city of Susa held a joyous celebration. 16 For the Jews it was a time of happiness and joy, gladness and honor. 17 In every province and in every city to which the edict of the king came, there was joy and gladness among the Jews, with feasting and celebrating. And many people of other nationalities became Jews because fear of the Jews had seized them.**

When Mordecai left the king, he wore the garment Xerxes had given him. Instead of wearing sackcloth and ashes, he now wore a blue and white royal robe. Grieving and fasting were replaced by joy and celebration.

It must have been a great comfort to the Jews of Persia to realize their queen was also a Jew. Many Gentiles felt this gave the Jews the upper hand, and as a result, many renounced idolatry and converted to Judaism. John Gill, Joseph Benson, and others believe only a limited number were circumcised.[333] There is no evidence anyone had tried to

2009, p. 498.
332     Dybdahl, Jon L, ed. "Esther." Andrews Study Bible: Light. Depth. Truth. Berrien Springs, MI: Andrews University Press, 2010. p. 621.
333     Clarke, Adam, Albert Barnes, Theodore Beza, John Wesley, John Trapp,

proselytize the pagans. Judaism, unlike Christianity, is not a missionary religion[334] (one which tries to evangelize, convert followers, or share their faith). There are no biblical records of any other people becoming Jews. Some scholars have speculated the Gentiles converted because they feared being killed by the Jews. This theory does not seem reasonable, since the only people in danger of death were those that attacked the Jews.[335] It is more likely they realized they would fight back if attacked. God was on the side of the Jews, so the wise choice was to join them. Standing against the people protected by God would be disastrous.[336]

Xerxes did not want the killing to go on endlessly, so he set a time limit of one day, the thirteenth of Adar, the same day Haman had set to massacre the Jews. They were not allowed to attack first, but they were permitted to defend themselves. They dispensed God's justice by taking vengeance on their enemies.[337] Mordecai's decree allowed the slaughter of wives and children of those who attacked them, because they had been included in Haman's order against the Jews. John Wesley, John Gill, Matthew Poole, and others state there is no evidence this carnage took place.[338]

---

Thomas Coke, John Gill, et al. "Esther with Book Summary Esther 8:17" Verse-by-Verse Bible Commentary. studylight. org. Accessed January 22, 2020. https://www. studylight. org/commentary/esther/8-17. html.

334     Buttrick, George Arthur. The Interpreters Bible (Vol 3) the Holy Scriptures in the King James and Revised Standard Versions with General Articles and Introduction, Exegesis, Exposition for Each Book of the Bible. Vol. 3. New York: Abingdon Press, 1954, p. 862

335     Tomasino, Anthony. "Esther." Zondervan Illustrated Bible Backgrounds Commentary. Edited by John H. Walton. Vol. 3. Grand Rapids (Mich.): Zondervan, 2009, p. 499.

336     Ritchie, Paul. "Esther 5-7 'Seeming Coincidences, Perfect Timing and an Irresistible Force'." Esther 5-7 'Seeming coincidences, perfect timing and an irresistible force', January 7, 2009. http://paulritchieblog. blogspot. com/2009/01/esther-5-7-seeming-coincidences-perfect. html.

337     Engelbrecht Edward A. "Esther." The Lutheran Study Bible: English Standard Version. Saint Louis: Concordia Publishing House, 2004. p. 771.

338     Clarke, Adam, Albert Barnes, Theodore Beza, John Wesley, John Trapp, Thomas Coke, John Gill, et al. "Esther with Book Summary Esther 8:11" Verse-by-Verse Bible Commentary. studylight. org. Accessed January 22, 2020. https://www. studylight. org/commentary/esther/8-11. html.

When Mordecai **"left the king's presence he was wearing royal garments of blue and white, a large crown of gold, and a purple robe of fine linen"** (Est. 8:15). The garment was an inner robe or tunic of blue and white striped linen; the crown was probably a large turban decorated with gold and jewels, and the royal robe was dyed purple with the blood of murex sea snails. It took 10,000 snails to produce one gram of dye, so all purple clothing was very expensive. (One pound of dye was worth three pounds of gold.)[339] Mordecai's destination when he left the king's presence is unknown.

Both Persians and Jews rejoiced when they saw Mordecai. He was a just and kind man who was much loved. To the Jews, he was a wonderful leader, and the pagans respected him as well. Mordecai was humbled by their love and adulation. Rather than take pleasure in personal recognition, he rejoiced in his people's deliverance. The once persecuted and condemned Jews were now honored and had a bright future. Everyone was thankful the wicked, unpopular Haman was dead. **"When the righteous thrive, the people rejoice; when the wicked rule, the people groan"** (Pr. 29:2).

---

339    Cartwright, Mark. "Tyrian Purple." Ancient History Encyclopedia. Ancient History Encyclopedia, April 28, 2020. https://www.ancient.eu/Tyrian_Purple/.

# ESTHER CHAPTER 9

## ESTHER 9:1-4

**1 On the thirteenth day of the twelfth month, the month of Adar, the edict commanded by the king was to be carried out. On this day the enemies of the Jews had hoped to overpower them, but now the tables were turned and the Jews got the upper hand over those who hated them. 2 The Jews assembled in their cities in all the provinces of King Xerxes to attack those determined to destroy them. No one could stand against them, because the people of all the other nationalities were afraid of them. 3 And all the nobles of the provinces, the satraps, the governors and the king's administrators helped the Jews, because fear of Mordecai had seized them. 4 Mordecai was prominent in the palace; his reputation spread throughout the provinces, and he became more and more powerful.**

There were now two contradicting decrees in force: the one issued by Haman, and the one issued by Mordecai. After the execution of Haman, Xerxes made Mordecai second in command beneath the king. The nobles and Persian officials chose to help the Jews, primarily because they were afraid of Mordecai. Since their new prime minister was a Jew, it would have been foolish to side with their enemies.[340]

---

340    Clarke, Adam, Albert Barnes, Theodore Beza, John Wesley, John Trapp, Thomas Coke, John Gill, et al. "Esther with Book Summary Esther 9:3" Verse-by-Verse Bible Commentary. studylight. org. Accessed January 22, 2020. https://www. studylight. org/commentary/esther/9-3. html.

Mordecai was one of Xerxes' counsellors as well as his prime minister. The king trusted the man who had saved his life and managed his affairs, and as a result, Mordecai became wealthier, more famous, and more powerful.

## ESTHER 9:5-11

**5 The Jews struck down all their enemies with the sword, killing and destroying them, and they did what they pleased to those who hated them. 6 In the citadel of Susa, the Jews killed and destroyed five hundred men. 7 They also killed Parshandatha, Dalphon, Aspatha, 8 Poratha, Adalia, Aridatha, 9 Parmashta, Arisai, Aridai and Vaizatha, 10 the ten sons of Haman son of Hammedatha, the enemy of the Jews. But they did not lay their hands on the plunder.**

**11 The number of those killed in the citadel of Susa was reported to the king that same day.**

This was the day Haman had planned to destroy the Jews, and it was now time for his evil edict to be enacted. The date was late February or early March, 473 BC in our calendar. Haman's decree and Mordecai's decree were to be carried out on the same day, the thirteenth of Adar. The pagans had the legal right to kill the Jews, and the Jews had the legal right to kill the pagans.[341]

The Jews' enemies hoped to defeat them with numbers and brute force. However, the Jews had a decree of their own allowing them to defend themselves.[342] The Jews did not try to eliminate everyone they did not like. They only fought the enemies that tried to harm them. With God's help, they were victorious in every battle. Every person who attacked them was defeated. To avoid the possibility of future revenge for the execution of their father, the Jewish warriors killed the ten sons

---

341     Engelbrecht Edward A. "Esther." The Lutheran Study Bible: English Standard Version. Saint Louis: Concordia Publishing House, 2004. p. 772.

342     Clarke, Adam, Albert Barnes, Theodore Beza, John Wesley, John Trapp, Thomas Coke, John Gill, et al. "Esther with Book Summary Esther 9:1" Verse-by-Verse Bible Commentary. studylight. org. Accessed January 22, 2020. https://www. studylight. org/commentary/esther/9-1. html.

of Haman.[343] Since they were blood enemies of the Jews, and they shared Haman's guilt, they were executed.[344] Their enemies were filled with terror as they realized Yahweh was protecting His people.[345] They realized it would be advantageous to be on the side of the winners.[346]

The Jews defended themselves on the thirteenth day of Adar.[347] They killed thousands of their enemies, but only those who attacked them. [348] This was the Lord's work. Not one Jewish fatality was recorded.[349] Xerxes' decree allowed the Jewish people to **"plunder the property of their enemies"** (Est. 8:11) however, the author was quite diligent in pointing out they never touched any of the spoils of battle (Est. 9:10, 9:15-16). There were probably two reasons for this self-control. First, the Jews did not want their enemies to believe their attacks were motivated by greed. They eliminated their enemies for self-preservation, not to gain their property. Second, this was a conflict between the Jews and the descendants of Amalek. Previously God had commanded His people to destroy the Amalekites' property, not take it with them. **"Now go, attack the Amalekites and totally destroy all that belongs to them. Do not spare them; put to death men and women, children and infants, cattle and sheep, camels and donkeys"** (1 Sa. 15:3). Even though that

---

343     Dybdahl, Jon L, ed. "Esther." Andrews Study Bible: Light. Depth. Truth. Berrien Springs, MI: Andrews University Press, 2010. p. 622.

344     Buttrick, George Arthur. The Interpreters Bible (Vol 3) the Holy Scriptures in the King James and Revised Standard Versions with General Articles and Introduction, Exegesis, Exposition for Each Book of the Bible. Vol. 3. New York: Abingdon Press, 1954, p. 868.

345     Clarke, Adam, Albert Barnes, Theodore Beza, John Wesley, John Trapp, Thomas Coke, John Gill, et al. "Esther with Book Summary Esther 9:2" Verse-by-Verse Bible Commentary. studylight. org. Accessed January 22, 2020. https://www. studylight. org/commentary/esther/9-2. html.

346     Engelbrecht Edward A. "Esther." The Lutheran Study Bible: English Standard Version. Saint Louis: Concordia Publishing House, 2004. p. 772.

347     Stamps, Donald C., and J. Wesley. Adams. "The Book of Esther." The Full Life Study Bible: New International Version (NIV). Grand Rapids, MI: Zondervan Pub. House, 1992. p. 701.

348     Clarke, Adam, Albert Barnes, Theodore Beza, John Wesley, John Trapp, Thomas Coke, John Gill, et al. "Esther with Book Summary Esther 9:5" Verse-by-Verse Bible Commentary. studylight. org. Accessed January 22, 2020. https://www. studylight. org/commentary/esther/9-5. html.

349     Clines, David J. A. "Esther." The HarperCollins Bible Commentary. Edited by James Luther Mays. San Francisco, CA: Harper San Francisco, 2000, p. 357.

command referred to a previous conflict, the Jews took no plunder from the Amalekites in this battle either.[350] They believed this bloodshed was God's judgment. They had merely carried out His vengeance. Some scholars believe the spoils went into the king's treasury.[351]

Even though verse 6 refers to the "citadel of Susa" (Shushan in some translations), the author probably meant the upper city, which covered more than one hundred acres, rather than the citadel itself. It is unlikely there were five hundred enemies living in the king's palace.[352]

The sons of Haman were named for Persian *daiva* (minor spirits or deities worshipped during Xerxes' reign). After Xerxes died, the *daiva* were regarded as demons, so their names would not have been given to children. This is one detail scholars use to verify Haman lived during the time of Xerxes. Such information is important when trying to validate the authenticity of a particular account.[353]

## ESTHER 9:12-15

**12 The king said to Queen Esther, "The Jews have killed and destroyed five hundred men and the ten sons of Haman in the citadel of Susa. What have they done in the rest of the king's provinces? Now what is your petition? It will be given you. What is your request? It will also be granted."**

350    Tomasino, Anthony. "Esther." Zondervan Illustrated Bible Backgrounds Commentary. Edited by John H. Walton. Vol. 3. Grand Rapids (Mich.): Zondervan, 2009, p. 500.
351    Clarke, Adam, Albert Barnes, Theodore Beza, John Wesley, John Trapp, Thomas Coke, John Gill, et al. "Esther with Book Summary Esther 9:9" Verse-by-Verse Bible Commentary. studylight. org. Accessed January 22, 2020. https://www. studylight. org/commentary/esther/9-9. html.
352    Clarke, Adam, Albert Barnes, Theodore Beza, John Wesley, John Trapp, Thomas Coke, John Gill, et al. "Esther with Book Summary Esther 9:6" Verse-by-Verse Bible Commentary. studylight. org. Accessed January 22, 2020. https://www. studylight. org/commentary/esther/9-6. html.
353    Tomasino, Anthony. "Esther." Zondervan Illustrated Bible Backgrounds Commentary. Edited by John H. Walton. Vol. 3. Grand Rapids (Mich.): Zondervan, 2009, p. 499.

**13 "If it pleases the king," Esther answered, "give the Jews in Susa permission to carry out this day's edict tomorrow also, and let Haman's ten sons be impaled on poles."**

**14 So the king commanded that this be done. An edict was issued in Susa, and they impaled the ten sons of Haman. 15 The Jews in Susa came together on the fourteenth day of the month of Adar, and they put to death in Susa three hundred men, but they did not lay their hands on the plunder.**

Since five hundred had been killed in Susa, it was reasonable to assume many more had died in other parts of the empire. Xerxes must have been shocked by the carnage, yet he made no effort to stop it. The king had granted Esther's first request. Amazingly, Xerxes seemed more interested in his wife's requests than in the deaths of many thousands of his subjects. He asked her if she had any more petitions. He was willing to do whatever she asked.[354] She requested his decree be continued another day so that any remaining foes could be eliminated. (The extended edict for Adar 14 applied only in Susa, not the rest of the empire.) It is possible she thought many of their enemies were in hiding, planning another attack the next day.

Esther also asked for Haman's ten sons to be impaled on poles. (It was not unusual for the Persians to display their enemies' corpses in this way.) This gruesome display was not just revenge upon her enemies. It was intended to terrify and discourage anyone else seeking to harm the Jews.[355]

Xerxes did as Esther requested. Even though Haman's ten sons were already dead (Est. 9:10), he had their corpses impaled on poles in clear view of his subjects. Xerxes never actually issued a death warrant for Haman. He spoke and it was done (Est. 7:9). However, he did issue an

---

354    Clarke, Adam, Albert Barnes, Theodore Beza, John Wesley, John Trapp, Thomas Coke, John Gill, et al. "Esther with Book Summary Esther 9:12" Verse-by-Verse Bible Commentary. studylight. org. Accessed January 22, 2020. https://www. studylight. org/commentary/esther/9-12. html.
355    Clarke, Adam, Albert Barnes, Theodore Beza, John Wesley, John Trapp, Thomas Coke, John Gill, et al. "Esther with Book Summary Esther 9:13" Verse-by-Verse Bible Commentary. studylight. org. Accessed January 22, 2020. https://www. studylight. org/commentary/esther/9-13. html.

order in writing for the sons' bodies to be impaled (Est. 9:14).[356] This act brought further disgrace upon the name of their notorious father. The Jews believed anyone impaled on a pike was cursed by God (Dt. 21:22-23).[357] Some historians believe Mordecai had warned Esther there were more enemies of the Jews still hiding in Susa. During battle, three hundred more enemies were killed, for a total of eight hundred.

None of the spoils were touched.[358]

## ESTHER 9:16-22

**16 Meanwhile, the remainder of the Jews who were in the king's provinces also assembled to protect themselves and get relief from their enemies. They killed seventy-five thousand of them but did not lay their hands on the plunder. 17 This happened on the thirteenth day of the month of Adar, and on the fourteenth they rested and made it a day of feasting and joy.**

**18 The Jews in Susa, however, had assembled on the thirteenth and fourteenth, and then on the fifteenth they rested and made it a day of feasting and joy.**

**19 That is why rural Jews—those living in villages—observe the fourteenth of the month of Adar as a day of joy and feasting, a day for giving presents to each other.**

**20 Mordecai recorded these events, and he sent letters to all the Jews throughout the provinces of King Xerxes, near and far, 21 to have them celebrate annually the fourteenth and fifteenth days of the month of Adar 22 as the time when the Jews got relief from their**

---

356    Buttrick, George Arthur. The Interpreters Bible (Vol 3) the Holy Scriptures in the King James and Revised Standard Versions with General Articles and Introduction, Exegesis, Exposition for Each Book of the Bible. Vol. 3. New York: Abingdon Press, 1954, p. 871.

357    Tomasino, Anthony. "Esther." Zondervan Illustrated Bible Backgrounds Commentary. Edited by John H. Walton. Vol. 3. Grand Rapids (Mich.): Zondervan, 2009, p. 500.

358    Clarke, Adam, Albert Barnes, Theodore Beza, John Wesley, John Trapp, Thomas Coke, John Gill, et al. "Esther with Book Summary Esther 9:15" Verse-by-Verse Bible Commentary. studylight. org. Accessed January 22, 2020. https://www. studylight. org/commentary/esther/9-15. html.

**enemies, and as the month when their sorrow was turned into joy and their mourning into a day of celebration. He wrote them to observe the days as days of feasting and joy and giving presents of food to one another and gifts to the poor.**

Xerxes was told 500 were killed in the capital (verse 6) and 75,000 were slaughtered in the countryside (verse 16). He took the information in stride and did not appear to be horrified or even concerned.

The Jews in the countryside defended themselves against enemies who wished them harm. The combined death toll in all the provinces was seventy-five thousand. (The Septuagint states the number killed was fifteen thousand.)[359] Once again, the Jews took none of their enemies' property.[360] Taking the plunder of battle was expected. The fact the Jews did not was observed and retold by friends and foes alike.

This was not blood lust or revenge. King Saul, ancestor of Esther, ignored God's command and failed to wipe out the Amalekites (1 Sa. 15:1-9). Because of his disobedience, the Jews were once again forced to face these enemies. This was a holy war in which the Jews executed God's divine judgment on their adversaries. After defeating their foes, they rested and celebrated on the fourteenth day of Adar.[361]

God used Mordecai and Esther as His hands and feet on earth to save His people from Haman's murderous plot. Notice, Mordecai did not instruct the Jews to celebrate their bloody triumph over their enemies. Rather, they were to honor the celebration held after the victory.[362] When Haman was in power as prime minister, Xerxes' kingdom was filled with despair and chaos. After the Jews' victory, people lived in peace.

359    Buttrick, George Arthur. The Interpreters Bible (Vol 3) the Holy Scriptures in the King James and Revised Standard Versions with General Articles and Introduction, Exegesis, Exposition for Each Book of the Bible. Vol. 3. New York: Abingdon Press, 1954, p. 869.
360    Clarke, Adam, Albert Barnes, Theodore Beza, John Wesley, John Trapp, Thomas Coke, John Gill, et al. "Esther with Book Summary Esther 9:16" Verse-by-Verse Bible Commentary. studylight. org. Accessed January 22, 2020. https://www. studylight. org/commentary/esther/9-16. html.
361    Engelbrecht Edward A. "Esther." The Lutheran Study Bible: English Standard Version. Saint Louis: Concordia Publishing House, 2004. p. 772.
362    Clines, David J. A. "Esther." The HarperCollins Bible Commentary. Edited by James Luther Mays. San Francisco, CA: Harper San Francisco, 2000, p. 357.

At the time the book of Esther was written, rural Jews celebrated on the fourteenth day of Adar, while those living in Susa celebrated on the fifteenth. Scholars believe this was due to the fact the battle ended on the fourteenth in the countryside, while fighting raged in the city until the fifteenth.

Festivals ordered by the Law of Moses involved sacrifices. Purim was a celebration without sacrifices. Since no sacrifices, prayers, or other religious activities were recorded, the early observances of Purim were apparently secular.[363] In verse 19, the NIV described people living in "villages." Some translations (KJV, ASV, AMP, CJB, NOG, and others) use the term "unwalled towns."

It was the custom in Persia for people to celebrate with their friends by feasting and drinking. They often sent gifts and food to the poor and those who were unable to join in the festivities. (Mordecai's letter commanded giving to the destitute.)[364] Modern Jews often take up offerings to share with the impoverished so they may buy the items needed for their own feasts. This money may not be used for any other purpose.[365]

Verse 20 states **"Mordecai recorded these events."** He wanted the Jewish people to remember God's faithfulness long after the present generation was gone. Some scholars believe this points to Mordecai as the author of the book of Esther. There is no evidence to either prove or disprove this theory. He also sent letters to all the Jews in the empire instructing them to celebrate this great deliverance every year.

363    Tomasino, Anthony. "Esther." Zondervan Illustrated Bible Backgrounds Commentary. Edited by John H. Walton. Vol. 3. Grand Rapids (Mich.): Zondervan, 2009, p. 500.
364    Buttrick, George Arthur. The Interpreters Bible (Vol 3) the Holy Scriptures in the King James and Revised Standard Versions with General Articles and Introduction, Exegesis, Exposition for Each Book of the Bible. Vol. 3. New York: Abingdon Press, 1954, p. 870.
365    Clarke, Adam, Albert Barnes, Theodore Beza, John Wesley, John Trapp, Thomas Coke, John Gill, et al. "Esther with Book Summary Esther 9:19" Verse-by-Verse Bible Commentary. studylight. org. Accessed January 22, 2020. https://www. studylight. org/commentary/esther/9-19. html.

To avoid any arguments over which date to observe, Mordecai specified the celebration should take place for two days, on the fourteenth and fifteenth of Adar.[366] (The fourteenth of Adar is sometimes referred to as "the day of Mordecai.")[367]

## ESTHER 9:23-28

**23 So the Jews agreed to continue the celebration they had begun, doing what Mordecai had written to them. 24 For Haman son of Hammedatha, the Agagite, the enemy of all the Jews, had plotted against the Jews to destroy them and had cast the pur (that is, the lot) for their ruin and destruction. 25 But when the plot came to the king's attention,** [or when Esther came before the king] **he issued written orders that the evil scheme Haman had devised against the Jews should come back onto his own head, and that he and his sons should be impaled on poles. 26 (Therefore these days were called Purim, from the word pur.) Because of everything written in this letter and because of what they had seen and what had happened to them, 27 the Jews took it on themselves to establish the custom that they and their descendants and all who join them should without fail observe these two days every year, in the way prescribed and at the time appointed. 28 These days should be remembered and observed in every generation by every family, and in every province and in every city. And these days of Purim should never fail to be celebrated by the Jews—nor should the memory of these days die out among their descendants.**

Verses 24 and 25 concisely retell the story of Haman's plot to destroy the Jews. He had cast lots (the *pur*), a type of divination (discerning the future using occult or supernatural means) to determine the best time

---

366    Clines, David J. A. "Esther." The HarperCollins Bible Commentary. Edited by James Luther Mays. San Francisco, CA: Harper San Francisco, 2000, p. 357.
367    Clarke, Adam, Albert Barnes, Theodore Beza, John Wesley, John Trapp, Thomas Coke, John Gill, et al. "Esther with Book Summary Esther 9:20" Verse-by-Verse Bible Commentary. studylight. org. Accessed January 22, 2020. https://www. studylight. org/commentary/esther/9-20. html.

to slaughter the Jews. God's people were not the victims of bad luck or accident. Esther came before Xerxes to plead for her life and the lives of her people. Haman's plan failed, and he, his ten sons, and his followers were killed.[368]

The Jews, proselytes (converts to Judaism), and their descendants have continued to celebrate this annual feast from ancient times to the present day with no interruptions, just as Mordecai commanded. The fact that Purim has been observed every year since the time of Esther confirms the truth of this account.[369]

The name Purim comes from the word *"pur,"* the lot Haman cast to determine the proper day to slaughter the Jews. (The plural of *"pur"* is *"purim"*)[370] Jews today follow the instructions, written in the letter by Mordecai (Est. 9:20). They observe the annual feast of Purim, just as they have for centuries, with gift giving, charity, and feasting. As part of the ceremony, the book of Esther is read, both morning and evening, from a sacred scroll.[371]

## ESTHER 9:29-32

**29 So Queen Esther, daughter of Abihail, along with Mordecai the Jew, wrote with full authority to confirm this second letter concerning Purim. 30 And Mordecai sent letters to all the Jews in the 127 provinces of Xerxes' kingdom—words of goodwill and assurance— 31 to establish these days of Purim at their designated**

368    Clarke, Adam, Albert Barnes, Theodore Beza, John Wesley, John Trapp, Thomas Coke, John Gill, et al. "Esther with Book Summary Esther 9:24" Verse-by-Verse Bible Commentary. studylight. org. Accessed January 22, 2020. https://www. studylight. org/commentary/esther/9-24. html.
369    Clarke, Adam, Albert Barnes, Theodore Beza, John Wesley, John Trapp, Thomas Coke, John Gill, et al. "Esther with Book Summary Esther 9:23" Verse-by-Verse Bible Commentary. studylight. org. Accessed January 22, 2020. https://www. studylight. org/commentary/esther/9-23. html.
370    Brettler, Marc Zvi., Carol A. Newsom, and Pheme Perkins. The New Oxford Annotated Bible: with the Apocryphal/Deuterocanonical Books: New Revised Standard Version. Edited by Michael David. Coogan. NIVed. New York: Oxford University Press, 2001, p. 719.
371    Clines, David J. A. "Esther." The HarperCollins Bible Commentary. Edited by James Luther Mays. San Francisco, CA: Harper San Francisco, 2000, p. 357.

**times, as Mordecai the Jew and Queen Esther had decreed for them, and as they had established for themselves and their descendants in regard to their times of fasting and lamentation. 32 Esther's decree confirmed these regulations about Purim, and it was written down in the records.**

Mordecai's first letter (Est. 9:20) was a recommendation. The Jews agreed to continue the observance of Purim (Est. 9:23). Had the letter been a decree, the people would not have had a choice in the matter. This second letter, penned by both Queen Esther and Mordecai, was a command that carried the binding force of law. The power of Queen Esther's authority was added to Mordecai's in establishing the new feast.[372] (Xerxes did not sign the letter because he was not a Jew, nor was Judaism the religion of the Persian Empire. No high priest or other religious official signed the document either.) Observance of Purim was now mandatory.[373] Copies of this letter were sent to every Jew in all 127 provinces of Xerxes' kingdom.[374] God had rescued His persecuted people. In verse 31, Mordecai and Esther also called for "fasting and lamentations" (earnest prayer). What appeared to be a secular observance now took on religious significance as well. Modern Jews observe the thirteenth of Adar as a day of fasting and supplication (petition humbly and sincerely before God) before the feast on Adar 14. Purim is now observed a month before Passover.[375] Adar 13 is sometimes called "Esther's fast."[376] Today,

372    Engelbrecht Edward A. "Esther." The Lutheran Study Bible: English Standard Version. Saint Louis: Concordia Publishing House, 2004. p. 773.

373    Clarke, Adam, Albert Barnes, Theodore Beza, John Wesley, John Trapp, Thomas Coke, John Gill, et al. "Esther with Book Summary Esther 9:29" Verse-by-Verse Bible Commentary. studylight. org. Accessed January 22, 2020.

374    Clarke, Adam, Albert Barnes, Theodore Beza, John Wesley, John Trapp, Thomas Coke, John Gill, et al. "Esther with Book Summary Esther 9:30" Verse-by-Verse Bible Commentary. studylight. org. Accessed January 22, 2020. https://www. studylight. org/commentary/esther/9-30. html.

375    Hayford, Jack W. "The Book of Esther." New Spirit Filled Life Bible (NKJV). Nashville, TN: Thomas Nelson Bibles, 2002. P. 641.

376    Clarke, Adam, Albert Barnes, Theodore Beza, John Wesley, John Trapp, Thomas Coke, John Gill, et al. "Esther with Book Summary Esther 9:31" Verse-by-Verse Bible Commentary. studylight. org. Accessed January 22, 2020. https://www. studylight. org/commentary/esther/9-31. html.

Jews celebrate Purim on the fifteenth of Adar in Jerusalem, and on the fourteenth everywhere else.[377] Purim was the first Jewish festival that was not decreed by the Law of Moses,[378] and the only Jewish ceremony in biblical history to be introduced by a woman (Esther).[379]

The Jews received the decree and promised to obey it. Esther's decree was recorded in the records (possibly The Book of the Chronicles of the Kings of Media and Persia, the Book of Esther, or a record book kept by the Jews).[380]

God used Esther and Mordecai to deliver His people from their enemies who tried to kill them. Even though they were both Jews, they became important officials in the Persian kingdom. This was a blessing to all the citizens and led to cooperation between the Jews and Gentiles.[381] Esther and Mordecai were delivered from death sentences to places of honor and power, and the homicidal Haman received the execution he had planned for Mordecai. **The righteous person is rescued from trouble, and it falls on the wicked instead** (Pr. 11:8).

377     Archaeological Study Bible: An Illustrated Walk through Biblical History and Culture: New International Version. Grand Rapids, MI: Zondervan, 2005. "Esther," p. 731.

378     Tomasino, Anthony. "Esther." Zondervan Illustrated Bible Backgrounds Commentary. Edited by John H. Walton. Vol. 3. Grand Rapids (Mich.): Zondervan, 2009, p. 500.

379     Brettler, Marc Zvi., Carol A. Newsom, and Pheme Perkins. The New Oxford Annotated Bible: with the Apocryphal/Deuterocanonical Books: New Revised Standard Version. Edited by Michael David. Coogan. NIV ed. New York: Oxford University Press, 2001, p. 709.

380     Clarke, Adam, Albert Barnes, Theodore Beza, John Wesley, John Trapp, Thomas Coke, John Gill, et al. "Esther with Book Summary Esther 9:32" Verse-by-Verse Bible Commentary. studylight. org. Accessed January 22, 2020. https://www. studylight. org/commentary/esther/9-32. html.

381     Clines, David J. A. "Esther." The HarperCollins Bible Commentary. Edited by James Luther Mays. San Francisco, CA: Harper San Francisco, 2000, p. 357.

# ESTHER CHAPTER 10

THERE ARE TEN BOOKS, COVERING APPROXIMATELY one thousand years, in the section known as the historical books of the Old Testament: Joshua, Judges, Ruth, First and Second Kings, First and Second Chronicles, Ezra, Nehemiah, and Esther. The Book of Esther is the tenth and last of these historical books. They describe God's involvement with the people of Israel.[382]

## ESTHER 10:1-3

**1 King Xerxes imposed tribute throughout the empire, to its distant shores. 2 And all his acts of power and might, together with a full account of the greatness of Mordecai, whom the king had promoted, are they not written in the book of the annals of the kings of Media and Persia? 3 Mordecai the Jew was second in rank to King Xerxes, preeminent among the Jews, and held in high esteem by his many fellow Jews, because he worked for the good of his people and spoke up for the welfare of all the Jews.**

Chapter ten is not part of a continuous story as are the first nine chapters. It might be called an addendum to the chronicle of Xerxes' Persia, covering the topics of taxation and the power and greatness of Mordecai.

---

382    "Historical Books of the Bible." TEL Library. Accessed April 29, 2020. https://tellibrary. org/lessons/historical-books/.

Haman's wicked plan was thwarted, and the Jews of Persia were spared. However, this is not a nice story that ends happily ever after. The self-centered, unpredictable Xerxes was still in power.

The Greeks united and posed a persistent threat to Persia. Wars with Greece were very expensive, so Xerxes levied new tribute (taxes) to add to his treasury. His popularity with his subjects declined as he increased their taxes on both land and the islands of the Aegean Sea, such as Cyprus, the island of Tyre, Platea, Aradus, and others. John Gill suggests he may have demanded tribute (protection money) from lands he did not actually control because the residents feared the power of Persia. John Trapp theorizes Mordecai's efforts may have spared Judaea from these taxes.[383] (The author never actually explained why these taxes were levied.)

In his later years, Xerxes refrained from military engagements, and concentrated on constructing impressive buildings, particularly in Persepolis, a ceremonial city built during the reigns of Cyrus the Great and Darius I.[384] His building efforts ended in 465 BC when his minister, Artabanus, murdered both Xerxes and his son Darius. In revenge, Artaxerxes, another son, assassinated Artabanus and took his father's throne. He continued Xerxes' building projects in his own name. [385]

Mordecai's accomplishments were recorded, just as those of Xerxes and Esther were. The Book of the Annals of the Kings of Media and Persia has been lost,[386] but the sacred writings of the Jews have been safeguarded and are studied worldwide. Earthly kingdoms rise and fall, but the Kingdom of God is everlasting.

---

383     Clarke, Adam, Albert Barnes, Theodore Beza, John Wesley, John Trapp, Thomas Coke, John Gill, et al. "Esther with Book Summary Esther 10-1" Verse-by-Verse Bible Commentary. studylight. org. Accessed January 22, 2020. https://www. studylight. org/commentary/esther/10:1. html.
384     Clarke, Adam, Albert Barnes, Theodore Beza, John Wesley, John Trapp, Thomas Coke, John Gill, et al. "Esther with Book Summary Esther 10:2" Verse-by-Verse Bible Commentary. studylight. org. Accessed January 22, 2020. https://www. studylight. org/commentary/esther/10-2. html.
385     Mark, Joshua J. "Xerxes I." Ancient History Encyclopedia, April 29, 2020. https:// www.ancient.eu/Xerxes_I/.
386     Engelbrecht Edward A. "Esther." The Lutheran Study Bible: English Standard Version. Saint Louis: Concordia Publishing House, 2004. p. 774.

Mordecai was second in rank to the king. Some have said he was prime minister (chief minister or highest officer appointed by a ruler), while others believe he was the grand vizier (chief officer of state).[387] Basically, the two terms are synonymous. He was a humble man who achieved greatness, although he showed no desire to become powerful. His main interests were preserving the safety of his people and honoring his God.[388] He was a kind, honest man who was loved and respected by Jews and Gentiles alike.

Esther began her life as a humble Jewish orphan, and by God's sovereign plan, became the Queen of Persia and the savior of her people.[389]

387     Crawford, Sidnie White. "Esther: Bible." Jewish Women: A Comprehensive Historical Encyclopedia. 20 March 2009. Jewish Women's Archive. (Viewed on April 25, 2020) <https://jwa.org/encyclopedia/article/esther-bible>.
388     Engelbrecht Edward A. "Esther." The Lutheran Study Bible: English Standard Version. Saint Louis: Concordia Publishing House, 2004. p. 774.
389     Spurgeon, Charles Haddon. "Esther's Exaltation; or, Who Knoweth?" Spurgeon, April 27, 1884. https://www. spurgeon. org/resource-library/sermons/esthers-exaltation-or-who-knoweth#flipbook/.

# CHAPTER 11: FINAL THOUGHTS

**A**ND WE KNOW THAT IN ALL THINGS GOD WORKS **for the good of those who love Him, who have been called according to His purpose** (Romans 8:28).

Dr. David Strain eloquently explained the ending to the story of Esther. "The wicked Haman's 'final solution' was to be the holocaust of the Jewish people"… However, by the grace of God "the Jews are delivered, their enemies are destroyed, giving rise to the annual festival of Purim, which is celebrated by the Jewish people even to this day.[390]

In 1874, Charles Spurgeon identified these six theses relating to the Book of Esther.

1. God places His agents in fitting places for doing His work… Every child of God is where God has placed him for some purpose.

2. God restrains His enemies.

3. God in His providence tries people… God's intent is to educate His people by affliction.

4. The Lord's wisdom is seen in arranging the smallest events so as to produce great results…. What a providence!

---

390     Strain, David. "Holy War." First Presbyterian Church, Jackson, Mississippi, July 28, 2013. https://www. fpcjackson. org/resource-library/sermons/holy-war.

5.  The Lord in His providence calls His own servants to be active… It is clear the divine will is accomplished, and yet, men are perfectly free agents.

6.  The Lord achieves the total defeat of his foes and the safety of His people.[391]

Pastor Stephen Blumer states, "A coincidence is God's way of performing miracles anonymously."[392] The book of Esther appears to be a series of fortunate coincidences and good luck, but that assumption would be inaccurate. It is far more than that. God was in control, and He orchestrated every incident that took place (see also Da. 2:21; Jer. 31:35).[393] It was God's will that His people would be preserved. Those who try to defeat God's divine plan will be defeated instead. He extends His favor towards those who seek to do His will. We serve an all-knowing God who will reward the faithful in His own good time. He worked miraculously in Esther's life, and He will do the same in ours.

The book of Esther is filled with preordained "coincidences." When we reject God's work as mere happenstances, we may miss God's magnificent design and the opportunities we are given to fulfill His purposes in our lives.[394] These are truly divine appointments. One lesson we may learn from the Book of Esther is to trust and obey God.

1.  Xerxes used a beauty pageant to choose a new wife, which was a practice never used before (Est. 2:17). Esther was the most beautiful young lady in the empire, and she became queen for the divine purpose of saving her people.

---

391     Spurgeon, Charles Haddon. "Providence–As Seen in the Book of Esther." Spurgeon, November 2, 1874. https://www. spurgeon. org/resource-library/sermons/providence-as-seen-in-the-book-of-esther—2#flipbook/.

392     Blumer, Stephen. "Is It Coincidence or God's Providence? (Esther 4:10-16)." Epiphany 2 – Jan–Risen Savior Lutheran Church. Risen Savior Lutheran Church, January 27, 2019.

393     Dybdahl, Jon L, ed. "Esther." Andrews Study Bible: Light. Depth. Truth. Berrien Springs, MI: Andrews University Press, 2010. p. 619.

394     Boylan, Robert. "'Designed Coincidences' in the Book of Esther." Scriptural Mormonism, January 31, 2019. http://scripturalmormonism.blogspot.com/2019/01/designed-coincidences-in-book-of-esther. html

2. A Jewish woman married a pagan Persian king, a practice disapproved of by both Jews and Persians. (Persian kings were to choose their wives from the seven noble families. The Jewish Esther certainly did not qualify.[395] Since Esther was forced to marry Xerxes, she was not criticized by the Jews.[396])

3. Mordecai overheard a plot to kill the king (Est. 2:21-22). God placed him in the right place at the right time.

4. Xerxes had insomnia. He commanded his servants to read to him. He was reminded he had not honored Mordecai for saving his life (Est. 6:1-2).

5. Haman came to the palace very early to ask Xerxes to kill Mordecai. Instead, Xerxes asked for his advice (Est. 6:4).

6. Haman planned a great reward for himself. Instead, Mordecai was rewarded (Est. 6:11).

7. Xerxes walked in just when Haman fell on Esther's couch (Est. 7:8).

8. Haman was impaled on the pole he intended for Mordecai (Est. 7:10).

9. The day Haman chose to annihilate the Jews, the thirteenth of Adar (Est. 3:7), was the day the Jews obliterated their enemies (Est. 9:1).

God-incidences occur today as they did in Esther's time. He had a plan for our salvation before He created the world. He placed Esther in the right place at the right time to save His people from the merciless plot of the homicidal Haman. It is no accident we were born when and where we were. The Lord Almighty chose us to be adopted into

---

395     Clarke, Adam, Albert Barnes, Theodore Beza, John Wesley, John Trapp, Thomas Coke, John Gill, et al. "Esther with Book Summary Esther 1:14" Verse-by-Verse Bible Commentary. studylight. org. Accessed January 22, 2020. https://www. studylight. org/commentary/esther/1-14. html.
396     Shurpin, Yehuda. "How Could Esther Marry a Non-Jewish King?" Judaism, January 23, 2008. https://www.chabad.org/holidays/purim/article_cdo/aid/628769/ jewish/ How-Could-Esther-Marry-a-Non-Jewish-King.htm.

His family through his Son, Jesus Christ. God can and does use plain, ordinary people to accomplish His divine purpose. One person who answers God's call can impact the lives of many. We are all in a particular place at a particular time chosen by God "for such a time as this."

**"For God so loved the world that he gave His one and only Son, that whoever believes in Him shall not perish but have eternal life. For God did not send His Son into the world to condemn the world, but to save the world through Him"** (Jn. 3:16-17).

**"For there is one God and one mediator between God and mankind, the man Christ Jesus, who gave Himself as a ransom for all people"** (1 Tim. 2:5-6a).

Esther and Mordecai are believed to be buried in Hamdan, Iran. It is the most popular location for Jewish pilgrims in that area. [397] The tomb is an impressive mausoleum, suitable for a queen and prime minister of ancient Persia.

From the Book of Esther, as well as other sources, scholars have found there is a significant connection between Jewish and Persian history. Jews living in present-day Iraq and Iran are the descendants of these ancient people.[398] They are known as "Esther's Children." Archaeologists have learned a great deal about Persian life during the reign of Xerxes, and many of the details in this book have been proven to be accurate.[399] As historians, archaeologists, and other scholars continue their important work, additional new discoveries may be found.

The Coptic Orthodox Church and the Eastern Orthodox Church recognize Esther as a saint. The Lutheran Church-Missouri Synod commemorates Esther as a matriarch.[400]

---

397    "Tomb of Esther and Mordechai." Wikipedia. Wikimedia Foundation, April 25, 2020. https://en.wikipedia.org/wiki/Tomb_of_Esther_and_Mordechai.

398    Yancey, Philip, and Tim Stafford. "Esther." The Student Bible. Grand Rapids, MI: Zondervan, 1996, p. 507.

399    Yancey, Philip, and Tim Stafford. "Esther." The Student Bible. Grand Rapids, MI: Zondervan, 1996, p. 513.

400    "Esther." Wikipedia. Wikimedia Foundation, March 8, 2020. https://en. wikipedia. org/wiki/Esther

# DIG DEEPER STUDY QUESTIONS

## Introduction

1. God was not mentioned in the book of Esther. How did the author show He worked in the lives of Esther, Mordecai, and the Diaspora Jews?

2. Why did Hadassah use the name Esther while in Xerxes' court?

3. Who is the hero of this book? Explain your answer.

4. Why did some biblical scholars believe Esther should not be included in the Bible?

## Chapter 1

1. What was the purpose of the king's banquet?

2. What did Persian leaders consume prior to discussing important topics? How might that affect their decisions?

3. What command did Xerxes give Vashti? What was her response? Why do you think she responded as she did?

4. What is a patriarchal society? How did that affect life in Susa?

5. What was Vashti's punishment and how did it fit into God's perfect plan? Why was her disobedience seen as a threat to the men?

## Chapter 2

1. What method was used to find Xerxes a new wife? How did this differ from the traditional practice? Was the young ladies' participation voluntary?

2. How was Esther related to Mordecai? Why had he adopted her?

3. What was done for a period of twelve months prior to the young women being presented to the king? Why was this preparation implemented for a full year?

4. What decision did Xerxes make concerning Esther? In what way was this part of God's plan?

5. Why did Mordecai tell Esther to hide her Jewish identity? What might have happened if her ethnicity had been revealed?

6. What vital information did Mordecai overhear at the king's gate? What did he do with this knowledge? Why was this report important to Xerxes?

# Chapter 3

1. In Esther's day, why was it sometimes difficult to determine a person's identity?

2. What did Mordecai do/not do to incur the wrath of Haman? What did Haman do as a result?

3. For what reason did Haman cast lots?

4. How did the Jews avoid contamination of their religion and customs?

5. What offer did Haman give to Xerxes?

6. What proclamation was made in Xerxes' name? What was the reaction of the Persians to this decree? What was the reaction of the Jews?

# Chapter 4

1. Why did Mordecai tear his clothes then wear sackcloth and ashes? Why did he refuse to wear the fresh clothes Esther sent him?

2. Why was it necessary for Esther to send Hathak, her eunuch attendant, to determine the reason for her cousin's distress?

3. What did Mordecai ask Esther to do? Why was this action dangerous?

4. What did Esther ask her fellow Jews to do before she faced her official visit with Xerxes? Do you believe prayer was a part of this request? Explain your answer.

# Chapter 5

1. Did Esther and Xerxes have a close, loving relationship? How did this affect Esther's willingness to obey Mordecai's request? What was the king's reaction when he saw his wife?

2. If Xerxes had rejected Esther's unbidden visit, what would have been the probable result? What sign did the king give to show he accepted his wife's presence?

3. What request did Esther make to Xerxes? Why was Haman included in this invitation?

4. What practice common at feasts might have clouded the king's judgment?

5. How did Esther's second invitation demonstrate her shrewdness?

6. In spite of two invitations to dine with the king and queen, Haman was still miserable. What event caused his despair? What advice did he receive from his wife and friends?

# Chapter 6

1. How was the king's insomnia part of God's plan? Do you feel the subject of the story read from the Book of Chronicles was coincidence?

2. How did Haman's arrival also fit into God's plan? Who did Haman think the king wished to honor?

3. What suggestions did Haman make to the king? What were his feelings when he discovered the truth?

4. What was Haman forced to do for Mordecai?

5. Why did Haman's wife and friends believe he would soon face disgrace and ruin?

# Chapter 7

1. What was Queen Esther's request at the second banquet? What was Xerxes' response? What was Haman's reaction?

2. In the midst of pleading for her life and the lives of her people, why did Esther discuss taxes with King Xerxes?

3. How would Queen Esther be affected by the death sentence faced by the Jews of Persia?

4. What crime did Xerxes accuse Haman of committing? Was he guilty of that offense? Why do you think Esther did not explain what actually occurred?

5. What happened to Haman as a result of the events at the banquet? Describe the irony of this outcome.

# Chapter 8

1. How did Haman's death affect the edict calling for the slaughter of the Jews? How did Xerxes handle the situation?

2. How did Esther acquire Haman's property?

3. In what ways did Mordecai's position in the kingdom change after Haman's execution?

4. Describe the edict authored by Mordecai? How was this different from Haman's edict?

5. Why did Xerxes set up a time limit on Mordecai's decree?

# Chapter 9

1. What was the significance of the thirteenth day of Adar to both the Jews and the Persians?

2. In what ways did King Saul's disobedience of God's command (1 Sa. 15:1-9) force the Jews of Persia to execute God's judgment on the Amalekites? How did the Jews show restraint during and after the battle? (Discuss the Jews' treatment of their enemies as well as their property.)

3. Why did Esther request an extension on Mordecai's decree?

4. What further humiliation did Esther request for Haman's sons? Why do you think she did this? Was it simple revenge?

5. Why do Jews celebrate Purim? How is Purim different from other Jewish observances?

# Chapters 10 and 11

1. Was Xerxes a wise ruler? Give reasons for your opinion.

2. Many people have marveled at the twists of fate in the book of Esther. How do you feel these "coincidences" demonstrated God's hand at work in the lives of His people?

3. Why did God place Esther when and where He did "for such a time as this"?

www.ingramcontent.com/pod-product-compliance
Lightning Source LLC
Chambersburg PA
CBHW051512120626
46551CB00012B/885